THE FOUR ARK ROYALS

The Four
Ark Royals

Lieutenant Commander
MICHAEL APPS, RN (Retd.)

With a Foreword by
Vice-Admiral Sir Michael Fell,
KCB, DSO, DSC

WILLIAM KIMBER · LONDON

First published in 1976 by
WILLIAM KIMBER & CO. LIMITED
Godolphin House, 22a Queen Anne's Gate,
London, SW1H 9AE.

© Michael Apps, 1976
ISBN 07183 0344 X

Photoset by
Specialised Offset Services, Liverpool
and printed in Great Britain by
The Garden City Press Limited,
Letchworth, Hertfordshire, SG6 1JS

Contents

Acknowledgements

A large number of people have been kind enough to help me in the preparation of this book. I would like to acknowledge their assistance with much gratitude. In particular I would like to thank the Staff of the National Maritime Museum at Greenwich; the library staff of the Royal Naval College, Greenwich; Lieutenant Commander L. Cox, R.N. Rtd., Curator of Fleet Air Arm Museum, Yeovilton; The Staff of the Ministry of Defence Reference Library, Empress State Building, London; Miss M. Joll; Photographic Records, Ministry of Defence, Foxhill, Bath; Mr Reg Longstaff, Department of Public Relations (Navy), Whitehall; Mr Bryan Jackson, (M.O.D.); Mr B.V. Cousens; Mr A.M. MacKinnon, Flight Lieutenant Merryweather, R.A.F. Rtd; Mr S. Gray, Mr Pat Oliver; Captain G.V.P. Crowden, O.B.E. R.N.; Commander G. Lee, R.N.; Fleet Chief Medical Assistant J. Dongworth; Roger Lyett, Lieutenant Commander P. Sheppard, R.N.; G.A. Halnan: Without the very kind co-operation, patience and the giving of their valuable time, the book could never have been written.

Lastly, I would wish to thank my very good friend Mr Desmond Wettern who provided so much of the information on *Ark Royal* IV, my son Timothy Apps who drew the maps and diagrams, my wife Anne who helped to edit, proof-read and index, and last but not least Mrs Pauline Talbot, the patient and long suffering typist who had to decipher and correct an almost illegible scrawl.

On behalf of all *Ark Royals*, past, present and future and the Fleet Air Arm: I would say a most sincere thank you.

List of Illustrations

Foreword

by *Vice-Admiral Sir Michael Fell, KCB, DSO, DSC*

What's in a name? A great deal, I suspect, and this is the story of four warships and a famous name – *Ark Royal*.

I am unreservedly an *Ark Royal* fan. It is a wonderful name which has a wonderful ring to it. It conjures up visions of involvement in great affairs. On several occasions during World War II I had seen the second *Ark Royal*, by then renamed HMS *Pegasus*, at sea. I served in the third *Ark Royal* during much of her time in the Atlantic and Mediterranean, leaving her shortly before she was sunk. I served in the present and fourth *Ark Royal* during three separate commissions, one of which was in command. In short, several years of my life have been spent in two ships of the name and they were the happiest, the most fun and the most rewarding of my time in the Navy.

From personal experience of the third and fourth *Ark Royals* I can testify to the remarkably careful and accurate research which has gone into this book. I found it much more than a simple account of four different warships. It is an historical and extremely readable story of life and warfare in the Royal Navy from 1588 up to the present date.

No new warship could get off to a better start than bear the name *Ark Royal* and this must surely come about in due course. When the time comes to chronicle the life of the fifth *Ark Royal*, I hope her story will be written by an author of the calibre of Michael Apps.

Introduction

In the sixty years of its existence, the Fleet Arm of the Royal Navy has become an integral part of the traditional older Navy of the dreadnought era. Another branch of the service, it was slow to be accepted, but nevertheless with ultimate acceptance and recognition came admiration and full support – the admiration and support that was given to a new branch with a surprising ability to adapt, to learn and to absorb the new lessons of the air war at sea.

The early courtship of the vigorous and boisterous air with a staid and conservative sea led to a tempestuous marriage, which in the late 1920s and early 1930s nearly ended in divorce by neglect. Happily its survival was to produce by the end of the Second World War – and in the busy years following the war – the dominating factor in naval operations. For there is no doubt that a detailed study of the naval war at sea during the Second World War provides striking and conclusive evidence – if evidence were needed – that the aircraft carrier was the vital component. Its proud achievements will stand both as an important lesson in sea warfare and grand strategy, as well as the basic argument for the retention of air power at sea into the future.

It is most fitting therefore, that the name of *Ark Royal* should have been chosen as the name of the first aircraft carrier completed in 1914. Today, in 1975, the third carrier and the fourth ship to bear the famous name *Ark Royal* steams into her last commission and the history books. But this famous and probably best known of all ship's names – next to Nelson's *Victory* – first appeared as a galleon in 1588 and was destined to become flagship of the Lord High Admiral of England, Lord Howard of Effingham, at the Battle of the Armada in the same year. She was in the battle from the first encounter with the Spaniards off Plymouth to the decisive battle of Gravelines, chasing the scattered and fleeing Spanish ships into the North Sea and beyond the Firth of Forth.

It was not the last time Lord Howard was to fly his flag in her, for in 1596 she was in the front line of the joint Army and Navy expedition against Cadiz, an interesting early example of combined service operations. The Spaniards only threatened England with invasion once more, in 1599, and *Ark Royal* was again commissioned as flagship. Perhaps the memory of her guns spoiled the Spanish appetite for action against her, for the threat died and *Ark Royal* never saw action again in her own name.

When James I acceded to the throne, he renamed her *Anne Royal*, in honour of his Queen Anne of Denmark. In 1625, under her own style and as flagship of Lord Wimbledon, she led another expedition against Cadiz, this time a disastrous one owing to the poor preparations made for it. The end came for the first *Ark*, or rather *Anne Royal* in 1636, as she was moving from the Medway for service as Sir John Pennington's flagship, when she stove in her timbers on her own anchor and sank. At a greater cost than her original purchase price of £5,000 she was raised and docked, but found to be beyond repair and broken up.

Three centuries passed before another ship called *Ark Royal* fought for Great Britain. She was in fact intended to be a merchant ship, but like her predecessor all those years before, history was to repeat itself when she was bought for the Royal Navy whilst still building in 1914 and converted into a sea-plane carrier. With the Mediterranean Fleet she served at the Dardanelles and the Gallipoli landings and, in 1918, in the Russian operations in the Black Sea, where in 1920 she was the evacuation ship for Russian refugees from the Revolution. After refitting in Rosyth and a period in reserve, she joined the Fleet again at Constantinople when trouble was brewing between Greece and Turkey. Returning to England in 1923, she joined the Nore Command and was renamed *Pegasus* in 1934. In the early days of World War II she was employed as a Fighter Catapult ship escorting convoys in the North Atlantic and on July 26th 1941, was relegated to catapult training duties in the Clyde area. In January 1944 the *Pegasus* was converted into an accommodation ship and surprisingly survived to be sold in 1946.

The third *Ark Royal*, a ship of 22,000 tons, was another aircraft carrier and was launched at Birkenhead in 1937. Perhaps the best-known and best-loved of all the ships in the Second World War, the third *Ark* was destined to carry some seventy-two aircraft and 1,500 officers and men into some of the most stirring battles in those early days of World War II. After taking part in the Norwegian Campaign in 1940, she joined the attacks on the French Fleet at Oran when France had fallen to the Germans. She then joined the famous Force 'H' based at Gibraltar and for fifteen months saw action in the Mediterranean, where she was a favourite target for the enemy, notably on the convoy runs to Malta. The sinking of the *Ark Royal* was a frequent German claim, and the enemy doubtless wished it were true when she played a crucial part in the great naval operation resulting in the sinking of the *Bismarck*. Her career was in fact ended early in the morning of 14th November 1941 when, having been torpedoed the previous day by a submarine, the 'old *Ark*' – as she is still referred to by many – turned over and sank within sight of Gibraltar.

In May 1943, the keel of the present *Ark Royal* was laid down at Cammell Laird's Yard, Birkenhead, by Princess Marina, Duchess of Kent, and in 1950 she was launched by Her Majesty Queen Elizabeth, now the Queen Mother. The ship has an overall length of 810 feet and has a deep displacement of 50,786 tons, the fourth ship to bear a famous name.

As she and her kind ousted the mighty battleships from command of the sea, so too, will other and new types of warships rise to challenge for the coveted title of 'the Queen of the Seas'. Hopefully, new types of aircraft will still be at sea in the next generation of ships, and the carrier's reign continue. But whatever the outcome of speculation, one thing is certain, the '*old Arks*' of yesterday and today will remember and say: 'She was always the greatest of them all'.

Chapter 1

Ralegh's Ark

By the year 1550, the sailing ship had come to be accepted in northern Europe as superior to the galleass, either as a warship or as a trading vessel. But in the Mediterranean there was still support for this compromise vessel; the galleass was an attempt to combine the manoeuvrability of oars with the thrust of sails. Twenty-one years later at the Battle of Lepanto, the last great sea fight between man-powered ships, the galleass routed the galley. However, it became generally recognised at this time that the ship relying solely on sail was the only vessel capable of long ocean voyages in a dual role of trading ship and man-of-war.

In spite of the threat from Spain and the lesson of the Armada, the end of the sixteenth century still saw England without a Royal Navy as an exclusive fighting force. Elizabeth I had insufficient money to build, equip or even maintain a permanent fleet. Commerce had to continue and the trading ships sparingly armed themselves with as small a sacrifice as possible of revenue-earning cargo space. In the face of piracy, merchant shipowners grouped themselves together in self-defence to form the first shipping company or shipping line.

Small trading ships of 120 tons were the most common type in use by the turn of the sixteenth century, but at the other end of the scale, there was the continuing obsession of monarchs to build big, prestige ships. In 1610 James I built the *Prince Royal* at Woolwich. Within ten years of each other Gustavus Adolphus of Sweden and Charles I of England built the *Vasa* and the *Sovereign of the Seas*, ships with very different fates.

The *Sovereign of the Seas* was the largest ship in the world of 1637. She was a showpiece, built without any thought of a budget and encrusted with elaborate decoration and carving. She carried 100 guns on three decks and was so much ahead of her time that she could have fought at Trafalgar. The *Sovereign of the Seas* survived for nearly sixty years, but in 1696, a candle accidentally overturned and caused a fire that destroyed her.

On 10th August 1628, there was an air of excitement at Stockholm in Sweden. Literally thousands of sightseers had turned out to watch the event of the decade – the maiden voyage of the *Vasa*. This great galleon, and near contemporary of England's *Sovereign of the Seas*, was much the same size – about 170 feet in length, but much narrower in the beam at less than 40 feet. At fourteen feet, her draught was five feet shallower than the English ship, but, far more serious, a vessel of these dimensions, fully rigged and equipped with an armament of forty-eight twenty-four-pounder guns, many of them placed high in the superstructure, sacrificed the essential factor of stability. The guns alone were said to have weighed eighty tons.

Preparations for the *Vasa's* departure from Stockholm were elaborate, with thousands crammed onto every vantage point to see the great ship towed from her berth into mid-stream to begin the forty-mile trip to the open sea. She had a total complement of 450 men, comprising 150 seamen and 300 military personnel, but by special dispensation they had been allowed to take their families with them as far as the outer reaches of the harbour, so this figure of 450 was probably more than doubled for the first part of the voyage.

Clear of the headlands, the *Vasa's* sails caught the wind and she began to make headway. Moments later she began to heel alarmingly; water rushed in through the lower gun ports and gradually the *Vasa* disappeared beneath the waters of Stockholm harbour. She righted herself as she went down and since most of the ship's company and their families were above decks for the departure, nearly all were picked up by the many harbour craft watching the event and the loss of life was no more than fifty.

If the *Vasa* made a short and spectacular voyage, she sank so evenly and gently in 100 feet of water that her hull rested upright on the sandy bottom. Three hundred and thirty-three years later, in April 1961, the hull of the *Vasa* was brought to the surface, cradled by pontoons. Previously abandoned as impossible, the salvage operation had been revived when the techniques of ship-raising had proved so successful at Scapa Flow. Here the patient salvage experts had managed to bring up the steel battleships of Germany's scuttled fleet from the First World War, and were soon to prove that with careful planning, even a fragile wooden hull could be brought up. Today the *Vasa* rests in a permanent berth in a Stockholm drydock, the most complete example of a perfectly preserved ship of the seventeenth century.

Eight years later, across the English Channel, a very famous English ship sank beneath the waters of the Medway, sunk by her own anchor stoving in her timbers. But though she was raised and docked at very great expense, she was found to be beyond repair and broken up. Thus ended the career of perhaps the most famous ship in the Navy up to that time – *Anne Royal* but originally named *Ark Ralegh* and then *Ark Royal*.

The Elizabethan ship, though her influence upon naval history is of a negative kind, deserves description at some length. Lacking everything that in naval architecture counts for efficiency, to the trained eye of a shipman she was at best an unlovely structure. To the layman she may appear otherwise, for in her lavish embellishment the gorgeous sense of colour characteristic of the age found a splendid means of expression. Indeed, efficiency was sacrificed to decoration, and much that might have been of good sea-service was denied to the seaman and his ship for the sake of artistic convention.

It would be unsafe to place too much reliance on the contemporary drawings, but by a careful comparison of the various pictures which have been preserved, by the study of the Swedish *Vasa* and much recent and detailed research from many sources, the ship of Elizabeth's navy can be reconstructed with tolerable accuracy.

The clumsiness which she shared with her foreign cousin, the galleon, was almost entirely due to the intense craze for over-elaboration. Her hull had a length from stem-post to stern-post approximately equal to three times her beam, and since from earliest times the chief mathematical problem in naval architecture had been one of simple proportion in thirds, the actual body of the ship should have been seaworthy enough. It was only when she was encumbered with towering upper-works that she became unstable. Full bodied, bluff in the bow, and square of stern, the hull was at all events staunch enough at sea, if nothing else.

Thus we have to start with, a blunt and beamy type of hull, with a broad and transom-stern. That is to say, that instead of the planking of the ship's sides curving in gradually to the stern-post and forming a symmetrical 'run' and 'tuck', the stern was cut off square and left almost as broad as the total beam of the vessel amidships. The hull was finished in box-like fashion by planking laid across from the rudder-post, hence giving the appearance of having been sawn off, and therefore seeming rather unwieldy. In terms of modern ship-building there is much to be said for this style of stern, and if the Elizabethan shipwrights had been content to let well alone, there could be no real criticism of this method of construction. The problems and difficulties arose when they began to build the upperworks on the stern.

The vessels grew higher and higher as they piled superstructure upon superstructure until finally, if the drawings of the period are to be believed, the overall height of the ship from taffrail to keel must have been greater than her length overall. From the waist or upper deck, a poop and top-gallant poop were constructed. There were never less than two poops in a 'great-ship' as they have sometimes been called – often there were three. The third frequently resembled a little roofed-in house perched right at the top of the towering mass and overhanging the sea. Forward there was the forecastle and top-gallant forecastle, equally ponderous, and a still more crazy appearance was imparted to the ship by the endeavour to compensate by an increase in length for the loss of breadth caused by the 'tumble-home' of the ship's sides. To explain this phrase it must be mentioned that the sides, instead of rising vertically up from the water-line, curved in, or 'tumbled in', considerably from the water-line to the deck rail. With the idea of balancing this decrease in width, the extreme bow and stern structures were made to project many feet outboard of the ship's sides. The net result of this grotesque and rather fantastic shipbuilding principle was that at sea, the vessel tended to roll and pitch excessively, and was almost entirely prevented from making any headway other than a very broad tack or running free before the wind. Indeed *Ark Royal* was noted for the fact that she tended to roll badly in any kind of sea.

An additional curious feature was the beak-head, or projection beyond the stem and above which the bowsprit stuck out like a finger pointing the way. This was added partly as an ornamental embellishment, partly for the purpose of breaking up the waves. So far from being of any real service, it was probably a source of considerable danger to the ship in a seaway, and there are several instances of the whole concern washing adrift or breaking up in storms.

Other remarkable features were the little round towers, resembling cages, which were placed at the break of the poop and

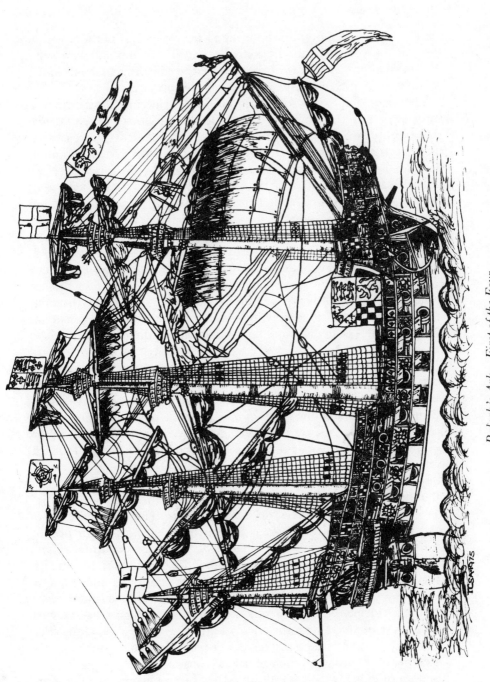

Ralegh's Ark – First of the Four

forecastle – i.e. the points where the latter rose up from the waist of the ship, – and often at the extreme end of the top-gallant poop. Their only comparable equivalent were the 'dickies', or small look-out shelters, which figured in the ships of Nelson's time.

The armament was of a varied kind, ranging from cannon throwing a solid ball of sixty pounds to the 'fawcons', which hurled shot of only two pounds. Other weapons included such minor sorts of projectile-throwers as demi-cannon, culverins, sakers, cannon-pesers, top-pieces, and hayle-shotte pieces. This miscellany of armament was mounted in the tops at the break of the poop and forecastle, and were intended for, as the historians of the day so quaintly put it . . . 'murthering near at hand'. The whole of the upper-works provided excellent positions for the sighting of these pieces of ordnance, and from a purely military – as distinct from a naval – point of view, the armament of these ships was excellent. However the heavy weight penalty was a serious matter, resulting as it did in a considerable top weight high up in the ship. Often the ship itself was badly overloaded, which meant that the heavier guns had to be taken out of her and her fighting efficiency thereby enormously reduced.

Certain guns of this period were breech-loaders. These were usually mounted in the break of the poop and forecastle, where they could be trained upon the waist of the ship, and executed fearful carnage and havoc in the ranks of any boarding party. The arsenal at Venice contains some extremely interesting examples of arms belonging to this period. From these we learn that the breech-loaders were mounted on pivots and could be fired as often as twenty and thirty times in an hour. The charge was contained in a separate iron chamber which was fitted into the breech of the gun and held in place by means of wedges driven tightly in. The chambers were loaded beforehand, and they were able to indulge in fairly rapid fire.

The type of gun most in favour with the Elizabethan seaman, however, was the thirty pounder. Judging by some of the results, its efficiency can have been very little less than that of similar guns in use as late as the Battle of Trafalgar, over two centuries later. The guiding principle of an engagement in those early days was to try to get to close quarters with the enemy and then, while lying alongside, literally to smash and pound his upper-works with ball and shot. To attempt to board him before such guns as he had capable of commanding his waist were disabled, was in the words of a Captain of the day, 'an enterprise fraught with too many risks to be lightly undertaken'.

Once an opportunity to place one's own ship alongside that of the enemy had occurred and been taken, the yard-arms were fitted with large iron hooks, 'so that they tangle with the sails and rigging of the enemy ship, holding him fast for the close range gunners and preventing him from escaping'. One can picture the gruesome and devastating carnage that followed!

In this, the story of *Ark Royal*, I feel that it is best to deal firstly with the ship and then with the men. Hopefully it will give the reader an accurate and lucid account of the hard life of the mariner nearly four hundred years ago, as well as painting a clearer picture of the first great sea battle in which *Ark Royal* was involved.

In 1586, a west countryman by the name of Sir Walter Ralegh placed an order with a Mr R. Chapman, a shipbuilder at Deptford, for a vessel of some 800 tons to be built for him and named *Ark*. To be strictly accurate, she was to be named *Ark Ralegh*, for it was common custom in Tudor Times, that privately ordered, armed ships were named after their gentleman owners, and he was presumably having her built for the colonisation of Virginia.

However in January 1587, alarmed by the growing menace of Spanish invasion and a shortage of ships to defend England, she was purchased by Queen Elizabeth I for the sum of £5,000 and renamed *Ark Royal*, and the cost of her purchase was deducted in 1592 from Ralegh's debt to the Crown. Like her namesake successors in their turn, the first *Ark Royal* was a formidable warship of her time and destined for great occasions. The well-known woodcut print made by Allen in 1767, and so often reproduced as *Henry Grace à Dieu* or *Great Harry* of 1514 – the first real battleship in the Navy – is almost certainly that of a ship of a later date. A complete refit in 1539 so altered her appearance that no reliance can be placed on the many impressions published in her time. Most historians now accept that it represents the galleon *Ark Royal* of 1588, and shows a lot of interesting detail. The vessel has two gun decks, double forecastle deck, quarter deck, half deck – and above the half deck further aft – a poop deck. An innovation was the balcony, the gallery which ran forward from the stern for a short distance on either side of the deck.

An experienced shipbuilder of the time, Matthew Baker, criticised the rig of these ships as being:

still inefficiently overburdened with lateen top and topgallant on the mizzenmast and topsail, but it may be that the remarkable lateen sails on the top and topgallant mast of *Ark Royal* and other larger ships were merely decorative, seldom if ever being used, to be hoisted when the new ships were paraded but soon to be removed, masts and all, by practical commanders.

Launched at Deptford on 12 June 1587, *Ark Royal* carried a crew of 125 soldiers and 300 mariners and displaced 692 tons. She was quite a large ship for those days and her armament comprised 4-60 pdr, 4-30 pdr, 12-18 pdr, 12-9 pdr, and 6-6 pdr making a total of 38 guns, but in fact she carried an additional 17 assorted guns of smaller size thus bringing her total armament to 55 guns. She was commissioned as the Flagship of Lord Howard of Effingham, Lord High Admiral of England, and of all her engagements, the most famous was to be her first and occurred within a few short months of her launching. Writing to Burghley on 26 February 1588 Howard says:

I pray you tell Her Majesty from me that her money was well given for the Ark Ralegh, for I think her the odd ship in the World for all conditions; and truly I think there can be no great ship make me change and go out of her.

The English, a nation of sea-rovers, with harbours on the Channel, the Humber, the Thames and the Bristol Channel, had in the words of an early Elizabethan historian; 'the love of the sea and the love of freedom in their souls'. Like their Portuguese and Spanish contemporaries, they embraced the dangers and the challenge of the seafarers' life, to seize upon the opportunities offered by the New World, to expand trade and to secure wealth, territory and freedom.

London, although a great market for traders of the time, was little more than a small town sprawling on both sides of the Thames: Liverpool was a village whilst Bristol was a small seafaring town with a population of perhaps 10,000 people.

In 1588, in the great reign of Elizabeth I, something happened in Europe that was to change dramatically this small island's destiny. England defeated the mighty Spanish Armada of Philip II of Spain through the leadership of those very sea-rovers, Howard, Hawkins, Frobisher and Drake, and who already, in the person of Sir Francis Drake and others, had explored distant oceans and sailed round the world and into history.

Born at Crowndale Farm near Tavistock, Devon about 1545, Francis Drake was the eldest of twelve children. His father, Edmund Drake had become a passionate Lutheran, but due to an over enthusiastic preaching and advocacy during the Prayer Book Rebellion of 1548, was forced to take his wife and three years old Francis to the relative safety of eastern Kent. There, it is said, 'that during the reign of Mary Queen of Scots, he lived with his multiplying family in one of the hulks on the river, in considerable poverty – and no little danger, since he read prayers and preached religious sedition to the seamen in the Queen's ships on the Medway'. Living as he was under constant danger and threat of persecution, this phase in young Francis' life was to have a lasting effect.

When only twenty-two he sailed with his cousin John Hawkins on the voyage to the West Indies which ended in the disastrous events of San Juan de Ulua, where warships of Spain, under the direction of Don Martin Enriquez, the new Viceroy of Mexico, having first given the small English fleet a promise of safe conduct, treacherously set upon them; with the result that the English returned home with a hundred and fifty men alive out of the six hundred who set out, and about a quarter of their ships.

From this point forward Spain became a practical and very hated enemy to Drake, 'the wolf with the privy paw', the embodiment of all that was worst in the Catholic faith. As the result of this intense hatred, his naval genius and a unique individualistic streak, he was able to gain a succession of brilliant victories over the Spaniards. In fact, he was so successful that they credited him with supernatural powers – powers of darkness of course – and felt they needed God's help when fighting him. In the years to follow, such superstition was to prove a considerable moral disadvantage for them.

As if to emphasise his 'supernatural powers', he captured one of Spain's richer prizes. He intercepted the *San Felipe*, the King's own caraque and the greatest ship in the Portuguese East Indian Trade, homeward bound with a cargo from the Indies. 'A magnificent caraque so richly loaded' it was said, 'that every man in the fleet counted his fortune made'. It was as if it had been sent on purpose for him and fell straight into his hands. There was no need for Drake to wait for more. It was only two months since he and his crew had sailed from Plymouth. Now they could go home after one of the most successful and profitable cruises in the history of seafaring. He had struck the King of Spain in his own stronghold. In the Spanish Port of Cadiz, he had disabled the intended Armada for one season at least, but to rub salt in the wound, he had picked up a prize on the way home worth half a million and almost as if by accident the prize would more than pay his expenses. He had cost nothing to his mistress Queen Elizabeth and had brought back a handsome present for her into the bargain. It is doubtful if such a naval estimate has ever been presented to an English House of Commons before or since! Perhaps more important, he had taught the self-confident Spaniard to be afraid of him, and he carried back his victorious crew in such a glow of triumph, that they would have fought Satan and the devil himself with Drake at their head. Perhaps the last word should be spoken by a Spaniard, Fernandez Duro: "There is not in the annals of England an expedition comparable to it."

The West Country annals still tell how the country folk streamed down in their best clothes to see the great *San Felipe* towed into Dartmouth Harbour. They needed something to give them a morale boost and Drake and his fellow sea-rovers were doing just that.

Of equal importance in the English Fleet – some would say even greater – was John Hawkins. A man of fifty-six at the time of the Armada, Hawkins had been born in Plymouth of a prosperous ship-owning family, and, almost more than Drake's, the history of his career traces the burgeoning of English maritime enterprise in the sixteenth century. Always well-dressed, unfathomable, courteous and charming, he claimed friendship with King Philip of Spain and argued that he was a loyal subject of Philip's, dating from the time of the King's marriage to Mary. Directly involved in the Ridolfi plot of 1571, which was one to assassinate Elizabeth and put Mary Queen of Scots on the throne, in which he was to provide naval cover for an invasion of Spanish troops under Alva, Hawkins had contrived to keep Elizabeth and Cecil informed of every step, and yet was adroit enough to avoid suspicion by the Spanish that he had betrayed them, even when the plot was uncovered and the main conspirators arrested.

Partly as a reward for these services, Elizabeth two years later had appointed him Treasurer of the Navy. With his considerable administrative talents, he was able to attack and control the many corrupt practices, which abounded at every level in the naval dockyards. In addition, it was largely due to his initiative and foresight, that the navy was built up with new vessels, which though half-crewed, poorly provisioned and short of powder and shot, were nevertheless, years ahead in design of any other ships in the world.

Charles Howard, Lord Howard of Effingham, Earl of Nottingham, as he was differently called at different stages of his long and eventful career, was Lord High Admiral of England at a time when England was first rising into eminence as a great maritime power. In addition, he was commander-in-chief of England's fleet in two of the most critical and important actions in our nation's history. Indeed, it has been said frequently that he was neither seaman nor commander-in-chief; that Drake defeated the Armada, that Ralegh led the fleet triumphantly into Cadiz; and that Howard was nothing more than a costly figure-head, placed in a high position by his relationship to the Queen and then kept in office by Courtly intrigues. Such a judgement is both unfair and incorrect, for a careful study of his career reveals that he had a considerable experience of maritime affairs; and though not trained to the sea from boyhood as was Drake, Hawkins and Frobisher, he had a more familiar and practical knowledge of the art of the sea warfare than many of his Elizabethan contemporaries.

At fifty-two years of age and personal friend as well as a cousin of the Queen, Howard of Effingham was first among the Admirals on the English side. As soon as Elizabeth came to the throne his good looks and ability, together with his kinship, had brought him advancement and high office. Ambassador to France at the age of twenty-three, General of Horse under the Earl of Warwick in putting down the northern rebellion, Member of Parliament for Surrey from 1563 to 1573, a Knight of the Garter, Lord Chamberlain of the Household, a commissioner at the trial of Mary Queen of Scots and one of the strongest advocates for her execution; a grandson of the second Duke of Norfolk, the victor of Flooden, he was, unlike many of the Howards, a staunch Protestant.

With the whole of the Spanish nation smarting under the indignity of the burning of the ships at Cadiz, Philip's warlike ardour had warmed into something like a fire. He had resolved at any rate, if he was to forgive his sister-in-law at all, to insist on more than toleration for the Catholics in England. He did not contemplate as even possible, that the English privateers – however bold or dexterous – could resist such a Fleet of Ships as he was preparing to lead up the English Channel. The Royal Navy, he knew very well, did not exceed twenty-five ships of all sorts and sizes. The Drakes of the time might be equal to sudden daring actions, but he would and must be crushed by such a fleet as was being prepared at Lisbon.

Philip of Spain's firm intention was to demand that the Catholic religion should be restored to its complete and exclusive superiority, and that additionally, certain towns in England were to be made over to be garrisoned by Spanish troops as security for Queen Elizabeth's good behaviour. As often happens with irresolute men when they have been forced to a decision, they are as too hasty as before they were too slow.

After Drake had retired from Lisbon, the King of Spain sent orders to the Prince of Parma not to wait for the arrival of the Armada, but to cross the Channel immediately with the Flanders Army, and bring Elizabeth to her knees. Parma had far more sense than his master. He represented that he could hardly cross without a fleet to cover his passage. For a start, his transport barges needed fair weather and calm seas. Then he would need to have protection and finally, he could take only about 25,000 men with him at the most. The English militia were in training and, though he would obey if His Majesty persisted, he recommended Philip to continue to amuse the English with the treaty till the Armada was ready. He ventured to suggest that if 'the English Queen Elizabeth would surrender the "cautionary" towns in Flanders to Spain, and would grant the Catholics in England a fair degree of liberty, then it would be in Philip's interest to make peace at once, without stipulating for further terms. After all,' he went on, 'His Majesty could make a new war against England at any time in the future that he wished, when circumstances might be more convenient and the annoying Netherlands revolt subdued.'

Perhaps the most surprising thing was that Elizabeth herself was inclined to this course of action. After all she said, the towns really belonged to Philip and she would only be returning his own to him. To surrender them to Britain's enemy Spain, and to make peace would have been an infamy so great as to have disgraced Elizabeth forever! Yet Elizabeth did not see it this way. She was advised that if she wanted peace, then she should send out Drake again to frighten the Spaniards and get more gold ships, capture more prizes.

Unfortunately she was in one of her ungovernable and hopelessly unpredictable moods, and instead of sending out Drake again, she ordered her fleet to be dismantled and laid up at Chatham. She even condescended to apologise to Parma for the burning of the transports at Cadiz, and said that Drake had done so against her orders.

All this was in December 1587 and only five months before the Armada sailed from Lisbon. Never had a Queen of England brought herself or her country so near to ruin. Though she did not know it, the entire safety of the Realm rested at that moment on the 'adventurers', on Howard, Hawkins, Frobisher and Drake alone.

Meanwhile, with enormous effort on the part of the Spaniards, the destruction at Cadiz had been repaired. The greatest fleet in history was pushed on, and in February Santa Cruz reported himself almost ready. Santa Cruz and Philip, however, were not in agreement as to what should be done. Santa Cruz was a fighting admiral, Philip was not a fighting king. He changed his mind as often as Elizabeth. Hot fits varied with cold. Unfortunately for Spain, Santa Cruz fell ill at the last moment – ill, it was said, with anxiety. Santa Cruz knew well enough what Philip would never know – that the planned expedition of the Armada would not be an easy venture. He had more than enough reason to be anxious if Philip decided to accompany him and tie his hands and embarrass him. Anyway, Santa Cruz died after a few days' illness and left Philip without an Admiral to lead his Fleet.

The sailing had to be suspended till a new commander could be found, but he had to be careful. He wanted to be sovereign of England again, but with the assent of the English Catholics. He did not mean, if he could possibly help it, to irritate the national pride by force and conquest. While Santa Cruz lived, Spanish public opinion would insist that he command, and Philip would have been forced to accompany him to prevent too violent proceedings. Now he had to find someone who would do as he was told, and thus his own presence would not be necessary.

The Duke of Medina Sidonia, named El Bueno, or 'The Good', was a grandee of highest rank. He was enormously rich, fond of hunting and shooting, a tolerable rider, for the rest a harmless creature getting on for forty, conscious of his defects, but not aware that so great a prince had any need to mend them; without vanity, without ambition, and most happy when lounging in his orange gardens at San Lucan. He had never been on any kind of active service. He was a Captain-General of Andalusia – an honorary prestige title – and had run away from Cadiz when Drake came into harbour; but that was all.

To his astonishment and to his dismay, he learnt that it was on him that the choice had fallen to be the new Lord High Admiral of

Spain, and commander of the so much talked about expedition to England. He protested his unfitness. He said that he was no seaman; that if he ventured out in a boat he was always sick, that he had never seen the English Channel; and that, as far as politics was concerned, he neither knew anything nor cared anything about them. In short, he had not one qualification which such a post required.

Philip liked his modesty; but in fact the Duke's defects were his recommendations. He would obey his instructions, he would not fight unless it was necessary, and would not enter into any rash adventures. All that Philip wanted him to do was to find the Prince of Parma, and act as Parma should direct. As to seamanship, he would have the best officers in the navy under him; and for second in command he should have Don Diego de Valdes, a cautious silent, sullen old sailor, a man after Philip's own heart.

The Duke took himself off to Lisbon and there he made his first mistake. He was a fussy, anxious little man; who decided that he could do everything himself, and meddled with things he could not understand and ought to have left alone. He should have left the details to responsible heads of departments, but it was not in his nature, he had to examine, to check, but because he could not understand what he saw, and didn't know what to look at, nothing was actually examined at all. To gauge some idea of his problem, which he alone insisted on taking on his shoulders, there were 130 ships, 8,000 seamen, 19,000 Spanish infantry, with gentlemen volunteers, officers, priests, surgeons, galley slaves – at least 3,000 more – provisioned for six months. Then he had to look at the ships' stores, arms small and great, powder, spars, cordage, canvas, and such other million necessities that ships need on an expedition of this enormous scale.

Perhaps the Duke had some justification for going into the logistic problem with such misplaced enthusiasm, for there is little doubt that everyone else's minds were taken up and absorbed with the higher spiritual needs of the expedition. It is said that for three years, a stream of prayer had been ascending from church, cathedral or oratory. Philip had emptied his treasury. All pains were taken to make this expedition spiritually worthy of its purpose. No impure thing, especially the ladies of easy virtue, was allowed to approach the yards or the ships. Swearing, quarrelling, gambling, all were prohibited under terrible penalties. Nothing could have been better prepared if only Medina Sidonia had listened to sound advice, but he did not and was unable to check on the validity of the information which any rascal, cheat or thieving supplier chose to give him.

At last at the end of April, he considered that all was ready. The invincible Armada suffered from one weakness, which was to prove its undoing – guns. There were twice as many as the English possessed; but they were for the most part nine and six pounders, and with only fifty rounds per gun. The Spaniards had done their fighting hitherto at close range, grappling and trusting to musketry. They were to receive a lesson about this before the summer was over.

With orders not to seek battle, but to proceed direct to North Foreland and communicate with Parma, the Duke set sail in the *San Martin* on 14th May, followed by the magnificent fleet. The carelessness or roguery of the contractors and suppliers soon became evident to the poor Duke. The water had been taken aboard three months before and not surprisingly, it was found to be foul, stinking and undrinkable. The salt beef, salt pork and fish were putrid, and the bread full of maggots and cockroaches. Cask after cask was opened with the same result and they had to be all thrown overboard. In the whole fleet the story was the same and as a consequence, the men went down in their hundreds with dysentery.

To add to their problems it came on to blow and the ships got scattered. The Duke with half the fleet crawled into Corunna, the crews scarcely able to man the yards and once ashore, trying to desert in their hundreds. Slowly they regrouped, repaired the damage, made good the losses in men and stores and after receiving another sacrament were 'all now well content and cheerful'.

Thus once more, on 13th July, the Armada in full sail was underway for England and streaming across the Bay of Biscay with a fair wind for the mouth of the Channel; religious fervour burning bright again, and heart and hope as high as ever. Three days later the Duke found himself at the entrance to the Channel with all his fleet around him. On Tuesday morning 16th July, the wind shifted to the north, then backed to the west, and blew hard. The sea got up, broke into the stern galleries of the galleons, and sent the galleys looking for shelter in French harbours. The fleet hove to for a couple of days, till the weather improved. On Friday afternoon, 19th July, they sighted the Lizard and formed into fighting order; the Duke in the centre, Alonzo de Leyva leading in a vessel of his own called the *Rata Coronada*, Don Martin de Recalde covering the rear. The entire line stretched to about seven miles – an awe inspiring and impressive sight.

On the English side, the situation had been equally frustrating. The Queen found fault with almost everything. She charged Drake with wasting her ammunition in target practice. She had it doled out to him in driblets, and allowed no more than would serve for a day and a half's service. She kept a tight hand on the victualling houses. April went, and her four finest ships – the *Triumph, The Victory*, the *Elizabeth Jonas*, and the *White Bear* – were still with sails unbent, 'keeping *Chatham church*' (in reserve). She said they would not be wanted and it would be a waste of money to refit them.

Again she was forced to yield at last, and the four ships were got to sea in time, the workmen in the yards making up for the delay; but she still had pitifully few ships available, even when her whole fleet was out in the Channel. Had it not been for the privateers, things could have turned out very differently when the final trial came. The Armada was coming now. There was no longer a doubt of it. Lord Henry Seymour was left with five Queen's ships and thirty London adventurers to watch Parma and the Narrow Channel. Howard, who had changed ships from *White Bear* and now carried his own flag in the *Ark Royal*, joined Drake sailing in the 500 ton *Revenge* at Plymouth with seventeen others.

Still the numbing hand of his mistress pursued him. Food supplies had been issued up to the middle of June, but he was left in no doubt that that was it, no more was to be allowed. The weather was desperate – the wildest summer ever known – and the south-west gales brought the Atlantic rollers right into the Sound. Drake lay inside, perhaps behind the island which to this day bears his name. Howard rode out the gales under Mount Edgecombe, frustrated and fed up, and as the days went by, so his vital provisions got less and less. The rations were cut down to make the stores last longer. Owing to the many changes, the ships crews had been hastily raised, but they were ill-clothed and ill-provided in every way. Incredibly they complained of nothing. They caught fish to supplement their meagre rations, and prayed only for the speedy coming of the enemy.

Even Howard's heart failed him now. English sailors would do what could be done by man, but they could not fight with famine. 'Awake, Madam', he wrote to the Queen, 'awake, for the love of Christ, and see the villainous treasons round about you.'

Finally he achieved success and goaded her into ordering supplies for one more month, but this was to be positively the last. The victuallers inquired if they should make further preparations, but Queen Elizabeth answered peremptorily, 'No'. The hope of England at that moment was in her patient suffering sailors at Plymouth. Each morning they looked out with hopeful, expectant eyes for the Spanish sails. For them, time was a worse enemy than the Spanish galleons. The six weeks would soon be gone, and the Queen's ships would have to leave the seas if the crews were not to starve. Drake had certain news that the Armada had sailed, but where was it? Once he dashed out as far as Ushant, but then turned back, in case it should pass him in the night and they would leave Plymouth undefended. Men died of starvation and privation and smaller grew the messes and leaner and paler the seamen's faces. Still not a man murmured or gave in.

It was now the last ten days of July, and Howard's Fleet had half-rations for only one more week, and powder for two days' fighting. That was all. On so light a thread such mighty issues were now depending.

As darkness fell on Friday night 19th July, the beacons were seen blazing all up the coast and inland on the tops of the hills. Down in Plymouth harbour, Howard realised just how narrow was the time margin if the fleet were not to be trapped in harbour, or still on the lee shore with a south west wind blowing and the Spaniards sailing up the Channel with the wind. For six hours from 3 p.m. to 9 p.m. on that fateful day, the full flood stream of the tide surged into Plymouth Sound and no ship could move against it. At the turn of the tide, all crews were aboard and ready and the laborious task of getting the ships to sea was started. Slowly and with great difficulty the English seamen managed to warp the ships out, either towing from rowing boats, or hauling them on cables from winches set up on Drake's Island and other suitable positions round the harbour.

By first light on the morning of Saturday 20th July 1588, most of the available English fleet of fifty-four ships were safely clear of the harbour, and had gained a vital day and tide. Howard wrote to Walsingham on 21st July:

Upon Friday, at Plymouth, I received intelligence that there were a great number of ships descried off the Lizard; whereupon, although the wind was very scant, we first warped out of harbour that night, and upon Saturday turned out very hardly, the wind being at

south-west; and about three of the clock in the afternoon, descried
the Spanish fleet, and did what we could to work for the wind,
which by this morning we had recovered . . .'

The Spaniards crept on slowly through Saturday, with reduced
canvas, feeling their way – not a sail to be seen. At midnight a pinnace
brought in a fishing-boat and they learnt that on the sight of the signal
fires, the English had manned all available ships and had come out
from Plymouth, during the morning of 20th July. Presently, when the
moon rose, they saw sails passing between them and the land. With
daybreak on Sunday 21st July, the whole scene became visible, and
the curtain lifted on the first act of the drama. The Armada was
between Rame Head and the Eddystone, or a little to the west of it.
Plymouth Sound was right open to their left. The breeze, which had
dropped in the night, was freshening from the south-west, and right
ahead of them, outside the Mew Stone, were eleven ships
manoeuvring to get to windward.

Towards the land were some forty others, of various sizes, and this
formed, as far as they could see, the whole English force. In numbers
the Spaniards were nearly three to one. In the size of the ships there
was no comparison. With these advantages the Duke decided to
engage, and a signal was made to hold the wind and keep the enemy
apart. The eleven ships ahead were Howard's squadron; those inside
were Drake and the adventurers.

With some surprise the Spanish officers saw Howard in *Ark Royal*
reach easily to windward out of range and join Drake. The whole
English fleet then passed out close-hauled in line behind them and
swept along their rear, using guns more powerful than theirs and
pouring in broadsides from a safe distance with deadly effect.
Recalde, with Alonzo de Leyva and Oquendo, who came to his help,
tried desperately to close; but they could make nothing of it. They
were out-sailed and out-cannoned. The English fired five shots to
one of theirs, and the effect was the most destructive because, as with
Rodney's action at Dominica, the galleons were crowded with
troops, and shot and splinters told terribly among them.

The experience was new and not agreeable. Recalde's division was
badly cut up, and a Spaniard present observed that 'certain officers
showed cowardice' – a snipe at the Duke, who had kept out of the
fire. The action lasted till four in the afternoon. The wind was then
freshening fast and the sea rising. Both fleets had by this time passed

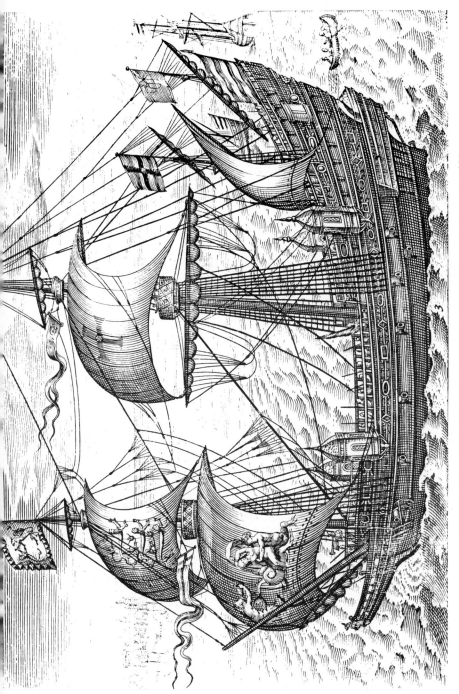

Ark Ralegh: launched at Deptford on 12th June 1587; she was broken up in 1636.

HMS *Ark Royal* (Dardanelles) in the Aegean in 1916; the photograph shows the first Short Type 166 being lowered into the water by steam crane.

A Short Folder Type 166 being hoisted out of the hold of HMS *Ark Royal*, the first vessel to be completed as an aircraft carrier in 1914. The use of aircraft with folding wings for close stowage in small ship hangars was devised for the light cruiser *Hermes*, fitted with a launching platform and two seaplanes for the 1913 Naval Review, but restored to her original condition before war broke out.

the Sound, and the Duke, seeing that nothing could be done, signalled to bear away up Channel, with the English following two miles astern. Recalde's own ship, *Santa Ana* had been an early casualty. She was observed to be leaking badly, to drop behind, and to be in danger of capture. Pedro de Valdez wore round to help him in the *Nuestra Señora del Rosario*, of the Andalusian squadron, fouled the *Santa Catalina* in turning, broke his bowsprit and foretopmast, and became unmanageable.

The Andalusian *Nuestra Señora del Rosario* was one of the finest ships in the Spanish fleet, and Don Pedro de Valdez one of the ablest and most popular commanders. She had 500 men on board, a large sum of money, and among other treasures, a box of jewel-hilted swords, which Philip was sending over to the English Catholic peers.

But it was growing dark. Sea and sky looked ugly. The Duke was flustered and unhappy with his first encounter with the English ships, so he ordered the Spanish vessels to continue up Channel and leave de Valdez to his fate. Alonso de Leyva and Don Miguel Oquendo – two of his commanders – rushed aboard the flagship *San Martin* to protest. It was no use and the Duke remained firm. Don Diego Flores de Valdes, the man in charge of seamanship and advisor to the Duke, said that the squadron could not afford to shorten sail or they would lose contact with the ships ahead. He added that the Armada would probably be scattered with night coming on, and in enemy waters it was imperative to keep together, even at the cost of abandoning one ship. The deserted *Nuestra Sẽnora del Rosario* made a brave defence, but could not save herself. With the jewelled swords, 50,000 ducats and a welcome supply of powder, she fell into Drake's hands. In company with the *Roebuck*, she reached Torbay on 26th July and de Valdes who stayed on board Drake's *Revenge* for ten days, was eventually sent to London with some of his officers pending arrangements for his ransom.

Earlier that day and off Start Point there had been an extremely unpleasant disaster, which had put everyone in the Spanish fleet in extremely bad humour. It has been alleged that during that first afternoon, a quarrel broke out between the soldiers and seamen aboard the *San Salvador* of Oquendo's Guipuscoan squadron. Suddenly an enormous explosion ripped the ship and rendered her into a helpless drifting wreck. Both stern decks were destroyed and two hundred men killed outright. She carried the paymaster-general of the fleet and a part of the King's treasure, so the ensuing alarm and chaos was considerable. Various reasons and theories have been put forward to account for the mysterious explosion, but the most popularly accepted is the one involving a Flemish gunner from the Netherlands whose honour was outraged by his captain, and so he threw a lighted torch into a nearby powder barrel and then jumped overboard.

The Duke of Medina Sidonia carried out a rescue operation and managed to save the treasure and some of the crew. The Spaniards then left the hulk and its grisly complement of dead and dying soldiers and seamen to its fate. Some reports suggest that the *San Salvador* was to have been scuttled, but Hawkins came up in his ship *Victory* and drove off the boats sent in to sink her. Lord Thomas Howard, captain of the *Golden Lion* and the Admiral's twenty-seven-year-old nephew, closed the helpless, rolling and abandoned wreck of the *San Salvador* together with the *Victory*, and was ordered to board one of *Victory's* skiff boats and examine the wreck . . .

> All the superstructure of the ship had been wracked by fire, and there were still aboard fifty men . . . who had been burned by the gunpowder and some languished, not yet dead, and the stench was so overpowering and the ship everywhere so filthy that Howard very soon left, forbidding his soldiers to board her.

The wreck was eventually towed to Weymouth after a very difficult salvage operation, which involved considerable risk to all concerned.

Two such accidents following an unsuccessful engagement did not tend to reconcile the Spaniards to the Duke's command. Pedro de Valdez was universally loved and honoured, and his desertion in the face of an enemy so inferior in numbers was regarded as scandalous. Although he was treated most courteously in England and eventually restored to Spain in honour and health, to the public at large he remained a victim and a sacrifice. Monday morning broke heavily for the Spaniards, for although the wind had died down there was still a considerable swell, and as elusive as ever, the hated English ships hull down and astern of the Spanish fleet.

All through the day, each fleet moved slowly up the Channel watching each other and preparing for the next move. They took advantage of the lull to repair all the damage and nail lead over the many shot-holes. De Recalde, in the *Santa Ana*, was moved up to the front centre of the formation to keep him out of harm's way and allow him to effect some very necessary repairs. Alonso de Leyva, in command of the land forces under the Duke moved over to the rear in the *Rata Coronada* and ordered all ships to keep tight formation. He added that any captain who failed to keep his proper station would be hanged and thus he aggravated the rift which already existed between the soldiers and sailors in the Spanish fleet. As the afternoon wore on, both fleets were in orderly fashion and sailing across Lyme Bay. The wind continued to fall and with it, the sea.

At sunset they were outside Portland. The English had come up within a league; but it was now dead calm, and they drifted apart in the tide. The Duke thought of nothing, but at midnight the Spanish officers stirred him out of his sleep to urge him to set his great galleasses to work; now was their chance. The dawn gave them a still better opportunity, for it brought an east wind, and the Spaniards had now the weather-gauge. Could they once close and grapple with the English ships, their superior numbers would then assure them a victory, and Howard and the *Ark Royal* being to leeward and inshore, would have to pass through the middle of the Spanish line to recover his advantage.

However, it was the same story. The Spaniards could not use an opportunity when they had one. New and designed to give manoeuvrability and superiority of speed when under sail, the English ships had the same advantage over the galleons as the steam-turbine cruisers would have over the old three-deckers or even clipper ships. While the breeze held they went where they pleased. The Spaniards were out-sailed, out-matched, and completely crushed by guns of longer range. To add to their frustrations, their own shot flew high over the low English hulls, while every English ball ripped and tore its way through their own towering sides.

This time it was the *San Martin* who was in the thick of it. Her double timbers were smashed and holed; the holy standard was cut in two; the water poured through the shot-holes. As the battle grew more fierce, the men lost their nerve, and in those ships . . . 'as had no gentlemen on board notable signs were observed of flinching'.

At the end of that day's fighting the English powder gave out. Two days' service had been the limit of the Queen's allowance, and though Howard had pressed for a more liberal supply at the last moment, he had received the characteristic answer that he must state precisely how much he wanted before more could be sent. The lighting of the beacons had quickened the official pulse a little, and a small amount of powder had been despatched to Weymouth or Poole, but no more could be done till it arrived. The Duke was left to smooth his ruffled plumes and drift on upon his way.

By this time it seemed England had woken up and fresh privateers, with powder, meat, bread, fruit, anything that they could bring, were pouring out from the Dorsetshire harbours. Sir George Carey had come from the Needles in time to share the honours of the last battle, 'round shot', as he said, 'flying thick as musket balls in a skirmish on land'.

The Duke had observed uneasily from the *San Martin*'s deck that his pursuers were growing more numerous almost by the minute. He had made up his mind definitely to go for the Isle of Wight, shelter his fleet in the Solent, land 10,000 men in the island, and defend his position till he heard from Parma. He knew that he might fight another battle; but, cut up as he had been, he had still only lost two ships, and those by accident. He held fairly high hopes that he would be able to force his way through – especially with help from above.

Wednesday, 24th July, was a breathless calm. The English were taking on their fresh supplies, and the Armada lay be-calmed and repairing damages. Thursday would be St Dominic's Day. St Dominic belonged to the Duke's own family, and was his patron saint. St Dominic he felt sure, would now stand by his kinsman, and it was about time he had a bit of help from above!

The morning broke with a light air. The English would be less able to move, and with the help of the galleasses he might hope to come to close quarters at last. Howard seemed inclined to give him his wish. With just wind enough to move, the Lord Admiral led in the *Ark Royal* straight down on the Spanish centre. The *Ark* outsailed her consorts and found herself alone with the galleons all round her. At that moment the wind dropped. The Spanish boarding parties were at their posts, the tops were manned with musketeers, and the grappling irons all prepared to fling into the *Ark*'s rigging.

At last they had the English Admiral in their grasp. But each day's experience was to teach them a new lesson. Almost before they realised what was happening, eleven boats dropped from the *Ark*'s sides and took her in tow. Then breeze rose again and she began to move. Slowly her sails filled, and she slipped away through the water, leaving the Spaniards as if they were at anchor and staring in helpless and frustrated amazement.

The wind also brought up Drake in *Revenge* and the rest of the English ships, and once more they commenced the terrible cannonade from which the Armada had already suffered so frightfully. That morning, it seemed to the poor Spaniards as if the English were using guns of even heavier calibre than on either of the preceding days. Of course the guns had not been changed, and the growth was a figment of their own frightened imagination.

The Duke had other causes for uneasiness. His own supplies of powder and shot were also giving out under the unexpected demands made upon them. One battle was the utmost which he had looked for. He had fought three, and the end was no nearer than before. With resolution he might still have made his way into St Helen's roads, for the English were evidently afraid to close with him. A report of the battle states that from the Duke's point of view . . . 'When St Dominic failed him too, he lost his head, then he lost his heart, and losing heart he lost all.'

In the Solent he would have been comparatively safe, and he could easily have taken the Isle of Wight; but his one thought now was to find safety under Parma's umbrella and make for Calais or Dunkirk. He presumed that Parma would have heard that he was coming and would be already embarked, with a second armed fleet, and ready for immediate action. He sent on another pinnace asking Parma for help, pressing for ammunition, and fly-boats to protect·the galleons. Ironically Parma himself was hoping to be supplied from the Armada, since he had no second fleet at all, but only a flotilla of river barges which in any case, would need at least a week's work to be prepared for the Channel crossing.

Philip had provided a splendid fleet, a splendid army, and the finest sailors in the world except for the English, but he had failed to realise that the grandest preparations are useless with a fool to command. Perhaps the poor Duke was more to be pitied and less to be blamed then his master Philip. An office had been thrust upon him for which he knew that he had not a single qualification. His one anxiety was to find Parma, lay the burden of responsibility on Parma's shoulders, and so have done with it.

On Friday, 26th July, he was left alone to make his way up Channel towards the French shore. The English still followed, but he counted that in Calais roads he would be in French waters, where they would not dare to meddle with him. They would then, he thought, go home and leave him in peace. As he dropped anchor in the dusk outside Calais on Saturday evening he saw, to his disgust, that the *endemoniada gente* – the infernal devils – as he called them, had anchored at the same moment half a league astern. His last desperate hope was in the Prince of Parma, and Parma at any rate, was now within reach.

On Saturday, 27th July, just one week after their entrance into the Channel, they dropped anchor in Calais Roads. Technically this was a breach of neutrality. But Medina Sidonia, with diplomatic adroitness, sent a message to the governor of the town, explaining that the Invincible Armada had 'swept the English out of its way, and, before proceeding to the punishment of heretics, came to greet with good wishes and felicitations the land of the most Catholic king'.

The Governor of the town came off in the evening to the *San Martin*. He expressed surprise at seeing the Spanish fleet in so exposed a position, but he was profuse in his offers of service. Anything which the Duke required would be provided, especially every facility for communicating with Dunkirk and Parma. The Duke thanked him, but said that he supposed Parma to be already embarked with his troops ready for the passage, and that his own stay in the roads would be a short one. On Monday morning at latest, he expected that the attempt would be made to cross the English Channel.

The Governor took his leave, and the Duke, relieved from his anxieties, was left to a peaceful night. He was disturbed on the Sunday morning by a message from Parma informing him that, far from being embarked, the Spanish army could not be ready for a fortnight. The barges were not in a sea-worthy condition, the troops were in camp, and the arms and stores were still stuck on the quays at Dunkirk.

Even if Medina Sidonia had been able to move at once, it is very doubtful whether he would have been in time. If he had bad luck and a north-wester should blow, on an open shoreline with shoals and sandbanks close under his lee, he would be very poorly placed. Nor was the view behind him calculated to give him much comfort. There lay the hated enemy almost within gunshot, who, though scarcely more than half his numbers, had hunted him like a pack of wolves. Worst of all, they were now in double strength; for the Thames squadron – three Queen's ships and thirty London adventurers – under Lord H. Seymour and Sir John Hawkins, had crossed in the night. There they were, between him and Cape Grisnez, and the reinforcement meant plainly enough that his situation was precarious and trouble was in the wind.

After such a trying week, the Spanish crews would have been glad of a Sunday's rest if they could have had it; but the rough mauling which they had gone through had thrown everything into complete disorder. The sick and wounded had to be cared for, torn rigging patched up, splintered timbers mended, decks scoured, and guns and arms cleaned up and got ready once more. No one could rest; so much had to be done, and so busy were the crews, that the usual rations were not served out and the Sunday was kept as a fast.

In the afternoon the stewards went ashore for fresh meat and vegetables and came back with their boats loaded, so the prospect seemed just a little less gloomy. Suddenly, as the Duke and a group of officers were watching the English fleet from the *San Martin*'s poop deck, a small, smart little pinnace, carrying a gun in her bow, shot out from Howard's lines, bore down on the *San Martin*, sailed round her and almost impudently fired a shot or two as she passed, then went off unharmed. The Spanish officers could not help admiring such airy impertinence. Hugo de Moncada sent a ball after the pinnace which went through her mainsail, but did no damage and the pinnace retreated to safety behind the English ships.

A Spanish officer described the scene, but English accounts make no mention of the pinnace, though she doubtless came and went as the Spaniard says, and for some very obvious reconnaissance purpose. The English too, were in a poor way, since their month's provisions had been stretched to last for six weeks, and when the Armada appeared only two full days' rations remained.

In the weeks leading up to the Armada, the Queen had changed her mind so often, first ordering the fleet to prepare for sea, then recalling them and paying off the men. So confusing was the situation, that those whom Howard had with him had been enlisted in a hurry, and had come on board as they were, so that now their clothes were hanging in rags on them.

Worse still, they were still being poisoned by sour beer and were on the very verge of starvation. Howard would have to do something quickly to settle the matter or he would be forced to go home in a day or two.

In that same Sunday afternoon a memorable council of war was held in *Ark*'s green-upholstered main cabin. There were green and yellow fringes to curtains and covers, and fine glazing in the windows. Under the fresh-guilded royal arms Howard, Drake, Seymour, Hawkins, Martin Frobisher and two or three others met to discuss the next move. As the lanterns swung gently to and fro, the men talked. Finally, they agreed to use fireships to dislodge the Spaniards, and Palmer was sent back to Dover to collect all the suitable vessels he could get and prepare them for the task. In the event and as soon as he was gone, it was pointed out that he couldn't possibly get back that night and the sooner the Armada was forced to sea again the better. A number of private owners of vessels in the fleet volunteered to provide their ships for the attempt, and eight were offered, selected and made ready. Pitch was poured on the decks, over the sides, on spars and rigging and then they waited for nightfall.

The quick sortie by the pinnace in the afternoon, which was assumed by the Spaniards to be sheer bravado, was probably a rapid survey of the Armada's exact position – in any event, Medina Sidonia was soon to get a nasty shock.

It was a dark moonless night with a strong flood tide running strongly to the eastward, directly from the English to the Spanish fleet. At midnight they set the fireships adrift and silently the small, shipboard parties steered their vessels towards the unsuspecting and anchored Spanish ships.

It is reported that:

'The Duke paced his deck late with uneasy sense of danger.' He observed lights moving up and down the English lines, and imagining that the *endemoniada gente* – the infernal devils – might be up to mischief, ordered a sharp look-out. A faint westerly air was rippling the water, and around midnight the watchers on board the galleons made out the dim outlines of several ships which seemed to be drifting down upon them.

The vague shapes drew nearer, and were almost among them when they broke into a blaze from water-line to truck and the two fleets were seen by the lurid light of the conflagration; the anchorage, the walls and windows of Calais, and the sea shining red far as eye could reach, as if the ocean itself was burning.

In the pitch blackness of the night the sight of them struck terror among the Spaniards, and created complete and utter panic. 'They came flaring on', wrote a Spanish Officer, 'spurting fire and their ordnance shooting, which was a horror to see in the night.'

A signal gun from the *San Martin* ordered the whole fleet to slip their cables and stand out to sea. It speaks well for the Spanish sailors, for their seamanship and courage, that they were able to get clear without too much mishap. Crowded together in an anchorage at midnight as they were, it is surprising that there were no collisions and they even buoyed their cables, which they cut or slipped in their haste to leave, and hoped to return the following morning to pick up.

The danger from the fire ships was chiefly imaginary, for they seem to have drifted through the scattering ships without doing any real damage. With the single exception of the flagship of the galleasses, the *San Lorenzo*, they all got away. One hundred and twenty four vessels entered Calais, and one hundred and twenty three escaped.

The *San Lorenzo* galleass, with Don Hugo de Moncada and eight hundred men aboard fouled her helm in a cable as she tried to get under way, collided with the galleon *San Juan de Sicilia*, broke her rudder and soon became unmanageable. The Galley slaves mutinied and as the tide ebbed, the *San Lorenzo* went aground on the sand banks, became stranded and rolled on her side.

At first light next morning, the sight of the lonely, stranded Spanish galleass was too much for Howard in the *Ark*. His theory was, as he said many times: 'to pluck the feathers one by one from the Spaniard's wing', and here was a feather worth plucking. The *San Lorenzo* was the most splendid vessel of her kind afloat and Don Hugo one of the greatest of Spanish grandees, though both were now helpless in the face of *Ark* and the dreaded sandbank.

In his greed and haste, Howard made two serious mistakes. Lowering *Ark*'s boats, it took three precious hours to subdue the enemy opposition and get aboard. Don Hugo was killed by a musket ball and resistance ceased. The *San Lorenzo* was captured and plundered and Howard's men prepared to salvage the vessel and take her off when the tide rose. Unfortunately the French authorities ordered him off, threatening to open fire, so after wasting the forenoon, he was obliged at last to leave her where she lay. Worse than this, he had lost three precious hours, and had lost along with them, in the opinion of the Prince of Parma, the honours of the great day.

Drake and Hawkins knew better than to waste time plucking 'single feathers'. The fireships had been more effective than they could have dared to hope. The enemy was broken up. The Duke had already lost more than half his strength, and had got under way still signalling wildly, and uncertain in which direction to turn.

His uncertainties were ended for him when he saw Drake bearing down upon him with the whole English fleet, except for those which were still loitering about the galleass. The English had now the advantage of numbers. The superiority of their guns he knew already, and their greater speed allowed him no hope to escape a battle. Forty ships alone were left to him to defend the banner of the crusade and the honour of Castile; but those forty were the largest and the most powerfully armed and manned that he had, and on board there were Oquendo, De Leyva, Recalde, and Bretandona, the best officers in the Spanish navy next to the lost Don Pedro.

Called the Battle of Gravelines, the scene of the action which was to decide the future of Europe was between Calais and Dunkirk, a few miles off shore, and within sight of Parma's camp. There was no more manoeuvring for the weather-gage, no more fighting at long range. A chance had fallen to Drake which might never return; not for the vain distinction of carrying prizes into English ports, not for the ray of honour which would fall on him if he could carry off the sacred banner itself and hang it in the Abbey at Westminster, but a chance so to smash the Armada so that it would never be seen again in English waters. They could deal such a blow to Philip of Spain that the Spanish Empire would reel under it and almost cease to exist.

The English ships had the same superiority over the galleons which modern ships have now over sailing vessels. They had twice the speed and perhaps more important, they could lie two points nearer to the wind. Sweeping round them at cable's length, herding and crowding them in against each other, yet never once giving them a chance to grapple, Drake and the English ships hurled in their broadsides of round shot. Short though the powder supply was, there was no sparing it that morning.

The battle raged almost without respite until six o'clock in the evening. Following the example set by Drake at Plymouth, the English selected the range to suit their big guns, and poured such murderous broadsides into the Spanish ships, that the scuppers ran with blood.

'Never on sea or land did Spaniards show themselves worthier of their great name than on that day,' wrote an eye witness. The *San Martin*'s timbers were of oak and a foot thick, but the shot 'went through them enough to shatter a rock'. The Duke looked at his splintered and battered ship, her deck was a slaughterhouse; half the ship's company were killed or wounded and no more would have been heard or seen of the *San Martin* or her commander had not the Spanish ships effected a timely rescue and enabled the crippled vessel to slip away under their cover.

It was said afterwards in Spain that the Duke showed cowardice. That he ordered his navigator to keep out of harm's way and then locked himself up in his cabin . . . 'buried in woolpacks'. Certainly, as an unwilling sailor, the Duke had his faults, but cowardice was not one of them and he drew the hottest fire in the midst of one of the most bloody and furious engagements recorded in the history of sea battles.

An English officer, admiring the courage of the enemy, ran up the bowsprit of his vessel and urged them to surrender and save their lives. For answer they cursed the English as 'cowards and chickens' because they refused to close the range. The officer was shot for his troubles, though his fall brought a last broadcast on them, which finished the work. They went down, and the water closed over yet another Spanish ship. 'Rather death to the soldiers of the Cross than surrender to a heretic.'

At noon, Howard and *Ark Royal* who had been lured away by the galleass joined in the battle, and claimed a share in a victory which was no longer doubtful.

Throughout the long day, the English fleet harried and damaged the Armada, keeping always to windward of it and shepherding it ever nearer the dangerous Zealand banks, where the shoal water was a prospect just as menacing as the English guns. By the evening the Armada seemed doomed, split up into small parties and ripe for capture. The English ships closed in for the kill and it seemed to the terrified Spanish sailors that even God had deserted them. But just at that moment a squall swept down, accompanied by driving rain that made gunfire impossible.

The English ships turned back into the face of the wind, but the Spaniards, too battered and weary by their experience at the hands of Drake and Howard, sailed on before it. By the time it was over three great Spanish ships had been lost, and the remainder were being driven to almost certain destruction onto the sandbanks.

It was in this condition that Drake left them for the night, not to rest or recover, but to collect from anywhere if he could, more food and powder. Over seventy ships comprising more than half the Armada were far away, and perhaps able to fight a second battle if they recovered heart. To follow the battered Armada was his most pressing task. Howard and Drake had to drive them onto the banks if the wind held, or into the North Sea, anywhere so that they left them no chance of joining hands with Parma again. The English sailors were famished and in rags; but neither Drake nor they had the time to think of themselves or worry about food and clothing. There was only one thought in their minds, and that was to chase the enemy ships, and Howard was as determined as Drake.

Fate had compelled the Duke to pick between the English and the shallows of the dangerous Zealand banks, and the shallows seemed to him to be the lesser of two evils and certainly more merciful. On Tuesday however, the wind which had so far befriended the English, suddenly changed sides. The Armada was temporarily saved, but a harbour had to be found and quickly.

Three possible alternatives presented themselves – Scotland, Scandinavia and Ireland. He decided against the heretic lands and headed for the rest and comfort of the Catholic Ireland. Beyond Scotland was the open ocean, and in the open ocean he would be safe from English guns and sandbanks, thus with all canvas crowded on, he sailed on before the wind. Howard in the *Ark Royal*, Drake and the rest of the English fleet shadowed the fleeing Armada until they passed the Firth of Forth, and thus ensured that there was no more threat from the Spaniards. On 13th August they saw the last of the enemy sails, turned south again and headed for the Thames.

But the story of the final fate of the great 'enterprise of England' (the '*Empresa de Inglateria*'), and the misery and tragedy of the final voyage home, almost defies description.

Gales dashed many of the ships on to the perilous and rocky coasts round the north of Scotland and Ireland, and 25 Spanish vessels met their fate in this way, while the total loss to the Armada for its abortive attack on England amounted to 64 ships and at least 10,000 men. 'The troubles and miseries we have suffered cannot be described to your Majesty,' Medina Sidona wrote to King Philip of Spain in his report of the ill-fated action, 'They have been greater than have ever been seen in any voyage before.' Those words did less than justice to what must have been an unending nightmare to the unfortunate Spanish crews.

Tragically, the misery and death caused by privations was to hit the victors as well as the vanquished. As the fleeing enemy ships reached the latitude of Newcastle-on-Tyne, Howard himself had problems and was forced to give up the chase. Apart from an acute shortage of supplies and powder, disease – typhus, dysentery and scurvy – was beginning to appear among the crew and it was vital to return to port as soon as possible.

It is perhaps worth digressing for a paragraph or two, to give the reader some idea of the horror of shipboard life in those disease ridden days – four hundred years ago. Lack of even the most basic hygiene enabled epidemics to gain hold and spread with lightning speed throughout a ship. The primitive advice to Captains of ships on how to control outbreaks of fire aboard a sailing ship of the 1580s makes illuminating reading:

> Chain two hogsheads to the sides of your ship for the soldiers and mariners to piss into that they may always be full of urine to quench fire with and two or three pieces of old sail ready to wet in the piss.

It wasn't until 1596 that slightly more hygienic advice appeared exhorting the Captains that:

> You shall give orders that your ship may be kept clean daily and sometimes washed; which, with God's favour, shall preserve from sickness and avoid inconvenience.

Just as dysentery was the result of poor hygiene and scurvy the product of poor victualling, so typhus was the direct consequence of inadequate clothing. It is a sad and sobering reflection that in the long and violent history of warfare, particularly on land, typhus has killed many more men than any other single agency. In the days of sail it was known as ship fever and since it is carried in the human body-louse, it flourished in the conditions prevailing aboard the typical man-o'-war. Conditions which provided for no washing water, no soap and more particularly no changes of clothing. If an infected man came aboard, an epidemic could spread round the crew in a matter of days, decimating the crew and rendering the ship helpless to defend herself or sometimes, even to move. Before serious official action was taken to improving the standard of cleanliness and general conditions on board ships, typhus was the commonest affliction in the Channel fleet of Tudor times.

A more vivid view of conditions at sea is described in a letter which Lord Howard (*Ark Royal*) wrote to Lord Burghley just after the action of the Spanish Armada:

My goode Lorde, Sickness and mortallitie begin wonderfullie to growe amongste us: and yt is a moste pitifulle sighte to see here at Margate, how the men, haveing no place to receive them into here, dye in the streetes. I am driven myselfe, of force, to come a-lande, to see them bestowed in some lodgeyinge; and the beste I can get is barnes and outhouses; and the relief is smalle that I cann provyde for themme here. It wolde grieve anie man's harte to see themme that have served so valiantlie to dye so miserabillie.

The *Elizabeth Jonas*, which hath don as well as eaver anie ship did in anie service, hath had a greate infectione in her from the beginning soe as of the 500 men which she carried out, by the time she had bin in Plymouth three weekes or a monthe, there were ded of them 200 and above, soe as I was driven to set all the reste of her men ashore, to take out the ballaste and to make fires in her of wett broom 3 or 4 daies together, and so hoped therebie to have cleansed her of her infectione, and thereuppon got newe men, verie tall and hable as eaver I saw, and put them into her; nowe the infectione is broken out in greater extremitie than eaver it did before, and they dye and sicken faster than ever they did, soe as I am driven of force to send her to Chatham we all thinke and judge that the infectione remaineth in the pitch. Sir Roger Townsend of all the men he brought out with him hath but one left alive; and my sonne Southwell likewise hath many ded.

It is like enough that the like infectione will growe throughout the most part of the fleete, for they have bin soe long at sea and have so little shift of apparell, and so few places to provide them of suche wants, and no money wherewith to buy it, for some have bin – yea, the most part – these eight monthes at sea. My Lord, I wolde thinke it a marvellous good way that there were a thousand pounds worth or two thousand marks worth of hose, doublets, shirts, shoes, and suchlike sent down; and I thinke your Lordshippe might use therein the Comptroller of the Navy and Waker, Mr. Hawkyns his man, who wolde use all expedicyon for the providing and sendynge away of such things; for else, in very short tyme, I looke to see most of the marriners go naked. Good my Lorde, let marriners be prest and sent down as soon as may be, and money to discharge those that be sicke here; and so in haste I bid your Lordship farewel.

In the next century, attempts were made to improve the situation and reduce outbreaks of typhus by the provision of extra clothing: – 'to avoid nastie beastlyness by continual wearing of one suit of clothes, and therebie boddilie diseases and unwholesome ill smells in every ship'.

A diary entry from Henry Teonge, Chaplain aboard the *Royal Oak* around the later 1670s and almost 100 years after the Armada, shows that conditions were still very bad. 'On March 22nd, I buried Francis Forrest as 'tis said eaten to death with lyce.' It was to be another hundred years before things could be said to have really improved.

To return once more to the luckless Spaniards: soon after the Firth of Forth was passed, the ships that had suffered most in battle were in the hideous grip of a water famine. Food was plentiful, but could not be taken without drink to wash it down. Even the sailors lost all semblance of health. Urgent repairs to masts and rigging went untended and uncared for. The seams of the vessels opened, and there were no working parties with strength enough to man the pumps. The droves of cavalry horses, intended to carry the conquerors in triumph into London, were pushed overboard to lighten labour. But all to no avail. Before the Shetland Islands were reached some of the ships were beyond all human help, and with careless indifference, they sailed to their doom, smashing themselves like matchwood on barren, rocky and hostile shores.

Every day that passed heightened and intensified the agony and the suffering. Even if Spain with all its havens and welcoming doors had been just a few yards away, some of the great galleons could not have stumbled to the threshold. When the Atlantic was reached, with its westerly winds blowing freshly but not unkindly, the fortitude of brave men could no longer endure. The ships foundered upon the cruel lee shore in batches of twos and sevens and tens. In one part of Ireland a five mile stretch of sand was heaped, from end to end, feet deep with broken wreckage. And no one in Ireland realized how utterly vanquished were the would-be victors of England. The garrisons butchered wasted men whose claim to pity was beyond all question, and the superstitious peasantry thought it quite natural to knock on the head shipwrecked men of strange speech, whose clothes and money attracted them.

De Leyva, the second in command, and close friend of Philip II, was cast away in his mighty ship, the *Rata Coronada*, off Erris Head in Mayo. Recalde, the third in command and the idol of the sailors, tottered into the Shannon and offered a galleon in exchange for permission to fill his water casks. He was refused, lost four vessels off the Cape of Clare, and staggered home to Corunna, to die almost as soon as he came ashore.

Medina Sidonia, alone of all the higher command, survived to earn the thanks of his monarch and the curses of all succeeding generations. He had set out from Lisbon with some 130 ships, and no more than fifty came home again. He had left Lisbon with 30,000 men, and had lost more than 10,000 by shipwreck alone, without counting those who had perished in battle, or come home to die of their wounds. No disaster in the annals of warfare was more pitiable or more complete.

Some eight years later *Ark Royal* was again selected for service as the flagship of the Lord High Admiral, Lord Howard of Effingham, who together with the Queen's new favourite, the Earl of Essex, as joint commanders in the new galleon, the *Due Repulse*, was to lead a new attack on the Spanish base at Cadiz. Together with Lord Thomas Howard (*Merhonour*) and Sir Walter Ralegh (*Warspite*) there was gathered in Plymouth a fleet of 110 ships, including a Dutch squadron under the command of Jan van Duyvenvoord, Admiral of Holland.

The expedition sailed finally on 3rd June and in an attempt to delay detection and maintain the secrecy of the target, *Ark Royal* and Howard led the fleet on course well out into the Atlantic. The great force of ships reached the latitude of Cape St. Vincent without the slightest suspicion by the Spaniards that they had even set sail. Here they captured a number of small craft and from them learned that a considerable naval force was concentrated at Cadiz, including the West Indian flota, some 40 or more carracks well laden with goods for the Spanish colonies across the Atlantic. Cadiz, then, was a prize well worth the capture.

In addition to the ships, Essex had raised an army of soldiers to accompany the expedition. Well drilled and excellently equipped, they numbered some 6,500 men and provided an early interesting example of 'combined service operations'. Of the whole expedition

Sir George Carew, a kinsman of Ralegh's and one of the military commanders, could write:

> They are strong enough at sea to abide the proudest fleet that ever swam, and by land our army, both in numbers and gallant men, is of strength to march and retreat in safety from a more puissant enemy than we are like to find.

So far all had gone wonderfully well and the stage was set for a complete surprise on one of Spain's greatest naval harbours. But on June 15th, as the ships rounded Cape St. Vincent, they were sighted from the shore with lightning speed. The news spread along the coast and the officers at Cadiz began to make their plans for defence. In the harbour were four great galleons of the Guard, known as the 'four Apostles', twenty war galleys, three Portuguese galleons, three strongly armed Levant ships, and three frigates, as well as the 40 carracks of the flota.

The town of Cadiz lies at the end of a long neck of land projecting out into the sea from the Island of Leon. The entrance to the outer harbour is guarded by Fort St. Philip, in Cadiz itself, and the Castle of Santa Catalina on the mainland opposite. The outer harbour narrows to a channel little more than half a mile across before widening into a great bay which forms the inner harbour, and Fort Puntal commands the channel. In the inner harbour lies the village of Carraca, on the bank of a long creek which connects with the sea again nine miles below Cadiz, thus forming the Island of Leon. Two miles south of Carraca the creek is crossed by the Punto Zuarro, a bridge which carried the main road from the mainland to Cadiz.

The English ships arrived off Cadiz on the morning of the 18th, three days after having been sighted near Cape St. Vincent. Early in the morning the *Ark Royal* captured an Irish bark which had just left Cadiz bound for Waterford, and from her captain Howard learned of the preparations being made to put the harbour in a state of defence. The news spread quickly through the English fleet that they would need to fight before they could capture the town.

> When this was once bruited in the army [wrote Dr. Marbecke, who was Howard's doctor in the *Ark Royal*], that there were so many ships, Lord God! what a sudden rejoicing there was. How every man skipt and leapt for joy, and how nimble was every man

to see all things were neat, trim, and ready for the fight, fearing all the way that they should never be encountered or have any 'sport', as they use to term it.

All that day the fleet sailed slowly towards the shore, making very slow progress in the light wind. And it was not until June 20th, at 5 a.m., that they reached a position from which they could contemplate a landing by the soldiers against the town. A council of war was called aboard *Ark Royal* and Essex – impetuous as ever – demanded to lead an immediate assault on the beach right under the walls of Cadiz. Howard called for caution and heeding the lessons of Drake, was all for attacking the ships first.

After a day of bitter wrangle and argument Essex's plan was adopted, with Howard to land a second and supporting force from seaward on the narrow neck of land joining Cadiz to the Island of Leon. Ralegh was to command an inshore squadron whose duty was to prevent the escape of any Spanish ships from the port, while half a dozen or so smaller vessels were ordered to prevent any attack by the war galleys.

Perhaps it is fortunate that fate took a hand and the wind freshened. In any event, Ralegh finally pointed out the impossibility of a seaborne landing and reconciled the two commanders. Howard agreed to sail *Ark* and the rest of the ships into the harbour, but because it was getting dark and no one – English or Spanish – relished the idea of night encounters, the ships lay off the town and just inside the outer harbour until morning.

Early the following morning, as the sun rose, a very curious state of affairs was revealed. So eager had been some of the commanders to lead the fleet into action that many ships had stolen secretly ahead during the night to get closer to the enemy. As they weighed anchor every semblance of order was lost and individual vessels tried to jockey the others out of the place of honour. Ralegh was first away in the *Warspite*, and as he closed the four great Spanish galleons drawn up in the narrows he anchored in mid-channel so that no other ship could, as he thought, squeeze past him. Vere, in the *Rainbow*, who had been engaging the galleys with the *Vanguard*, managed to get ahead over the shoal water, so that for a time he was in the van. Next, Lord Thomas Howard in the *Nonpareil*, to which he had removed from the *Merhonour*, forced his way past the *Warspite* and took the lead.

Ralegh was furious and weighing anchor, managed to drift up the channel ahead of the *Nonpareil* again, and again anchored, once more nearest the enemy. Next it was the turn of Essex. He barged his way through the ships and, after an exciting few minutes when he fouled the *Dreadnought*, dropped anchor a ship's length ahead of Ralegh. Vere in the *Rainbow*, seeing another chance to get ahead, sent off one of his boats with a hawser which he made fast to the *Warspite*, hoping to haul himself up alongside before his trick was noticed. Unfortunately for him, Ralegh discovered what was happening and ordered the rope to be cut.

As if all this were not sufficient, Howard himself, who had been busily engaged against the Cadiz forts, decided to take a hand. His own ship, the *Ark Royal*, drew too much water to have any chance getting up within range of the Spanish galleons, so he had himself rowed to the *Merhonour*, where with his own hands he laid and fired the guns.

It seemed complete and utter chaos and should have provided every advantage for the Spaniards, who were able to take the English attackers.

'The shooting of ordnance was great,' wrote Vere, 'and they held us good talk by reason their ships lay athwart with their broadsides towards us, and most of us right ahead, so that we could use but our chasing pieces.' Such was the accuracy and power of the English gunnery that, after about three hours, the Spanish fire began to slacken and Ralegh managed to get a warp out to one of the Spanish ships, the *San Felipe*, hauling himself up alongside in an attempt to carry her by boarding. Essex and Lord Thomas Howard followed his example and the four galleons, unable to face the fury of the attack any longer, slipped their cables and tried to retire inside the inner harbour.

Almost at once all four of them ran aground. The Spanish crews gave way to panic and began desperately to abandon ship. 'There could be seen tumbling into the sea', wrote Ralegh in his report, 'heaps of soldiers, so thick as if coals had been poured out of a sack in many ports at once, some drowned and some sticking in the mud.' Boats from the fleet raced in to capture the four galleons, but before they could reach them, two, including the *San Felipe*, had been set on fire and were burning fiercely. The other two, the *San Andreo* and the *San Mateo*, were captured intact and towed out as prizes.

There was a pause in the fighting as the two Spanish ships burned.

The spectacle [says Ralegh] was very lamentable on their side; for many drowned themselves, and many half burnt leapt into the water, very many hanging by the rope ends by the ship's side under the water even to their lips, many swimming with grievous wounds strucken under water and put out of their pain. And withal so huge a fire and such tearing of the ordnance in the great 'Philip' and the rest, when the fire came to them, as if any man had a desire to see Hell itself, it was there most lively figured.

As Spanish resistance on water ended, it was Essex who decided to launch an attack on the town of Cadiz. Without waiting to consult Howard, his joint commander, he ordered his soldiers into the boats and, drawn up in an exact and precise formation, led them to the shore. It was a wonderful and awe-inspiring sight. They rowed ashore in strict silence except for the beat of drums, which gave time to the rowers. Every boat was in its station and ahead of them was Essex in his barge, flying his banner. They landed near the Puntal fort, and the meticulous exactness of their advance so terrified the Spaniards that they abandoned the fort without firing a single shot.

The town was taken that night after fierce fighting and given over to the sack. Yet such was the discipline among Essex's troops that their behaviour was exemplary and all prisoners were treated with the greatest consideration.

The success of the mission was unquestioned, but in spite of Essex's pleas to exploit their victory, by holding on to Cadiz or hunting for Spanish ships, the fleet came home to England.

Ark Royal was once more called upon to be the flagship as the dying Philip of Spain sailed his third and last Armada against England on 9th October. As in 1588, so in 1597, the gales played a decisive hand and the third Armada was finished before it could even enter the Channel. The badly manned galleons floundered into a fierce northern gale and were left scattered and sinking. The disorganised fleet crept back into its ports. King Philip was kneeling in his chapel in the Escorial praying for his ships and success, but before the news of their ignominious return could reach him, he suffered a paralytic stroke.

It was the end of his hopes and dreams and he died early in the following year, an unloved despot who had through his obsessions reduced Spain from the richest country in the World to the very depths of poverty.

In the early hours of the morning of March 24, 1603, Queen Elizabeth died and thus ended the Tudor dynasty. For the Great English Navy it was the start of a steady and tragic decline and for *Ark Royal* the beginning of the end.

She never saw action again under her own name. James I acceded to the throne in April 1603 and a very battered *Ark Royal* was rebuilt at Woolwich some five years later. As soon as the task was finished she was launched and renamed *Anne Royal* by the new King, in honour of his own wife Queen Anne of Denmark.

In 1625, under her own style and as flagship of Lord Wimbledon, she led yet another expedition against Cadiz – this time a disastrous one owing to the poor preparations made for it. When men were being raised it was said: 'the number of lame, impotent and unable men unfit for actual service is very great'. A letter from the *Anne Royal* suggests that better pay was what was required.

> Those in this action were the worst that ever were seen, for they are so out of order and command and so stupefied that punish them or beat them they will scarce stir. Their ordinary talk being that his Majesty presseth them and giveth them so little means that it was better to be hanged, or serve the King of Spain or the Turk

– which many of them did, like the notorious Captain Ward and his fellow renegades in the service of the Barbary Pirates, or in later years those that served the Dutch.

One other major factor which affected the outcome of this calamitous voyage was the old and inevitable problem of sickness aboard ship. Although common in Elizabethan times, the first really serious epidemic occurred on the Cadiz expedition of 1625. It is fact that a plague was raging throughout England at the time the ships set out on their voyage that year, and it is known that thousands of people were dying from a form of bubonic plague. But it is also true to say that the symptoms of bubonic plague were so well known by this time, that if the sailors had been suffering from that dreaded disease, then that word would have been used to describe their sickness. All the evidence available suggests that once again, the men were afflicted with a very virulent form of typhus, though at the time many records ascribed their illness to 'corrupt and stinking victuals'.

A quarter of all the men were either dead or dying before the force reached Cadiz and after only 21 days at sea. When the ill-fated ships returned to West Country ports, over five thousand casualties were reported and the ships themselves were in a terrible state. Few of them had sufficient healthy men left in the crew to man the pumps or trim the sails. In the *Anne Royal* there were 130 dead and over 160 sick and incapable of doing anything – well over half the crew. The stench and filth was unbelievable, and one Captain complained that his crew had a 'miserable infection and they die very fast', while another said . . . 'they stink as they go, and the poor rags they have are rotten and ready to fall off'.

Thus ended the last account of the voyages of the old *Ark* as she was always called. The slow decline of the Elizabethan navy continued and was not to be arrested for nearly one hundred and fifty years.

The end came for the famous *Ark*, or rather *Anne Royal* in April 1636, as she was moving from the Medway for service as Sir John Pennington's flagship, when she stove in her timbers on her own anchors and sank. At a cost greater than her original purchase price of £5,000 she was raised and docked, but found to be beyond repair and broken up.

Perhaps it is fitting that the last word should be about the sailors, who built up the legend of that first *Ark Royal* and helped to shape the traditions of our modern navy. However much we might wish to glorify and paint the Elizabethan sailor's life in rosy colours, there is a mass of contemporary evidence which tells a different story. The cruelty, disease, appalling and rotten food, poverty, lack of hygiene and the foul smell of the ships themselves. As Peter Kemp in his biography of the British Sailor[1] says:

> That he endured them with, on the whole, little more than good natured grumbling is little short of remarkable. That when the necessity arose he could rise to the heights of glory in spite of them is little short of a miracle.

[1] *The British Sailor*, J.M. Dent.

CHAPTER 2

The First Aircraft Carrier

Ark Royal II

Three centuries passed and many changes occurred before the name of *Ark Royal* was to be selected for another ship of the Royal Navy. During that time, the face of warfare at sea had changed dramatically, with the large, ponderous, ironclad dreadnought battleships assuming the predominant role in all operations. Battleships had replaced the galleon, steam and gun had made the sail and cannon obsolete – but now, the advent of the aeroplane would add a third dimension to war and change men's thinking yet again.

Today, in 1976, it is hard for us to look back something like sixty-five years and to really appreciate the problems that faced those early pioneers of aviation. Sophistication and automation are the new all-embracing words used to describe the highly technical and complex aircraft – both military and civilian – which can now fly at two and three times the speed of sound. Military aircraft can launch and direct their weapons from many miles away with accuracy on to an unseen target, whilst the giant 400 to 500 seat passenger aircraft are quite able to make automatic flights with only pilot monitoring.

Yet in 1914, just over sixty years ago a naval pilot wrote in his log book:

I flew back home almost on the surface of the water to cheat the wind of some of its strength. It took us nearly an hour to cover 16 miles. As a passenger I would have been sick. The bumping was severe. Another aircraft went up to 2,000 feet to avoid the bumps: that took over an hour longer to do the 16 miles.

This pilot was describing his flight in a seaplane during a gale in the Thames Estuary. After he had landed safely and while the aircraft was being pushed and manhandled into the hangar on its beach trolley, the seaplane was lifted by the wind and smashed against the jetty like a toy.

Indeed some of the toys in those early days were far more robust than aircraft. The pioneer flying machines were for the most part, flimsy affairs of wood, fabric and struts, with open cockpits and clumsy, unreliable pusher engines of less than 50 horsepower. Three amusing although quite serious Flying Safety tips of the time make interesting reading:

> *Horizontal Turns* To take a turn, a pilot should always remember to sit upright, otherwise he will increase the banking of the aeroplane. He should *never* lean over.

This was followed by advice on *Engine Noises*:

> Upon the detection of a knock, grind, rattle or squeak, the engine should be at once stopped. Knocking or grinding accompanied by a squeak indicates binding and lack of lubricant.

Finally, the pilot was given some sound advice on *Crash Precautions*:

> Every pilot should understand the serious consequences of trying to turn with the engine off. It is much much safer to crash into a house when going forward than to sideslip or stall a machine with engine troubles. Passengers should always use safety belts, as the pilot may start stunting without warning. Never release the belt while in the air or when nosed down to land.

From the pilot's point of view, it was an everlasting battle against lack of knowledge, unreliability and the elements. The early pilots thought themselves extraordinarily lucky to achieve a height of thirty feet before reaching the airfield boundary, and curious spectators threw themselves flat on the ground until they were sure the aircraft was safely off. As for aircraft armament, revolvers were carried for the 'aerial dogfights', and bombs were literally thrown over the side.

The development of naval aviation prior to the First World War owed much to the personal initiative of individuals of a pioneering cast of character, both in and out of the service. For example, Lieutenant G.C. Colmore, RN, learnt to aviate and qualified (Aviator's Certificate No. 15) on 21st June 1910, entirely at his own expense. Some six months later, the Admiralty selected four pilots to undergo flying training, but this decision was taken only after a civilian member of the Royal Aero Club had made the offer of the loan of two aircraft and the Club's facilities at Eastchurch, Isle of Sheppey. Even the tuition was free! The first official naval flyers, Commander C.R. Samson RN, Lieutenant A.W. Longmore RN, Major E.L. Gerrard RMLI and Lieutenant R. Gregory RN obtained their Certificates (Nos. 71, 72, 75 and 76 respectively) in April 1911, and afterwards the Admiralty purchased the two aircraft on which they had qualified, as well as two new aircraft. This created a unique precedent of one aeroplane for each qualified flyer with no reserves of the latter for crew attrition.

A fruitful collaboration developed between the Short Brothers – manufacturers of the aircraft – and those first naval pilots. Its efforts were directed in the first instance towards adapting the aircraft to alight on water by means of flotation bags attached to the undercarriage. The first successful landing was made by Lieutenant Longmore on 1st December 1911. However, such an arrangement did not permit take-off from water and this (earlier) achievement lies to the credit of private enterprise. Commander O. Schwann, RN, purchased a 35 hp Avro, fitted it with floats and flotation gear and made a successful first take-off from the water (by a British flyer) on 18th November 1911, at Barrow-in-Furness. He crashed on landing, but his design of wooden floats was adopted for the first Short seaplane, the S.41. Irony of ironies, five months later in April 1912, Commander Schwann qualified as a pilot!

While Schwann was making his contribution to the development of the seaplane, Samson's ingenuity was directed to another aspect – take-off from the deck of a ship. On 10th January 1912, he took off in a Short S.27, fitted with flotation bags, from a launching ramp built on the forecastle of the battleship *Africa* at anchor in Sheerness. He repeated the performance five months later during a Royal Fleet Review. This time he flew from the deck ramp of the cruiser *Hibernia*, in Weymouth Bay, but with the added achievement of taking-off while the ship was underway. On the same day, the float-equipped Short S.41 made its debut, taking-off from and landing on the water.

In May of 1912, naval and military flying units were officially brought together in the form of the Royal Flying Corps, which consisted of a Naval Wing and a Military Wing, together with a Central Flying School based at Upavon. Although the Central

Flying School was supposed to train all service pilots, the Royal Navy maintained its school at Eastchurch and commissioned seaplane stations at the Isle of Grain, Calshot and Felixstowe in 1912 and 1913. In 1913, (November) the Naval Wing was made responsible for the operation of airships, which had hitherto been operated exclusively by the Army, with the exception of the period between 1908 and 1911, when the rigid airship 'RI' was being built for the Admiralty by Vickers Limited. In September 1911, it was wrecked while being taken out of its shed during trials, thus more than living up to its unofficial nickname of 'Mayfly'. During the two years following the formation of the Royal Flying Corps, the Admiralty continuously pressed for the complete control of its own aviation, but this was not achieved until the 1st July 1914 – the eve of war – with the formation of the Royal Naval Air Service.

On 18th July 1914, the naval might of the greatest seafaring nation in the world, represented by over 200 ships ranged in neat lines over 40 miles in length, was anchored between Southsea and Lee-on-Solent for the Royal Review. For the first time in history, a handful of seaplanes anchored inside Gilkicker Point were to fly past to add their own salute to their King. For as *The Aeroplane* of 22nd July 1914 reported in its columns:

> For the first time in its brief history the Royal Naval Air Service carried out on Saturday last a job of work as an integral part of the Royal Navy . . . flying back round the Royal Yacht and down the centre line of ships in the evening 'at a height not exceeding 500 feet', according to orders.

'The significance of the air fleet,' said *The Times* in a leader on 20th July, 'none can miss ... This, after all, is the great, new, outstanding feature of the immense display.'

One month later, hostilities opened between England and Germany and for a while there was little for the Royal Naval Air Service to do. At once they flew a system of coastal air patrols to counter German mine laying off the Suffolk coast, and followed this with reconnaissance patrols to cover the passage of the cross-Channel Expeditionary Force to France. One of the early lessons to come out of these first few tentative uses of air power in support of the fleet, was that the seaplanes – still in the early stages of development – lacked the necessary range for scouting or reconnaissance ahead of the British battlefleet.

The answer lay in a ship capable of taking those seaplanes with it to sea, and the proof was provided by Commander Samson when he had flown from a special platform built over the bows of the old cruiser, HMS *Hermes*. She was able to carry and launch two seaplanes on trolleys from her short flying deck, but so successful had the experiments been that, late in 1913, the Admiralty took over an old trampship which was being built and still lying in frame on her building slip at Blyth Shipyard in Northumberland.

The merchant ship was fitted with a large launching platform built over her bows, and converted into a seaplane carrier of some 7,080 tons, thus was born the first aircraft carrier in the world. Given the name HMS *Ark Royal*, she was launched on 5th September 1914 and commissioned at Blyth on 9th December 1914 and under the command of Commander R.H. Clark-Hall, RN. She left Blyth on 10th January 1915, and calling at Harwich and Chatham, arrived at Sheerness at the end of the month. On 13th January 1915, the day that the Government decided on the naval attack on the Dardanelles, she was ordered to prepare to take part in that operation.

On 2nd August 1914, before Great Britain and Germany were at war, a secret agreement was drawn up in Constantinople between the German Government and the leaders of the Turkish Committee of Union and Progress, who undertook to do all that they could to bring the Ottoman Government into line with the Central Powers. The first sign of the influence of the pro-German Turks came on the 10th August, when the German cruisers *Goeben* and *Breslau* were allowed to pass up the Dardanelles Straits to Constantinople, where they were nominally purchased by the Ottoman Government.

Further, early in October, the Turks began to assemble large forces in Palestine, whence they posed a direct threat to the Suez Canal and Egypt. Consequently a British naval squadron was concentrated at Tenedos on 27th October, when the Turkish fleet steamed into the Black Sea to attack Russia by bombarding her ports. On 30th October 1914 an Allied ultimatum was presented at Constantinople, and the following day the British Government issued orders for hostilities against Turkey to begin.

Historians argue that two fundamental errors preceded the actual commencement of the Dardanelles operation. On 3rd November the squadron at Tenedos led by the battle cruiser *Inflexible* bombarded the outer forts of the Dardanelles for ten minutes, partly as a

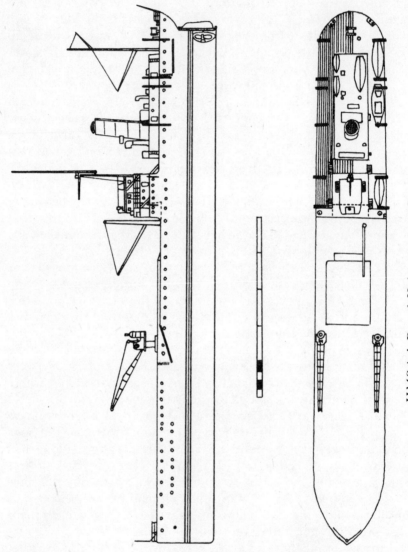

HMS Ark Royal II, later renamed Pegasus

demonstration and partly to test the effective range of the Turkish guns. According to the Turkish commander this action caused more damage than any subsequent naval bombardment, but although the actual damage caused was slight, it had the adverse effect of causing the Turks to strengthen the defences. Further operations against the Dardanelles were then for the time being suspended. The second basic error was the belief that slow minesweeping trawlers could clear a passage up to and through the Narrows to enable the British fleet to reach the sea of Marmara.

The year 1915 was but two days old when a request from Russia re-opened the question of whether to continue with another attack in the Dardanelles. The Russians were at this time being pressed in the Caucasus, and a hope was expressed that to relieve this pressure, a demonstration against the Turks might be made in some other quarter. Many critics of the Dardanelles saga both then and since have condemned the conception of a purely naval enterprise as the gravest mistake, which stemmed from the badly worded War Council recommendation to the Government which they accepted on 13th January, that the Admiralty would prepare for a naval expedition in February to bombard and take the Gallipoli Peninsula, with Constantinople as its objective.

Three days later, the First Lord of the Admiralty received a minute from the Chief of the War Staff, Vice Admiral H.F. Oliver and endorsed by Mr. Churchill.

FIRST LORD

Submitted that directions may be given for the Pilots and Observers, who will accompany the sea planes to the Mediterranean in "Ark Royal", to be attached to the Army in France as soon as possible for practical training in observing artillery fire.

They should go as soon as possible as they will require to leave for Medn. by the end of January.

Wireless telephones will be required for the sea planes and the ships receiving messages from them.

In her day the *Ark Royal* was something of a 'Wonder ship', and indeed marked a great advance in the employment of ship-borne aircraft. Unfortunately her aircraft (1 short, and 2 Wight seaplanes (200-h.p. Canton-Unne engines), 3 Sopwith seaplanes (100-h.p.

Monosoupape engines) and 2 Sopwith Tabloid aeroplanes (80-h.p. Gnome engines) were, with the exception of the one Short Seaplane, 'sadly inefficient for the work they would be called upon to do'.

An Admiralty paper unsigned and undated but probably written in 1915 gave details of the new carrier. With a complement varying between 140 and 180, this 7000 odd ton carrier had a Triple Expansion, 3000 h.p. engine which drove the ship at the maximum speed of 10.6 knots. Her armament consisted of 4-12 pounders and of course, up to 10 seaplanes. The paper then went on to outline her equipment and the capabilities of the aircraft.

SEAPLANE EQUIPMENT

Ship has a large hold in which are at present stowed six seaplanes and four land machines. There is a well-equipped workshop for their maintenance and repair. The seaplanes stow below with their wings folded back. To send them away, they are hoisted up by one of the cranes, swung round and landed on the forecastle where their wings are spread and they are then joisted up again, swung out by the crane and lowered into the water.

If the engine has been previously run on the same day, this operation takes about ten minutes, but otherwise the engine is usually run while the machine is on the forecastle which will add another ten minutes or more to the time . . .

It is not possible for the seaplanes to fly off the forecastle of the ship.

The four land machines have so small a wing span that they can be hoisted in and out with their wings spread. They can be flown off the deck of the ship but they cannot be landed on deck and can only be landed in the sea at considerable risk to the pilot and with practical certainty of seriously damaging – if not completely wrecking – the machine . . .

For use from a shore base, these four land machines are suitable and they can be landed without difficulty in the ship's boats.

The same author went on to say that the capabilities of *Ark*'s seaplanes were:-

(1) They fly at a speed of about 60 knots in still air.
(2) They carry fuel for about three hours.
(3) The engines are by no means reliable and the chances of

breakdown increase greatly as the length of any given flight increases. In other words the chances of engine failure during a three or four hours flight are more than three or four times as great as they would be during a one hour flight, and consequently long flights to seaward are not desirable as a matter of routine.

(4) Wind up to 30 or 40 miles an hour is no deterrent to flying and only a drawback inasmuch as it reduces the range of action of the machines. Seaplanes however, can only be relied on to get off the sea when the surface is moderately calm, a Number 3 sea or short waves of over 2 or 3 feet high being often sufficient to render this impossible.

(5) All seaplanes carry a passenger (in addition to the pilot) who can be used either for observing, operating the wireless or aiming bombs.

(6) Seaplanes can be towed in fine weather by destroyers or submarines at a speed up to 15 knots.

Strange reading for a person used to seeing a modern jet or hearing about Concorde!

Now, with her 8 aircraft safely embarked and stowed, the new and very unworked up carrier *Ark Royal* sailed from Sheerness on 1st February 1915 en route for Malta, where she arrived on the 12th. From there, she sailed eastwards to Tenedos and war.

The Turkish defences at the Dardanelles consisted of four principal elements: the forts, the minefields, torpedoes and floating mines. The last two were of secondary importance and this left the forts and the minefields as the major threat. The intention was to bombard the forts and suppress them with naval gunfire, then sweep up the mines, thus opening up a route for the main fleet to reach Constantinople.

It was just before ten o'clock on the morning of 19th February 1915, that the first shot was fired by the pre-dreadnought battleship, HMS *Cornwallis* at Fort Orkanie. Two days earlier, in the late afternoon on 17th February, the forts of the outer defences and the coast for three or four miles up the Straits had been reconnoitred from the air by a seaplane from *Ark Royal*. She arrived at Tenedos just after lunch on 17th and within a couple of hours, one of her seaplanes was airborne and busily carrying out a reconnaissance.

On the morning of 19th February the *Ark Royal* weighed anchor and proceeded to steam to a position just to the south of the Island of Mavro, anchoring just after nine. Before she left Tenedos she had hoisted out the Short seaplane to reconnoitre the coast from Besika Bay, eight miles south of the entrance, to Gaba Tepe, twelve miles north of it. The seaplane flew back to Mavro at 9.15 that morning, and the observer's report told the Admiral the exact position of the barracks and fort at Helles (Fort Number 1). More important, he confirmed that the guns at Cape Tekke could not fire northward of north-west, and so they would not be able to engage the *Triumph*, positioned and ready to bombard the Helles fort. At 11 o'clock a Wight seaplane left to spot on to Orkanie for HMS *Cornwallis*, but before it got into position the battleship ceased fire and the pilot was ordered by searchlight signal to make an examination of the damage done by the morning's bombardment. The observer's report showed that the guns were still intact in Orkanie, Kum Kale and Sedd el Bahr.

Later in the afternoon, the Admiral ordered the ships to close and attempt to smash the forts with a short range bombardment. While this was being carried out, two more seaplanes from *Ark* were over the fort at Helles trying to spot for the battle cruiser HMS *Inflexible*, but both were having trouble with their wireless. In one, the trailing aerial got completely fouled and tangled up whilst in the other the transmitting set short-circuited.* So many ships were firing on the same target, however, that in any case spotting would have been impossible, and the seaplanes were encountering fairly heavy ground fire.

It is perhaps worth discussing the Air side of the operations at this point, to give the reader a little more information about the 6 seaplanes and the 2 aeroplanes which formed the 'armament' of *Ark Royal*. In a contemporary document it said:

> Seaplanes can be used for scouting, for controlling gunfire or for offensive work. Under favourable conditions they may be able to locate submarines or even mines.
>
> Scouting. The range of action of the seaplanes carried varies according to their fuel capacity.

* The *Ark Royal* had brought out two Sterling wireless sets. The Sterling set at that time was hardly out of its experimental stage, and, in fact, had been supplied to the carrier before it had been put into war service in France.

Commander Charles Rumney Samson, RN, one of the first naval officers to qualify as a pilot at Eastchurch, Kent, 1911; in 1915 he played a distinguished part in Dardanelles operations in command of No 3 Wing. In 1929 he made his last recorded flight. In 1931 he died at Cholderton, Thruxton, Wilts, aged 47.

Cromaty Seaplane with the wings taken off being lifted aboard HMS Ark Royal after trials at the Scilly Islands 1922-23 prior to going back to the Isle of Grain.

HMS *Pegasus* (ex-*Ark Royal*) at Spithead in 1937. She still has the ramp built on the stern and used for the Hein Canvas Mat trials some four years earlier. Completed in 1914, *Ark Royal* was renamed HMS *Pegasus* in December 1934 and sold out of the service in 1947.

HMS *Pegasus* in her new role as a catapult trials and training ship after her short spell as an anti-aircraft (Q) ship. In nine convoys between 3rd December 1940 and 26th July 1941 she launched a Fulmar Fighter on three separate occasions against FW 200 shadowers and made one interception. In April 1950 she was sold to the British Iron and Steel Company and broken up at Grays Yard in Essex.

(opposite) The problem of finding a satisfactory and quick method of recovering seaplanes was still being investigated in 1933. A Hein Canvas was one of the methods tried and in the three pictures facing a Fairey IIIF attempts a landing on the canvas mat towed by HMS *Ark Royal* astern. The system was not successful and was later abandoned.

Job 1012 completed and ready for launching on 13th April 1937. Sixty thousand people watch the third *Ark Royal* launched by Lady Maud Hoare, wife of the First Lord of the Admiralty, after the official blessing by the Reverend W. Webb, vicar of St. Mary's, Birkenhead.

Three large 200 H.P. seaplanes are carried which have a fuel capacity for 4 hours flying. Their speed is about 60 knots in still air, which under ideal weather conditions gives them – allowing a certain amount for errors in steering a course – a range of action of about 200 sea miles when equipped for scouting only.

If equipped with bombs for offensive work, less fuel can be carried and the range of action is correspondingly reduced. One of these large seaplanes is fitted with 250 Watt Renzet Wireless Set working on an 830 foot wave which has a range of 50 miles. The equipment is only for transmitting. The wave length is sufficiently near that used by T.B.Ds for the messages to be picked up by T.B.Ds.

Three lighter 100 H.P. Sopwith seaplanes are also carried. When equipped for scouting only, these have a fuel capacity for $4\frac{1}{2}$ hours flying, and have in consequence a maximum range of about 225 miles. These seaplanes are not fitted with long distance wireless installation but can carry a light W/T transmitting set which is effective up to 10 miles. This set works on a 700 foot wave which can be received by T.B.Ds.

All these six machines may be used for controlling gunfire. Control of gunfire by wireless is at present being used with considerable success by our Army in France and a report on the methods in use there is attached. [Not reproduced].

Naval requirements are different and so far little or no experience on the subject has been gained. For the bombardment of forts, military lines of communication and bases of supply near the coast – when the fall of shot could not very well be seen from the ships – it might prove of great value.

In the more aggressive role, *Ark*'s aircraft could carry bombs, darts and machine guns. The document went on . . .

(1) *Bombs* – Accurate practice in dropping these cannot be relied on. As a rough guide to the accuracy that can be expected, it may be taken that a large target such as a dockyard would be hit from any height, but a battleship might very well be missed from so low as 1000 feet. If the target aimed at has slight or ineffective anti-aircraft defence, lower altitudes can be flown at and consequently greater accuracy obtained.
Two types of bombs are available viz:–

(1) (a) 100 lb. bombs containing 40 lb. of T.N.T. These are about equivalent in explosive effect to a 9.2 (inch) lyddite shell. The three larger seaplanes can each carry two of these.
(b) 20 lb. bombs containing 7 pounds of T.N.T. These are not quite equal in explosive effect to six-inch shell. All the seaplanes and aeroplanes are fitted to carry these bombs, the number carried varying from four to eleven.

(2) Steel Spikes or Darts (Flechettes) – These are intended for dropping on bodies of troops. The method of dropping them distributes them over a considerable area. They weigh 50 pounds per 1000 and can be carried as an alternative to a similar weight of bombs.

(3) Lewis Guns – These are machine guns firing the ordinary .303 ammunition. Two of the large seaplanes can be fitted to carry these and would then be available either for the attack of other aircraft or of troops on shore. The last named might be of value against troops in camp or on the march along a road near the sea coast, but the flying of seaplanes inland for more than two or three miles is not desirable, as in the case of engine trouble – if the seaplane cannot regain the sea on its glide down – it will be completely wrecked on landing on the ground.

(4) Incendiary Bullets – fired from a rifle for igniting the hydrogen of airships are also provided.

LAND MACHINES

The four aeroplanes carried,* have a speed of 85 to 90 miles an hour and a fuel capacity of $3\frac{1}{2}$ hours. They carry a pilot only and no passenger. They will carry four 20 lb. bombs or 1000 steel spikes. In order to utilize these aeroplanes, a suitable base on land with level ground for 400 yards in every direction is required, but as before mentioned, they can be flown from the deck of the ship.

To return once more to *Ark Royal*. At 5.30 p.m. the bombarding fleet withdrew, and at 7.05 p.m. the carrier hoisted in her seaplanes and returned to the anchorage at Tenedos.

* As already mentioned, *Ark* carried only 2 Sopwith Tabloid aeroplanes at this time.

The weather, which had been brilliant on the opening day, broke during the night, and for four days no operations were possible. On the 25th the bombardment in which the battleships *Queen Elizabeth* and *Agamemnon* took part, met with greater success, and the only four long range Turkish guns were put out of action. Although many efforts were made to get seaplanes off the water, the sea proved too choppy, and spotting for the bombarding ships on this day was done by other vessels.

They were experiencing some of the early frustrations and limitations of the unreliable and inflexible seaplane. 'The heavy and cumbersome floats over-taxed the low-powered engines, and we were constantly pre-occupied with keeping our machines in the air', reported the Senior Flying Officer in HMS *Ark Royal*, Lieutenant Commander H.A. Williamson, during the critical first weeks of the operation. Indeed the Aegean weather was anything but kind for more than a few days each month. As explained earlier, the seaplanes could get airborne only under virtually flat calm sea conditions, and even if they could climb to height, frequently they were being forced to return with engine trouble.

On the other side of the coin however, in modern terms, air superiority was complete and the fact that the Turks had neither aircraft nor effective anti-aircraft guns, went some way towards counterbalancing the seaplanes' inherent disadvantages.

It is perhaps surprising that Vice Admiral S.H. Carden, who commanded the squadron at the Dardanelles, and who considered aerial reconnaissance and spotting as essential, did not insist on some basic work-up practices. In the event, precious flying hours were squandered on non-productive flights, which added nothing to the success either to the campaign nor to the gunnery efficiency of the fleet.

On the afternoon of 26th February, the outer forts having been abandoned by the Turks, demolition parties were put ashore on either side of the Straits. An observer in *Ark*'s Short seaplane who had reconnoitred the area, earlier in the day, reported that three guns at Sedd el Bahr, three at Kum Kale, and one at Helles, appeared intact, but all other guns on these forts, as well as those at Orkanie, appeared to be 'out of place', although not necessarily destroyed. The demolition parties rapidly destroyed the armament at Sedd el Bahr and Orkanie, but had no time to deal with Kum Kale before dusk set in.

The following day a further party was landed at Sedd el Bahr and destroyed six modern six-inch howitzers on the cliffs to the east of the fort, and on 1st March, they turned their attentions to Kum Kale. Here the demolition party found only one out of the nine guns unserviceable and quickly destroyed all of them. Six 12-pounders to the westward and four Nordenfeldt guns, as well as a motor searchlight, were also blown up before the party re-embarked.

For something over seven hours, the *Ark Royal* had aircraft flying over the demolition parties, supported by the marines. This 'waste of time and effort' and 'an unnecessary and useless job' in the opinion of Williamson, meant that most of the valuable aircraft were unserviceable or temporarily out of action when they were most needed.

The bombardment of the inner defences began on 5th March, and the battleship, HMS *Queen Elizabeth*, the flagship, and the only one with sufficient range to fire the 14000 yds, was expected to take a leading part in their destruction by indirect fire across the Gallipoli Peninsula. For this, she would need efficient aircraft spotting, since she could not see the target and the gunlayer would correct for range and bearing as directed from the aircraft sitting overhead. The spotting for her was to be done both by seaplanes and by battleships inside the Straits. At 10 a.m. the *Ark Royal* closed the *Queen Elizabeth* in her position off Gaba Tepe, hoisted the seaplane out – a Sopwith – and an hour later it was airborne.

Ark had prepared four aircraft for this very important bombardment, but because of the requirement to fly in the preceeding few days, 5th March was to prove a disaster! Lieutenant-Commander Williamson was to do the spotting, and his Captain told him to take any machine and any pilot he liked. He took the best one available; his own special machine had been hit and damaged on the 'useless job' on the 4th. (Contrary to Admiralty regulations, on the way out from England he had altered this machine, exchanging the positions of pilot and observer to give the latter the best possible view for spotting.) Had they not 'wasted' those seven hours the day before, he would have had his own good aircraft. At the appointed time on the 5th the aircraft was hoisted out. Williamson has recorded:

It was a perfect day, with just the right amount of wind for taking off from the water, and we were soon in the air. It was an exhilarating moment. There below was the *Queen Elizabeth* with her eight 15-inch guns ready to fire and trained on the coast. The conditions were ideal; stationary ships and stationary target, only eight miles apart, and perfect visibility. I believed that there was every prospect of destroying the Forts, and that the Fleet would be able to go through the Straits and accomplish the object of the campaign by appearing off Constantinople. Few junior officers have ever been in a position so favourable and of such importance, and I was thrilled with confident expectation. We soon reached 3,000 ft. and were ready to cross the peninsula to the target . . . Then it happened. In a moment the machine was out of control and we were hurtling towards the sea.

For some unexplained reason the propeller had disintegrated and the aircraft went completely out of control. Moments later the machine hit the water and practically smashed itself into matchwood. Miraculously, both Williamson and his pilot survived the crash, badly shaken and with minor injuries, and were picked up by a destroyer. Another Sopwith was sent up immediately, but unable to gain much height over the peninsula, the pilot was hit in the leg by a rifle bullet and forced to return. Another pilot took over the controls and for the third time, the Sopwith went away again just after 2 p.m. This time the observer was able to signal a few observations before the battleship ceased fire owing to bad light. Although she had put quite a few of her enormous 15-inch shells into the forts, as was afterwards learned, no guns had actually been damaged, and operations were suspended until next day.

A further attempt was made next day, but no seaplane could get off, and the enemy succeeded in partially jamming the radio signals from the spotting ships. Indirect fire having failed, an attempt was made to use the *Queen Elizabeth* inside the Straits on 8th March. A seaplane was sent up in squally weather to spot for her, but the observer could see nothing owing to low clouds and once again the sortie was abortive. Observation from ships was equally handicapped, and this attempt, the last before the concentrated attack on 18th March, also ended in disappointment.

Between the vital period of 17th February and 5th March during which no less than fifty hours were available to Admiral Carden, most if not all were frittered away in wasteful sorties.

Even had things gone better, would the spotting of the *Ark Royal's* pilots have been of much use, given their lack of experience? Lieutenant Commander Williamson continues:

> It was, of course, true, that at that time neither I, nor anyone else, had ever spotted for ships firing at a shore target. (A good reason for doing a little practice before attacking the forts.) But it had never struck me that the spotting required would present any difficulty. With good visibility, no hurry, no interference by enemy aircraft or anti-aircraft guns, and a target which was stationary, in no wise camouflaged and very conspicuous, it would have interested me to know in what way it was thought that I would go wrong. This point is connected with an obsession which was strong in the Flagship. A conviction that they wanted aeroplanes and not seaplanes. I do not know whose idea this was, but it was so strong that within a few hours of the *Ark Royal* joining the Fleet a party from the Flagship, including the Flag Captain, came to us in a picket boat wanting an opinion on the suitability of a landing ground which they had chosen on Tenedos Island.

Obviously in some respects and under certain conditions land aeroplanes would have been more suitable than *Ark*'s seaplanes. Their major advantages were that they would be unaffected by sea state and without the heavy, cumbersome floats they would be able to fly faster and higher and out of small arms range. It was not made clear to Williamson or the other aircrew, why aeroplanes should have been better for spotting and observing.

Although *Ark*'s seaplanes had little or no chance for offensive operations until it was decided to land a military force, there were one or two nuisance raids on Turkish installations and ships. They were but small, irritating pinpricks rather than serious military attacks, nevertheless some damage was caused when a 100-pound bomb hit the main hangar of an enemy aerodrome at Chanak and destroyed a German aeroplane inside it. By far the most important work during these first few early days was the daily photographic flights over the peninsula which, pieced together, formed a composite picture of every defensive position in the area.

With the limitations of *Ark*'s seaplanes firmly fixed in the Admiral's mind, and since he considered reliable aerial reconnaissance essential to the plan to force a way for his fleet through the Dardanelles, he sent an urgent request to England for

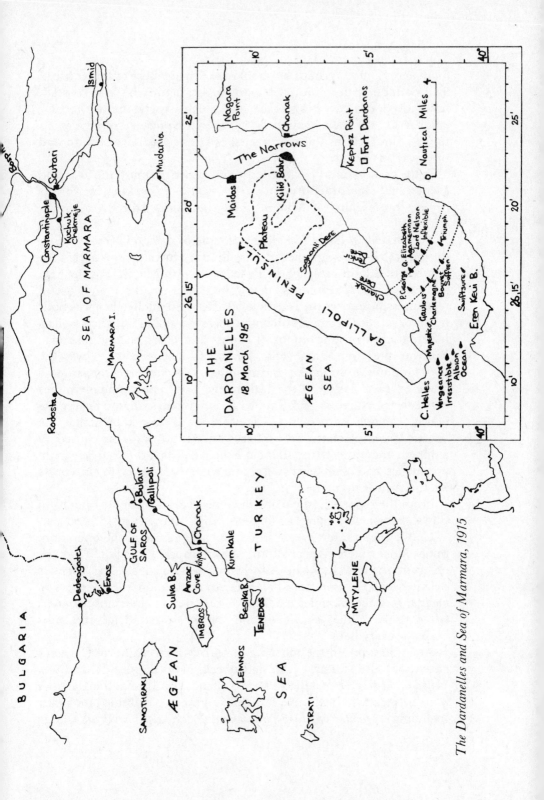

The Dardanelles and Sea of Marmara, 1915

more aeroplanes. Perhaps he should have made more or better use of his existing resources in *Ark* but to be fair, neither he, nor his staff, nor indeed the Navy, knew or had much experience of the new fangled air. He knew enough to realise that he needed more aircraft to give him a chance at the Straits, but that was in the future and time was on the enemy's side.

In the event Admiral Carden lost his chance to smash the forts and silence the guns, thus preventing the fleet from making the Straits before the fateful 8th March when the Turks laid their barrier minefield.

The *Ark Royal*, after spending a couple of days off Xeros Island, during which two seaplanes reconnoitred the fortifications across the isthmus of Bulair, returned to Tenedos on 12th March. For the next four days, her seaplanes flew often and made many useful reconnaissances over the Dardanelles. Detailed intelligence was built up and gun emplacements on both shores were pinpointed, as well as information on the locations of camps and other enemy positions. But the most important work, for much depended on it, was the searching of the Straits for enemy mines. Minefield reconnaissances made on each day from the 13th to the 17th reported many mines between the Narrows and Kephez Bay, but surprisingly, nearer the entrance, none were seen or reported. It is now known that the serious losses which the fleet suffered on 18th March were caused by a minefield parallel to the shore in Eren Keui Bay, that is to say in an area which had often been swept, and which, according to air reports had been clear up to the 17th.

From the reports in the Turkish General Staff account, Eren Keui Bay was sown with mines again on the night of the 17th-18th March.

Unlike the first few weeks in the opening phase of the operation, mines indeed were now providing the all important factor. Thus the object of the attack on the 18th March was to silence the Narrows defences and the minefield batteries, so as to allow the sweepers to clear a passage unmolested. The observation of the ships' fire was left entirely to the *Ark Royal*, and she was ordered to send up a seaplane every hour.

At 11.30 a.m. on the morning of 18th March, Admiral Carden's successor, Vice Admiral J.M. de Robeck, in his flagship HMS *Queen Elizabeth* ordered the Allied Fleet to silence the forts in the Narrows and the attack to begin. No less than eighteen battleships took part including: *Agamemnon, Lord Nelson* and *Inflexible*, as well as a large number of cruisers and destroyers.

An hour later a Wight seaplane from *Ark Royal* was flying over the Turkish positions and reported by wireless, that four of the forts at the Narrows were all manned and firing rapidly, but that the one known as Chemenlik (No. 20) did not appear to be occupied. The shooting by the big ships was good and three of the forts were being repeatedly hit, but owing to the volume of smoke and dust no estimate of the damage was possible. The forts at Mount Daranos and at Kephez Point also appeared to be empty and unmanned, but many mobile batteries around the area were active. Before the Wight landed, a Sopwith relieved him and took up the observation.

The bombardment continued for most of the day, and in cloudless, fine blue skies, the droning, orbiting and ever present seaplanes watched and reported back to the ships. Most of their messages carried only routine information, but others gave some cause for optimism. A number of the Turkish guns had been knocked out and others half buried along with their crews under tons of rubble and dust. Indeed the Turks themselves stated later on 'that they had to cease firing for considerable periods to clear dirt and grit from the guns due to hits on the parapets of the forts.'

By early afternoon, the intense enemy return fire and the well-laid defensive minefield began to make their mark. The French battleship *Bouvet* was hit as she turned at speed in a wide arc, slewed and shook under the blast of a violent underwater explosion, then capsized and sank with the loss of over 600 lives.

The first victim of the minefield. The battleship *Inflexible* was the next casualty. Soon after 4 p.m., she whipped and shuddered as a mine exploded under her keel, and although crippled and listing badly, she limped back to the safety of Tenedos. Three minutes later there was more drama. By this time only Hamadieh I (Fort No. 19), south of Chanak, was observed to be firing with real and effective determination. From the air, all the Fort's guns were seen to be in action and though shells from the ships were exploding in the centre of the fort, they were doing little or no damage to the Turkish guns. Indeed, almost at once, this fort concentrated her fire on the *Irresistible* which, after being hit and developing a slight list, also struck a mine and had to be abandoned. At five minutes past six, a third battleship, HMS *Ocean*, was also mined as she was withdrawing and she too, floundered and had to be abandoned after drifting helplessly for hours.

As soon as it became blindingly obvious that the area had been insufficiently swept, the engagement was broken off, and the ships withdrew. Despite the comparatively favourable air reports, we now know that very little permanent damage had been done to the forts, and that the Allied fleet had paid a very high price for almost negligible results. Three battleships sunk, a number of small ships including the *Gaulois* and *Suffren* badly damaged, and over seven hundred officers and men killed or drowned. To quote an official report: 'The day had ended in a very serious set-back, and the whole plan of operations had to be reconsidered.'

The Turkish defensive minefields had completely tipped the scales and achieved a remarkable success. The minesweeping trawlers had failed to clear the area in spite of an assurance by the commander of the sweepers that he had done so. In addition, *Ark Royal*'s aircraft had also spent many hours on minehunting sorties. A statement in the subsequent Mitchell Report quotes: 'On 14th–16th March seaplanes [from *Ark Royal*] had made a careful search for mines in the bombarding area and reported it clear of mines.'

De Robeck was fatally wrong in accepting their evidence at face value. Trials on 15th March had determined that seaplanes could locate a moored mine down to 18 feet when flying at 3,000 feet. But the experiment smacked of the bogus, the Mitchell Report observing wryly (p. 83), 'There is something misleading about this experiment, for no such satisfactory results would seem to have been since achieved ...' Under certain limited conditions of sun angle, water clarity, colour of mine and bottom of sea, etc., mines can be seen. But it was a grave mistake to rely entirely on it under all conditions. It is possible that the trial was done on a mine moored on a sandy bottom: there was a lot near Tenedos, which is where the *Ark Royal* used to anchor. In clear water it is easy to see one's anchor and cable on the bottom in 30 feet of water on a sandy bottom. The Dardanelles with its current would have a rocky bottom, which looks brown or grey, and the mines would not have shown up.

The failure of the sweepers and the doubtful value of the aircraft conspired to produce a totally misleading and false picture. The outcome for the Allied fleet was both tragic, unnecessary and disastrous.

Even before the ill-fated attempts by the battleships to subdue the Turkish guns, it had become increasingly apparent that even if the Navy succeeded in forcing the Dardanelles, the provision of military forces would be necessary to occupy the Peninsula. As early as 16th February it was decided that a force should be massed in the Eastern Mediterranean, and on 11th March General Sir Ian Hamilton was appointed in command. He arrived in the Dardanelles with a large body of troops, no agreed plan of campaign and the farewell words of Lord Kitchener to add encouragement: 'I hope you will not have to land at all; if you do have to land, why then, the Powerful Fleet at your back will be the prime factor in your choice of time and place.'

After the failure of 18th March it was quickly realised that the object of the campaign could only be attained by the strong co-operation of the Army, and then only by landing troops in strength. However, the military forces were not yet ready to undertake such an operation, and it was not until the third week in April that the landings were carried out. On 24th March the advance party of No. 3 Aeroplane Squadron of the Naval Air Service, which had left Dunkirk at the end of February, arrived at Tenedos, but owing to a gale the aeroplanes could not be got ashore until the 26th and 27th. Some days later the balance of the personnel and equipment arrived. The squadron comprising of eighteen aircraft of six different types had been asked for by Admiral Carden after the earlier fiasco on 5th March. They operated from an airfield which had been prepared for them by *Ark Royal* on the island of Tenedos. The air strength in the Dardanelles area was now boosted by eleven pilots, three observers, four ground officers and one hundred men, to maintain and fly: eight Henri Farmans, two BE2c's, two BE2's, two Sopwith Tabloids, one Breguet bi-plane and three Maurice Farmans.

Admiral de Robeck had decided to use the aeroplanes for reconnaissances of the Straits and surrounding neighbourhood, and to send the *Ark Royal* with its seaplanes to harass the enemy away from the area of Tenedos. This decision meant that land planes could not be used effectively except close to base, so the carrier, reaping the advantages of sea power, went off to distant coasts to the Gulf of Adramyti, to Smyrna, Enos and Bulair.

At Tenedos, the first aeroplane flight was made on the 28th March, and from now on the pilots of No. 3 Squadron were over the Peninsula at every opportunity which the trying weather afforded. Systematically the officers plotted the enemy positions; they controlled the ships' fire against enemy batteries, especially those hidden in the difficult country on the Asiatic side of the peninsula; they photographed the landing beaches and the ground in the area and wrote descriptions of the beaches as they appeared from the air; they corrected the inaccurate maps; and they dropped bombs on the batteries and camps. The reconnaissance information was the more important since air photography was at this time more or less crude and experimental. Most of this early photography was done by one officer, Flight Lieutenant C.H. Butler, with a small folding Goertz Anschutz camera. A better apparatus was then borrowed from the French squadron, which came out in May, and Butler fixed this alongside his seat outside the nacelle. By the end of June when he was badly wounded, he had exposed in all some 700 plates. These were then pieced together in groups to form maps of each important area, which were then passed on to Army Headquarters.

It was not until July that the enemy air activity in this theatre caused much concern, and even after this, the average number of aeroplanes in use during the latter half of 1915 was only eight, together with a solitary seaplane.

Whilst the naval aeroplanes were watching the enemy in the southern half of the Peninsula, the seaplanes of the *Ark Royal* were helping to divert the minds of the Turks to other possible landing places. On 31st March the carrier accompanied a small Allied squadron to Mitylene, where her seaplanes reconnoitred the northern coast of the Gulf of Adramyti. After returning to Mudros to refuel and take on a new Wight seaplane, she proceeded to the Gulf of Smyrna, and on 4th April, launched two flights to map the Turkish defences. In fact, in the two to three weeks leading up to the Gallipoli landings, *Ark Royal* and her seaplanes ranged far and wide in an effort to distract and confuse the enemy. On 6th April, after visiting Tenedos, the carrier sailed north to the Gulf of Enos and launched a seaplane reconnaissance of the town of Enos which preceded a feint landing on the 7th.

On the following day the *Ark Royal* returned to Mudros, embarked two Sopwith 'Schneider Cup' seaplanes, and then sailed for the Gulf of Xeros. She arrived on the 12th, and on 16th April one of her seaplanes, spotting for the battleship HMS *Lord Nelson*, helped to blow up a section of the magazine at Taifur Keui. On the same day, two Sopwiths reconnoitred Gallipoli and dropped bombs on the Turkish battleship *Turgud Reis*, which was anchored in Gallipoli Liman. On 17th April the *Ark Royal* returned to Mudros, and all flying over the peninsula ceased until the day of the landing, planned to take place one week later.

From the Turkish side, it also became increasingly obvious that an allied landing was inevitable. As day after wasted day of indecision went by, the thankful Turks repaired and strengthened their defences. On 26th March, the German General Liman Von Sanders arrived in Gallipoli to take command of the Turkish Fifth Army. Immediately he demanded more infantry, heavier artillery and a squadron of aircraft. Time was running out, but 'the British', he wrote later, 'allowed us four good weeks of respite . . . before their great disembarkation.'

By this time the air service had been augmented by the kite balloon ship *Manica*, which had left England on 27th March with a balloon section equipped for work either ashore or afloat. The ship arrived at Mudros on 9th April, and on the 15th her balloon made a first successful trial flight. The kite balloon had many advantages over any other form of observation. It could remain aloft all day and, since the observer was in uninterrupted communication with the firing ship, fire control was as nearly perfect as it could be. The *Manica* did her first spotting for the armoured Cruiser, HMS *Bacchante* on 19th April.

For the landing operations, the Army was ready at its bases about the third week in April waiting for a spell of fine weather. With the object of concentrating on the capture of Kilid Bahr and the reduction of the forts at the Narrows, Sir Ian Hamilton decided to land his whole force on the southern half of the Peninsula. The places chosen for the landings were: a group of four small beaches about Cape Helles; a broken cliff some three miles up the coast; and a beach (Anzac) north of Gaba Tepe, from where it was hoped the force might strike at the enemy's communications at their most vital point.

It was arranged that the landings should be made in towed, open boats except at Sedd el Bahr, where in view of the strong defensive position, the bulk of the troops were to be run ashore in the old collier, *River Clyde*. To cover the advance of the troops from the collier to the shore, across a bridge of lighters, eleven maxim guns were mounted on the forecastle of the ship. These maxims were provided and manned by No. 3 Squadron of armoured cars of the Naval Air Service which, together with No. 4 Squadron and No. 10 Motor Cycle Machine Gun Squadron, had been sent out to the Mediterranean to give a helping hand to the Army.

Before dawn on 25th April, the landing of the troops on the

Gallipoli Peninsula commenced. The Cape Helles landing was made by the 29th Division, supported by part of the Naval Division and later by a French Division. At the right and left-hand beaches of the Cape Helles landing, the troops were got ashore with little loss, but in the centre met with severe opposition. The *River Clyde* was run in at the pre-arranged spot, but unhappily the shore shelved more gently than had been expected, and the foremost hopper which was to form part of the bridge, grounded before it was high enough for the flying gangway to reach the beach. To add to the confusion, the connecting lighters broke free and swung away, leaving a gap between the *River Clyde* and the hopper. It was not until eight o'clock that a naval party, working under a murderous fire, got the lighters into a correct position for getting the bulk of the troops ashore.

During the whole of this chaotic episode, the entire weight of the Turkish fire power was concentrated on the hopper and lighters, and attempts to land ended in tragic and bloody disaster. The supporting battleships could do almost nothing to keep down the Turkish fire, and with the lethal hail of bullets inflicting terrible casualties, no landings were possible until nightfall. All day the Naval Air Service machine gunners in the *River Clyde* had kept up a duel with the enemy marksmen; not a gun went out of action despite the fact that in at least one casemate every man of the gun crew was wounded. The beach was littered with dead and dying; smashed boats, riddled with bullets drifted away in sinking condition; the sea turned red with blood and overall hung the dreadful reek of death and destruction.

Meanwhile the Australian and New Zealand troops had made good their landing north of Gaba Tepe and soon had the Turkish defenders on the run. They had begun to land just after four in the morning, and by half past eight advanced troops were entrenched about a mile inland. By two in the afternoon the whole Australian Division and two batteries were ashore, and holding a position with its right about a mile north of Gaba Tepe. During the afternoon and night, further troops, guns and stores were landed, but the opposition had now become very stiff and determined, and repeated attempts were made by the Turks to push the invaders back into the sea. It was very bad luck that bombs dropped by five aeroplanes on Maidos on the 23rd had been so effective that they caused the Turks to transfer two reserve battalions that were in the town to a nearby camp. This was some miles closer to the Anzac beach, and these troops were rushed up to the battle area at the first warning.

During the night of 25th April, the troops were at last got ashore successfully from the *River Clyde* and immediately pushed forward to the village of Sedd el Bahr. On the following day, in conjunction with the troops landed at the beaches to the right and left of them, the advance was continued to a point north of the village, where the position was consolidated.

From the first moment that the landings took place, the naval aircraft were in constant demand for support of the infantry.

The aeroplanes of No. 3 Squadron under Wing Commander E.L. Gerrard co-operated with the landings at Helles, while the seaplanes of the *Ark Royal* under the command of Wing Commander C.R. Samson and the *Manica*'s balloon worked at Anzac. In weather which was ideal for flying, the aeroplanes were up without a break throughout the day. The first aeroplanes were over the coast at dawn with others to spot for the ships covering the landing, and to direct their fire on to any Turkish batteries that were seen firing. As soon as the Turks opened fire, the aeroplanes had no difficulty in picking up targets, and soon urgent wireless signals were being passed to the waiting ships below. Unfortunately the covering ships paid little attention to them in the early stages, since they had more than enough targets already staring them in the face. Once the troops were actually established ashore however, the Navy had more leisure to deal with aircraft spotting information, and the aircraft were required everywhere. Throughout the long day, they kept up a never ending shuttle service as one relieved another over the Cape Helles area, and another replaced its predecessor over the Asiatic coast. Opportunities occurred for the aircraft to carry out more offensive operations, and they bombed guns, camps and troop concentrations whenever a chance presented itself.

In the beginning, steel spikes or darts (*flechettes*) were sometimes carried for use against personnel, but without much success. 'They were carried in boxes of 500, the boxes being fitted with shutter lids,' recalls Squadron Leader Teasdale.

The darts were about the size of a pencil, and were intended for dropping on formations of troops or cavalry; indeed, it was claimed that they were capable of passing clean through a man and horse. The containers were secured to the side of the fuselage clear of the lower wing, so that when the lid was withdrawn, the darts scattered away point downwards to the target. In fact they were found to be quite useless, as they tended to wobble during their descent, depending on the weather conditions; and when they wobbled they would not penetrate anything.

The seaplanes from *Ark Royal* and the balloon which watched the Anzac area were handicapped by the very broken nature of the terrain, although the Narrows and part of the Sea of Marmara were within view. The balloon had gone up at 5.21 a.m., on the day of the landing and fourteen minutes later, when the advanced troops were scrambling over the cliff tops below, the observer spotted the Turkish battleship *Turgud Reis* in the Narrows. He reported her position to the *Triumph*, which opened fire, forcing her to retreat over the horizon.

Soon after nine she reappeared again and commenced to bombard the Anzac transports. These in turn were forced to move out of range, but the *Triumph*, spotted for by the balloon, once more engaged the Turkish battleship and forced her to depart so that the disembarkation could continue. It was not until after 2.00 p.m. that the balloon was hauled down for the first time. For nearly nine hours the same observer had been on constant duty watching the Anzac's right flank, spotting on the Turkish positions in the area, and working in close co-operation with the *Triumph*.

Ark's seaplanes had greater dificulty in finding the Turkish batteries, which were well concealed in the scrub. This was made particularly difficult because the gunners held back their fire whenever a seaplane came near them. To take full advantage of these unexpected and enforced silences, General Birdwood asked that as far as possible, the seaplanes should try to remain in the area of the front lines, especially while movements of friendly troops were being made. This was done and the volume of Turkish fire kept down, thus easing to some extent, the pressure on the infantry.

On the air side, a letter from Wing Commander C.R. Samson to Commodore M.F. Sueter dated 2 May 1915, probably from the *Ark Royal* at Mudros, makes fascinating reading . . .

Dear Commodore Sueter:
So far we have had wonderful luck. Up to to-day our mileage is 18,851 miles, which is pretty nearly a record as the average number of machines is six. Information from a prisoner states that one of our 100 lb. bombs killed 23 soldiers. I had the luck also to

hit a big howitzer full and square with a 100 lb. bomb.

We live in the air all day and it is taking it out of our machines. I am not too keen on the BE 2c, as they climb rottenly carrying a passenger, and we have a lot of passenger work to do. Some more M. Farmans, 100 Renaults or sister machines to 1241 are urgently wanted. 1241 Engine has only about 10 hours to do now to beat the world record. She has not been taken out of the machine. The way it runs is greatly due to the Mechanic, Dessoresor's, whom I have frequently recommended for promotion to CPO but he has not been promoted.

A steady supply of 100 100-lb. bombs a month is rather essential. I can get rid of them as quickly as they are supplied. We generally do a before breakfast bomb attack. Lieut. Butler has taken wonderful photographs of the German positions which have proved of great value to the Army.

Just this minute one of the Farmans has come back and reported that she spotted with great success, that the *Agamemnon* completely destroyed 3 out of 4 howitzers in a battery that has been annoying the fleet and landing place. We did 2400 miles the first day the Army landed.

I am still of opinion that the only war machines are fast Pushers with good climb. The M. Farman with 100 Renaults and 1241 are absolutely splendid. Other types of machines cannot compete at all.

Avros, etc. are just so much waste money. These M. Farmans can do 75 m.p.h., carry wireless and 2 100-lb. bombs, therefore they can spot, reconnoitre or attack, whatever is wanted. They can also fight. Their only drawback is that they turn slowly and wallow about in a wind. It was rotten seeing the soldiers get hell at the landing places. Knowing the defences I did not believe they would be able to get ashore. These Turks are devils to the wounded. We are giving them no rest with bombs. One of our machines got two 100-lb bombs in a divisional camp and blotted out over 18 tents and their occupants. They must have killed over 100 men. We also got a lot of good hits on Maidos and Chanak, the day before yesterday and the day before that, a big camp near Bogheli. I have two very good Army Officer observers and two Midshipmen. Everyone seems quite satisfied with the work we have done. One of the BE2c's chased the German to-day, but could not catch him.

We will soon shift to the mainland but it is not free from shells yet and it is not worth risking all our machines as they can reach our new landing ground quite easy. The German dropped bombs here and made good shots twelve days ago. I sent two units in return, and we laid him up for ten days. He only escaped to-day by the skin of his teeth, as an M. Farman and myself on No. 50 were just between him and home, and we never saw him as we were busy dropping bombs. He must have passed within a quarter of a mile of me, running away from Ormond on the BE2c.

The Breguet is ready now. I urgently require three or four more good carpenters. The kite balloon appears to be jolly useful only he has to be too far away.

I got hit right along the propeller by a rifle bullet the other day.

I think the job will be a great success soon, as although the Turks and Germans have got awfully strong positions our men have got their blood up, as the Turks are such devils to the wounded.

Aeroplane spotting I really consider has helped a devil of a lot, as now we can get batteries silenced right away. Practically always now the batteries cease fire when an aeroplane gets over the top of them. I honestly believe that our aeroplanes have given the Turks a healthy feeling of dread.

With kind regards to Mrs. Sueter.

I am, Sir . . .

In fact, Commander Samson was a most gallant officer who did more with his aircraft than his orders allowed. Frequently his idiosyncratic methods and flagrant disregard for convention and orders, led him into direct conflict with higher authority. He led his aircraft far and wide over the battle area, engaging in unauthorised raids and carrying out a private war of his own. Towards the end of 1915, he was recalled to the Mediterranean and later to England. He did much to develop anti-Zeppelin tactics in the North Sea in the air defence role and in 1918, nearly lost his life when he made the first attempted flight in a Sopwith Camel fighter from a lighter towed by a destroyer.

During the last days of April and the beginning of May, several attempts were made in the Helles area to push forward north-eastwards to Krithia. Although the attacks were pressed home with determination, they resulted in very little gain, and it soon became clear that strong reinforcements would be required before Sir Ian Hamilton could hope to clear the defences which dominated the Straits. As these could not begin to arrive until the middle of July however, the minor attacks at Helles were continued and the stalemate dragged on. The Turks on the other hand, decided to take the offensive, and on the night of the 18th-19th May, they again made a determined attempt to push the Anzacs into the sea.

A lucky and chance discovery of the enemy plan was made by Flight Commander R.L.G. Marix, whilst making a routine patrol on the look out for enemy aircraft on the morning of the 17th. His attention was attracted by unusual activity in the port of Ak Bashi Liman, and a large camp inland from the port already filled with troops. When Marix returned with his valuable piece of intelligence which pointed to the arrival of a new division – actually the 2nd Division from Constantinople – a bombing raid on the camp was planned for that afternoon.

Loading one 100 lb. and fourteen 20 lb. bombs on the Breguet, Marix went up with Commander C.R. Samson in the observer's seat and carried out a highly successful raid on the port creating panic amongst the dock hands and killing or wounding fifty-seven soldiers. The aviators then made a detailed reconnaissance which confirmed the strength of the reinforcements. When their reports were received at GHQ, it was concluded that an early attack on the Anzac position was likely, and General Birdwood was warned accordingly.

The news of the probable attack was received in the trenches at 10 p.m. on the 18th, and as the Turkish soldiers crept forward to make the assault, the allied troops were ready and waiting. The attack was pressed relentlessly, but the chance discovery from the air had robbed the enemy of surprise, and by 24th May, the ground was so thick with enemy corpses that a temporary armistice had to be granted to enable the Turks to bury their dead.

Early in May a rough aerodrome had been constructed on Cape Helles so that observers could land to report urgent information direct to corps headquarters. However, the landing ground had many disadvantages, the chief of which was the fact that it was under observation from the Turks on Achi Baba, and was heavily shelled whenever aeroplanes remained on it for any length of time. Nevertheless, the aerodrome saved much valuable time, especially before and during the renewed attack from the direction of Helles on 4th June.

In this attack the Naval Air Service's armoured cars of Nos. 3 and 4 Squadrons were used for the first time on Gallipoli, but owing to the rough nature of the roads and tracks, the cars could do little to help the infantry and after a few hours' fighting they were withdrawn. However, on the credit side, ten dismounted machine guns of No. 10 Motor Cycle Squadron did good work in the forefront of the battle.

A remarkable victory in the air was achieved on 22nd June, when a German aeroplane was shot down near Achi Baba by Captain C.H. Collett (pilot) and Major R.E.T. Hogg (observer) flying a Voisin and armed with a rifle. Firing his rifle with extraordinary accuracy, Hogg managed to hit the enemy aeroplane in the engine and bring it down in a forced landing. Then the French Air Service located its position and called up its own artillery, who obtained a direct hit and completely destroyed it.

Towards the end of the month a second attack was made against the Turkish right at Helles, which resulted in five lines of trenches being won and held. The aeroplanes co-operated by directing 60-pounder batteries on to the enemy infantry and ammunition columns and by dropping small bombs on troops and batteries. Aeroplane observers saw considerable movements of enemy troops in front of the Anzac position on the 28th, where a subsidiary British attack was being made. This Turkish concentration heralded heavy counter-attacks made on the night of 29th-30th June, which again met with no success and proved to be the last effort of the Turks against the Anzac position.

At the end of the month the Helles aerodrome was given up except for emergency bombing – since the airfield was almost under constant shell fire and three aeroplanes had been hit and wrecked.

Meanwhile, towards the end of May, the Allied naval position was seriously threatened by the arrival in the area of Lieutenant Commander Hersing in his submarine *U.21*. On the day the British troops landed on the Peninsula, he had left the Ems and, proceeding north of the Orkneys, down the west coast of Ireland and through the Straits of Gibraltar, arrived at Cattaro on 13th May. A week later he left the Adriatic for the Aegean, and on the 25th torpedoed and sank the battleship *Triumph* off Ari Burnu, and two days later the *Majestic* off Sedd el Bahr. Hersing then made the passage of the Dardanelles and thence to Constantinople.

Other submarines, mainly small boats put together at Pola,

followed in Hersing's wake, and the menace became so serious that the larger of the supporting ships were withdrawn. The *Ark Royal*, too, was not considered fast enough to avoid the menace of torpedoes or to operate in unprotected waters. She was withdrawn and remained at Kephalo Bay, Imbros, where she became, in effect, a harbour depot ship for seaplanes. However, her seaplanes did continue to carry out routine spotting, photography and reconnaissance sorties from a base in Aliki Bay, Imbros, but at the end of October the *Ark Royal* was again ordered to move.

This time, the seaplane base was broken up and after visiting Jero Bay, Mitylene, and carrying out reconnaissance over Smyrna, the carrier left the Dardanelles area for Salonika arriving on 8th November.

The Royal Naval Air Service continued to operate in support of the hard pressed troops and on November 19th, Squadron Commander R. Bell Davies won the second Victoria Cross to be awarded to a member of the RNAS. Nevertheless the end of the misery, suffering and hardship was near, for with close of the year 1915, the stalemate of Gallipoli was ended and the Allied forces withdrawn. Now it remained only to count the cost of failure, which amounted to a staggering quarter of a million men sick, killed or wounded on each side.

On the brighter side, the embryo Royal Naval Air Service had sharpened its teeth in action and proved its worth under the worst possible conditions. The valuable lessons would further the expansion and development of ship-borne aircraft in the next few years of war, and the small but modest part played by *Ark Royal* would influence that progress.

Ark Royal remained in the area of Salonika carrying out the solid, but unspectacular routine of reconnaissance flying until 27th March 1916. The sudden, unexpected and rather spectacular arrival of *U.21* in the area of the Dardanelles in late 1915, had caused considerable concern over the safety and protection of shipping, and the main pre-occupation had shifted to submarine hunting.

The Admiralty were being pressed to provide more seaplanes for anti-submarine patrol work in the Eastern Mediterranean, but the problems were considerable. So important an issue did the matter become, that it prompted Mr. A.J. Balfour, the then First Lord, to send a memorandum dated 22nd January 1916 to the First Sea Lord. It is one of the very few occasions in fact, that he made a suggestion regarding operations to his naval colleagues:

I desire to suggest for consideration an extended and organised use of seaplanes in the Aegean for the purpose of hunting submarines. This is an ideal area in which to use this method for detection and attack. The seaplane-carrier can always find an island under whose lee it can safely lie, and from whose waters the seaplane can easily rise. Neither seaplane-carriers nor seaplanes have practically anything to fear from hostile aircraft or hostile destroyers. The track of a submarine with only its periscope showing is scarcely visible from a ship, but is fairly easily detected from the air. The lives of submarines might, I think, be made quite intolerable by a carefully arranged patrol by seaplanes of these relatively narrow waters; and if they are in the habit of using secret sources of supply to fill themselves up with oil or provisions, these sources could scarcely fail to be detected when the seaplanes had had experience of the submarine routes.

It should be noted that our earlier seaplanes, which do not mount very quickly, nor find it easy to rise from a lumpy sea, and have no great fighting power would be quite fitted for the kind of scouting which I am suggesting; – although they are becoming antiquated for patrol purposes in the North Sea.

I should be glad if this suggestion, which at first sight seems to me of value, could have early consideration.

The answers came back next day:

Three of the 6 Seaplane Carriers we possess are now in the Eastern Mediterranean, – *Ben-my-Chree* and *Empress* under the orders of C-in-C. East Indies to work on the Syrian Coast, and the *Ark Royal* under VAEMS [Vice-Admiral, Eastern Mediterranean Station] at Salonika.

With only the one ship, *Ark Royal*, VA East Med. is not in a position to do much seaplane work hunting submarines as the few seaplanes have Salonika and the Dardanelles to attend to.

Ben-my-Chree and *Empress* are both required for the Syrian coast where they bomb the Turkish depots and carry out scouting flights.

Engadine can be sent out to E. Med. if required as there is little suitable flying weather at the Forth until about May.

It must be borne in mind that seaplane pilots are far more difficult to train than aeroplane pilots, particularly when civilians have to be used.

We already have very large calls on us in this respect, and only to-day a wire has been received from C-in-C, East Indies, for an additional 15 pilots for seaplanes for *Ben-my-Chree* and *Empress*, a demand which we are not in a position to meet in its entirety.

An alternative suggestion was submitted by Captain Murray F. Sueter that:

A number of small stations, each consisting of one Bessonneau Tent and three or four seaplanes with very small personnel might be placed on a number of islands in the Aegean. *Ark Royal* might act as headquarters and repair ship at some submarine safe harbour (Milo?). *Engadine* or some other fast carrier could then visit these stations periodically, giving them new machines and taking the old ones back to *Ark Royal* for overhaul . . .

(3) A reference to the chart suggests stations at Samos, Nikaria, Mykoni, Tinos, Andros, and possibly on the mainland at Cape Mandili, but such a scheme must of course be worked out in considerable detail, and with a knowledge of what has already been done or proposed in the way of netting, trawler, and motorboat patrol work etc. It would also be necessary to consider the routes in use, use of the airships now at Mudros for night work, number and type of seaplanes which could be spared for this duty etc. etc. At some places aeroplanes might be preferable to seaplanes. For watching a narrow channel a kite balloon on shore might be of value.

(4) It is considered that such a patrol efficiently carried out would form a very strong deterrent to hostile submarines if backed up by the airship patrol, and supported by a few large armoured motor-launches.

(5) Presumably any shore bases selected would need some form of gun armament in view of the fact that most of the German submarines now carry guns.

At all events, *Ark Royal* was dispatched back to Mudros, firstly as part of the Mediterranean Fleet and latterly until 3rd April 1918, as part of the British Aegean Squadron. Three incidents served to brighten an otherwise 'quiet' war, when she was attacked by enemy aircraft in November 1916 and September 1917, and a Zeppelin bombed her in March 1917. She was at Syra from April to October 1918 and when on 11th November 1918, the guns on the Western Front finally fell silent after more than four years of fighting the 'War to end all Wars', *Ark Royal* was at Piraeus – arriving back at Mudros on the last day of 1918.

On 1st April 1918 (All Fools' Day), with the formation of the Royal Air Force, the Admiralty lost control of its own aircraft. It was to be twenty years of bitter wrangling before that control was fully regained. Almost at the stroke of a pen, the Navy transferred nearly all its officers and men experienced and trained in the complex art of aviation from ships at sea. In all, 2,500 aircraft and 55,000 officers and men were transferred to the new Service, and there was no nucleus left on which to build at a later date.

Air Force contingents comprising both aircrew and servicing crews were provided by the RAF. Although the vessels from which they operated were still under Naval command. These seaborne RAF units were poorly trained, inexperienced in carrier operations and worse still, they were given aircraft by the new RAF that were either obsolescent or totally unsuitable for carrier work.

As World War I ended, the Admiralty wrote to the newly created Air Ministry proposing that all personnel connected with naval air operations afloat should be drawn from the navy, though the RAF would still be responsible for their training. Regarded with open hostility by senior RAF officers, the proposal produced the first angry exchange in a 'verbal war' that was to last until the summer of 1937.

Oblivious to the political squabbles in high places, Flight Lieutenant A.C. (Merry) Merredith left home the day after Armistice, 12th November 1918, and headed for his new appointment – HMS *Ark Royal*. He travelled overland by train to the famous Italian Naval Base of Taranto, then by sea in the SS *Maple* through the Corinth Canal and the Bosphorus to Constantinople.

Together with the CO of the RAF unit, Flight Lieutenant Abbot, and six other officers of the detachment, 'Merry' Merredith made his way to their temporary home in the old Sultan's Palace near Constantinople. 'It was a magnificent and impressive building from the outside', recalled Merry, 'but we had to use mosquito nets to stop the rain of bugs and other insects which kept falling down from the ceilings.'

Their stay was a short one and soon they were on their way again across Turkey to the port of Bartumi on the Turkish Russian border in South Georgia. Here they embarked in *Ark Royal* and got a first glimpse of their new 'home' aboard a naval seaplane carrier. As part of the Allied Intervention Force fighting on the side of the White Russians against the increasingly victorious Red Army in the Revolution of 1919, *Ark Royal* had received secret orders to proceed to Sevastopol in the Crimea.

The surroundings and traditions were strange to Merry and his fellow officers. He recalls that

When I first got aboard *Ark*, the Captain came into the Wardroom and offered us all a drink. I downed mine and asked the Captain if he would like another gin. He eyed me up and down for a moment or two and then I learned my first lesson in naval etiquette when he growled . . . 'I never have *another* gin Merredith! Steward bring me a double gin and put it down to Mr. Merredith'.

Early in the New Year of 1919, *Ark Royal* left Bartumi and headed north west towards the Russian port of Novorriysk and then on to the Crimean port of Sevastopol. One of the new pilots, Lieutenant Lea Forrest, had never flown seaplanes before, so the opportunity was taken to give him an early familiarisation flight. Merry Merredith was selected to check him out and had to sweat it out in the back cockpit, without the comforting reassurance of dual controls. Merry took off from Novorriysk and flew westwards to Yalta, landed and then it was the turn of Lieutenant Lea Forrest. They exchanged seats, got airborne and headed back for Novorriysk and *Ark Royal*. Merry Merredith remembers that 'the actual flight was OK but the landing – that was a bit tricky!'

As if he hadn't had enough for one day, the Rear Admiral Black Sea – known to everyone by his initials RABS – had been notified that a seaplane was missing – Flight Lieutenant Merredith received a logging. The stay at Sevastopol was largely social, although by mid 1919 the Bolsheviks had reached Odessa and were too close for comfort. Picking up refugees, who included a so-called White Russian Princess, *Ark Royal* headed down through the Black Sea for Malta.

The RAF unit left the ship on her arrival in Grand harbour, though Flight Lieutenant Merredith was unaware that he and *Ark* would meet again.

Europe was now at peace but wars went on. Small, sporadic actions involving British forces extended far beyond to the Middle East and North West Frontier. As early as February 1920, in Somaliland twelve DH 9s were dispatched from the United Kingdom in *Ark Royal* to support a small force of Camel Corps in a final effort to end the career of the 'Mad Mullah', who had defied authority for twenty years. The sight of the aeroplanes in what was obviously a demonstration of authority and power was enough, and the task was concluded in three weeks.

Turkey was defeated in World War I, but Turkish Nationalists, under Mustafa Kemal, refused to accept the terms of the 1920 peace treaty, particularly as part of Turkey was occupied by Greece – an age-old enemy. As a result Kemal seized effective power in Turkey. By September 1922 the Greeks had been defeated and the victorious Kemal threatened the Straits of the Dardanelles leading to the Sea of Marmara, where of the Allies only Britain had small forces in Constantinople and Chanak to maintain the neutrality of the area.

The British Commander, General Harrington, had warned of the impending invasion by the Turks, and in mid-September the British Cabinet decided to re-inforce the area with naval, army and air force units. At the same time Kemal was to be warned of the threat to European peace if he invaded the Straits area. Nevertheless, Kemal's forces lurked just south of Chanak, and at one time were well inside the neutral zone.

The first reinforcements in the area were naval ships, including the carrier HMS *Argus* with No. 203 Squadron RAF on board. On 11th September No. 203 Squadron at Leuchars had been re-equipping one Flight with Nieuport Nightjars (deck landing versions of the Nighthawk). She sailed from Portsmouth on the 18th and after a stop in Malta to pick up six Fairey IIIDs arrived in the Dardanelles on the 25th.

The World War I seaplane-carrier HMS *Pegasus* (3,000 tons) was already in the area with her RAF unit of five Fairey IIID seaplanes aboard, and one of her first tasks was to evacuate an army outpost to the main garrison at Chanak on 9th September. Thereafter her RAF aircraft maintained daily patrols in the IIIDs over the Neutral zone around Chanak, and General Harrington was therefore kept informed of the Turkish movements on this front.

Meanwhile mobilisation orders had been issued to RAF Squadrons in Egypt and England to stand by to leave for the

Dardanelles. Squadrons worked round the clock to crate their aircraft, pack stores and get their kit ready. Such was the enthusiasm in packing that stores were thrown into the boxes without any regard for the order in which they would be required. There was no indication of the contents of any box. Indeed all Squadrons that were shipped out had similar experiences and No. 25 Squadron in the country, packed exactly the correct number of split pins, with the result that some of their aircraft could not be assembled in Turkey when some pins were dropped in the mud.

Shipping was arranged in Egypt and England to transport the Squadrons to the Dardanelles area. Many ships were totally unsuitable and notably, the SS *Podesta* used to transport No. 208 Squadron from Egypt to the Straits. This gallant ship had lain on the bottom of Alexandria harbour for five years from 1915 until she was raised in 1920. She had not completed her refit by the time she was required by the RAF in September 1922 and worse still, she had insufficient hold space for the crated aircraft. Undaunted by these minor considerations, the crates were dumped on deck and the ship set sail – even swinging the compass on leaving harbour. To everyone's unbelievable astonishment, the SS *Podesta* arrived in the Bosphorus on 30th September and docked at Constantinople. One of the RAF crew of that voyage still believes in miracles!

During the period mid-September to mid-October the political and military situations were very obscure and confusing. A Turkish attack was expected daily, even after meetings with their leaders had started at Mudania on 3rd October. During the meetings, the RAF aircraft kept up a complete reconnaissance over both sides of the Straits, and reported dispositions and movements of Turkish troop concentrations via W/T link 150 miles away to RAF Headquarters at Constantinople. Such was the efficiency of the intelligence and reconnaissance, that the Turkish representative at the peace talks remarked that General Harrington was better informed about Turkish dispositions than he was.

No. 4 RAF Squadron of Bristol fighters was based at Farnborough – commanded by Squadron Leader C.H.B. Blount, MC, the Squadron F 2b embarked in HMS *Ark Royal* in Portsmouth on 19th September 1922. The aircraft were lifted aboard – fuselages complete with Rolls-Royce Falcon III engines and top and bottom sections – but the mainplanes, stores and equipment were stowed in packing crates. Mr S.A. Gray was one of the RAF Maintenance members of No. 4 Squadron and he recalls:

> We arrived in the Dardanelles on October 8th. We transferred
> the aircraft and components to the aircraft carrier *Argus* flying
> deck, where we erected the aircraft and they were flown off the
> carrier by our own pilots on October 11th to Kilia aerodrome.
> The pilots had never flown an aircraft off a carrier before.

In fact *Ark Royal* – who operated her own 6 Fairey III seaplanes –
had no flight deck, so she tied up alongside *Argus* on arrival and the
partially erected 'Brisfits' were transferred across. Final assembly
was completed on the deck of *Argus* by floodlight during the night of
10th–11th October. During the following afternoon *Argus* steamed
into wind and all twelve Bristol fighters (Brisfits) were flown off. The
successful reinforcement by *Ark* raised the total number of
serviceable aircraft in the area from twenty-six to thirty-eight.

Three days after *Ark*'s arrival in the area, the Turks acceded to the
British demand to respect the neutral zone, and an agreement was
duly signed. The latter part of October and November 1922 was an
anti-climax. It was necessary to see that the Turks honoured the
agreement and at the same time, to make sure that our actions did
not antagonise them. The British Commander staged a mass
formation over Constantinople and planned for 10th November. In
the event the weather went sour and it was not until the 21st, that the
fifty-one aircraft led by Group Captain Fellowes was able to fly over
the city.

The peaceful atmosphere around the Straits area was still liable to
deteriorate as the local peace treaty, concluded at Mudania in
October 1922 was only an interim settlement pending a full
conference later. It was considered that up to the successful
conclusion of a full peace treaty, the Turks could give trouble at any
time and therefore RAF Squadrons would be required to remain in
the area. They actually stayed until after the signing of the Peace
Treaty in September 1923.

HMS *Argus* left the Dardanelles for the UK on 20th December
1922, while the other two sea-plane carriers *Ark* and *Pegasus*
continued to operate in the area of the Dardanelles and the
Bosphorus; returning briefly to Malta for a short refit early in 1923.
Ark returned again to the Dardanelles in April 1923 with its own
flight of five of the first new Lion-engined Fairey IIIDs (N9567-71).

During the following five months, the aircraft and ships operated a more leisurely routine and normal training was resumed.

In August an 'At Home' air pageant was organised at San Stefano, attended by the Embassy Staffs in Constantinople. Mr. Gray continues:

HMS *Ark Royal* and *Pegasus* co-operated more closely with land stations than I think has been possible before. At the pageant it was an awe-inspiring sight to see the Fairey IIIDs haring across the aerodrome whilst participating in a land relay race.

On 5th September 1923, No. 4 Squadron again embarked in *Ark Royal* for the passage home to Portsmouth. It was uneventful and she arrived in UK at the end of the month. After their disembarkation, Mr Gray says 'that all units that had taken part in the operation, got together and produced a small record of the tasks undertaken and lessons learned'.

Certainly the most significant development during the joint operations in the Dardanelles in 1923, was the standardisation of the methods employed by the Army and Navy in bombardment spotting with the RAF. Previously the Navy's guns had been controlled by the IIIDs using one system, and the Army's artillery by the 'Brisfits' using another. The shortage of aircraft to co-operate with the Navy led eventually to the evolution of a common bombardment spotting system for all three services.

Ark returned to England at the end of 1923 and spent the rest of her service in the Reserve Fleet at Chatham. But in early 1924 she was ordered to go to the Scilly Islands to act as the support ship for the ground maintenance and aircrews of the Flying Boat Development Unit. With one Cromaty seaplane and three F 2a flying boats, Squadron Leader Maycock and the unit which included Flight Lieutenant Merredith flew down for trials. It was an uneventful period and the last time 'Merry' would see his old carrier.

She continued in reserve and as a catapult trials ship from 1924 onwards. Between the wars development continued in finding suitable Catapults for mounting in Capital ships. Apart from carriers, and those aircraft consisted of reconnaissance and torpedo planes, single seat fighters and seaplanes.

The increased demand for aircraft at sea led to the development of suitable Catapults for mounting in Capital ships. Apart from providing 'more baskets for the eggs' since there were many aeroplanes available and too few carriers, the scheme offered attractive financial savings. The cost of mounting Catapults in capital ships was estimated to be about £40,000 for two aircraft, while the provision of the same two aircraft operated from a carrier was reckoned at between £100,000 and £150,000 depending on the carrier's size. Indeed, so long as there were insufficient carriers to meet even the most important requirements of the Fleet and its detached units, the catapult policy was pushed on.

In a memorandum to the Board in 1928, the Naval Staff expressed the view that, pending further experience in operating carrier aircraft, the building of a new carrier could be delayed until the 1932-33 Programme, but that 'Catapults were essential in all capital ships and cruisers in the future'. In 1934 the number of catapult aircraft authorised was more than a quarter of the whole Fleet Air Arm strength.

To whatever extent the use of 'one shot' catapult aircraft might be pushed in wartime, it was always the policy that in peacetime all such aircraft should be capable of a safe landing and recovery. Commanding officers of ships developed the technique of slewing their ships to make a relatively calm patch of water (slick) for the aircraft to land on, but most damage was done usually at the moment of hooking on and hoisting.

About 1933 a German called Hein endeavoured to exploit an idea for making this hooking-on operation safer and easier by means of a towed mat. This was tried out by the Admiralty in the trials ship *Pegasus* (late seaplane carrier *Ark Royal* but renamed in December 1934), and eventually discarded. The idea was used by the Germans however, for the recovery and refuelling at sea of the large mail-carrying seaplanes, which they employed on the trans-South Atlantic mail route.

The renamed *Pegasus* continued in her role of trials ship for catapults, aircraft recovery and training, and it seemed only a matter of time before she too would go the way of all good ships and be broken up. Surprisingly though, this old, slow and veteran carrier would find herself once more in action and at war – her semi-retirement would be short lived and rudely awakened.

In Europe, the clouds of war which had been darkening the horizon for many months moved overhead and suddenly erupted in the long awaited storm. At 0530 on the morning of 1st September

1939 German troops surged over their borders to invade Poland and in fulfilment of their pledge, Britain and France entered the war just two days later.

Although the early days of World War II on land were described as the 'phoney war', at sea the Germans at once opened a campaign by submarine and mine to destroy allied and neutral shipping. As this war gathered momentum, England became more and more isolated, shipping losses increased and soon she became solely dependent upon her seaborne links for survival.

Towards the end of 1940, the growing shipping losses prompted urgent counter measures to be taken by the Admiralty. The Germans were using the long range Focke-Wulf Condor (FW200) to seek out our shipping and pass position reports to the waiting U-Boats. Anti-aircraft cruisers and convoy escorts were needed to defend the hard pressed shipping on the South and East coasts, there were just not enough to re-inforce the convoys in the Atlantic.

The Naval and Air Staffs decided in November and December that a new means of countering the threat had to be found. The outcome of their joint meetings and the two earliest projects to be put into operation was firstly a specially fitted anti-aircraft 'Q' ship, HMS *Crispin* and secondly, the veteran seaplane-carrier *Pegasus*.

It is perhaps worth mentioning a few details about these two ships, for their fates were very different and they were indeed the first of many. The 'Q' ship *Crispin* was fitted with one six inch low angle and one 12 pounder high angle gun, four Oerlikon and four single-barrelled two pounder pompoms. The following extract from her original operation orders show the nature of her employment:

. . . *Crispin* is expected to be ready to sail from the Clyde on or after 21st December . . .

OBJECT – The object is the destruction of Focke-Wulfs.

EXECUTION – *Crispin* is to fly the red ensign and is not to disclose in any way that she is one of HM Ships. The crew are not to wear uniform. She is to be sailed with the first convenient outward bound convoy from Clyde . . . return with the next corresponding inward bound convoy.

When in the area where air attack is likely *Crispin* is to act as a 'straggler', keeping not more than four miles from the rear of the convoy, rejoining before dark. If, however, there is information that a U-Boat is near the convoy *Crispin* is to remain in convoy . . .

HMS *Pegasus* was provided with three Fulmar fighters and directed on 3rd December 1940, to join Convoy OG 47 outward bound for Gibraltar from Liverpool. Her orders included the following points:

She was in no sense a 'Q' ship, but her 'object' was the same as in *Crispin's* orders – namely the destruction of German Focke-Wulfs.

EXECUTION – *Pegasus* is to be stationed in the rear position of one of the centre columns of the convoy. One additional sloop will be detailed to join the A/S (Anti-Submarine) escort; she is to screen HMS *Pegasus* while flying operations are in progress . . .
The decision whether to fly off aircraft is at the discretion of the Commanding Officer HMS *Pegasus*. Aircraft may land on any convenient aerodromes in Northern Ireland or in the sea if circumstances justify it.

The employment of these two ships did not produce any immediate results, though it is certain that the presence of fighter aircraft, clearly visible to all in any convoy sailing on the Atlantic routes at this time, made an important contribution to the morale of the Merchant fleet.

Crispin operated with six convoys in the Western Approaches after her first escort duty with Convoy OB 266 on Christmas Day 1940. She was torpedoed by a U-Boat and lost on 3rd February 1941 while changing over between an outgoing and incoming convoy in the Atlantic, and before she had had the opportunity to make effective use of her guns against any German aircraft.

Pegasus on the other hand was more fortunate, though she was employed for many months as a convoy escort, before she was able even to find an enemy Focke-Wulf and Catapult her Fulmar fighters. There is little evidence to suggest that she was an effective deterrent to the enemy shadowing aircraft, though it may well have been the case. Compared to the later generation of Catapult ships, she was sadly deficient in direction finding and communications equipment.

Nevertheless, in the nine convoys in which she provided the invaluable and morale boosting fighter cover between 3rd December 1940 and 26th July 1941, she launched a Fulmar on three separate occasions against FW 200 shadowers and made one interception.

On 7th July 1941, while escorting Convoy HG 63, her aircraft

Ark Royal, commissioned 16th November 1938, had a total complement of 1575 officers and men and could carry five squadrons amounting to sixty aircraft. First Commanding Officer, Captain A.J. Power, CVO, RN.

One of *Ark*'s first assignments was a shake-down cruise in the Mediterranean before joining the Home Fleet in the spring of 1939. The photograph shows a Swordfish turning downwind prior to landing on.

February 1939. Swordfish aircraft of 820 and 821 Squadrons range on *Ark Royal*'s flight deck prior to the spring exercises.

Skua fighter dive bomber landing on *Ark Royal*. One of our principal fleet fighters from 1938 to 1941.

Swordfish of 821 Squadron flying out to join *Ark Royal* in the spring of 1939 prior to her first work-up in the Mediterranean.

Fulmar Fighter of 808 Squadron taking off for patrol duties from HMS *Ark Royal*. This squadron replaced the Skuas of 803 Squadron in October 1940 and remained with the carrier until she was torpedoed in November 1941.

Ark gets her first. The first enemy aircraft to be destroyed in World War II by any service was this Dornier 18 flying boat, shot down by a Skua from *Ark Royal* on 26th September 1939 in the North Sea. Photograph 1 shows the crew of three preparing to launch their rubber dinghy. Photograph 2: the crew paddle away. Photograph 3: two stranded airmen about to swim to HMS *Somali*. Photograph 4: HMS *Somali* delivers the coup de grace after rescuing the crew.

managed to drive off an enemy shadowing FW 200 and it was not seen again. The pilot landed safely in Belfast. One month later and this time with Convoy OG 67 she again launched a fighter. This time he failed to intercept and flew back to Ireland. Tragically the pilot crashed into a hillside in bad visibility and was killed.

On 26th July 1941 *Pegasus* returned to her routine catapult training duties in the Clyde area, and survived the war to be finally sold in 1946.

It was estimated that between August 1940 and the end of January 1941, long range aircraft in the Atlantic had sunk 53 ships totalling over 210,000 tons while 125 other ships were attacked and many suffered damage. Without the old *Ark Royal*, these totals would have been possibly much higher. She was the forerunner of a project which provided the escort carriers and MAC ships, and whose operations later contributed so much to the improved safety of Atlantic convoys.

Now the world was at peace and as the thousands of men left the services to return to civilian life, Barracks and Air Stations became deserted and hundreds of ships paid off. *Pegasus* after thirty-two years of service and two wars was sold on 18th October 1946, and as *Anita I* sailed for another three years, but now registered in Panama and sailing under the Panamanian flag. Her engines were tired and her frame battered and dented. Time was indeed running out for this remarkable little ship. In 1949, she was reported to be up for sale and available for scrap and as such, she was purchased by a Dutch company called Boomse Sheepss Boujen. It seems from the records in Lloyds Library, that no immediate decision was taken to break up *Anita I* and that some months later, in April 1950, she was again sold to the British Iron and Steel Company. This time she was taken to a small yard at Gray's in Essex and broken up.

As the men clambered over the rusty, decrepit and old fashioned hulk that was once the pride of the fleet, the first and last thing in aircraft carriers – *Ark Royal* – perhaps they smiled tolerantly and wondered that anything so old and ugly could have been a carrier.

Her successor had already gained immortal fame and the fourth *Ark Royal* was on the slipway. Yes, she could bow out gracefully and her name would live on.

CHAPTER 3

Ark Royal III

Where is 'Ark Royal'?

The 16th September 1935 was a very important date in the life of one little girl – Wendy Johnson, twelve-year-old daughter of the Managing Director of Messrs Cammell Laird, Birkenhead. At her signal, a large rusty plate was lowered onto the slipway blocks and the first keel plate of the third *Ark* was laid.

During the next twenty-two months, two thousand men were employed continuously on her construction – Job Number 1012 – the very latest thing in aircraft carriers. After HMS *Hermes* completed some ten years earlier, she was the first ship to be planned and built as a carrier, and she embodied all the improvements suggested by well-tried and proven experience.

Ark Royal III was a far cry from her two predecessors, for at a cost of £2,330,000 – it was the most valuable contract the Admiralty had given out since 1918 – she was the longest ship ever built on Merseyside. She had a total of nine decks. Her armoured and iron flight deck was no less than 800 feet in length and had a beam of 94 feet. It lay like a gigantic flat lid over the vast honeycomb of compartments in the new vessel.

The final sketch design for this new and revolutionary aircraft carrier received Board of Admiralty approval on 21st June 1934 and her specification looked impressive – capable of carrying sixty aircraft in two vast hangars extending almost the full length of the ship below the flight deck, and linked to the flight deck by three large aircraft lifts. The 'island' superstructure – a dominant feature of all aircraft carriers today – rose amidships above the starboard side of the flight deck to give the ship a curious lop-sided appearance.

In the island were the navigating bridge, gunnery control positions, mast, funnel and some of the light anti-aircraft guns. The Captain's sea-cabin was immediately below the bridge, with the Chart room, Air Intelligence office and Wireless Control office close at hand. The main gun armament consisted of sixteen 4.5 guns, mounted in eight twin turrets and sited just below flight-deck level. In addition she carried four multiple pom-poms and eight multiple machine guns. Three screws giving 32,000 horsepower on each shaft gave the ship a speed of 30.75 knots and her fuel endurance exceeded that of any previous carrier.

Ark Royal III was a welcome piece of news for the hundreds of men who had been on the dole for years, for she represented work, security and an end to the misery and poverty which had hit so many families in the Merseyside area.

On 13th April 1937 the third *Ark Royal* was launched by Lady Maud Hoare, wife of the First Lord of the Admiralty. It was a great and festive occasion with gaily coloured bunting fluttering from the ship herself and the shipyard buildings. Work had ceased all round the yard as hundreds of grimy men and boys crowded every vantage point. Under the title 'Most up-to-date Carrier', *The Times* Special Correspondent reported the event in the paper next day – 14th April:

They mounted a special platform for the launching ceremony. After a delay of about half on hour while the tide was rising, and after a brief religious service, Lady Maud Hoare stood forward to perform the ceremony. 'We have come here today', she said, 'to launch this great ship and to wish her Godspeed. No words of mine can be adequate to express our feelings of pride and thankfulness in the magnificent achievement. I name this ship . . . *Ark Royal*. May God guide her and guard and keep all who sail in her'.

After the official blessing by the Rev. W. Webb, Vicar of St. Mary's, Birkenhead – Lady Hoare launched the new ship in the presence of a crowd of some estimated 60,000.

She then took the bottle of wine, which hung from a bollard high above, and flung it against the plates of the stem. The bottle rebounded unbroken (probably because it was covered with some material to prevent the scattering of splinters), and because of this it had to be flung three times more before it broke and the champagne flowed down the bows of the ship.

The the *Ark Royal* began, slowly but surely, to move down the slipway. To cries of 'She's off!' the great ship gathered speed until, without a tremor, she entered the water and slowly swung upstream on the tide. The enveloping cloud of tugs began to draw in the cables thrown out from the vessel, and by the time the visitors had assembled at the moulding floor for luncheon the new carrier had been brought safely to her moorings in the fitting-out basin.

Twenty months later on 16th November 1938 *Ark Royal* III was commissioned as a naval ship under the command of Captain A.J. Power, CVO. She ran her trials in the Clyde and was finally completed and taken over from the shipbuilders, Messrs Cammell Laird on 16th December 1938 – a few short months before the start of World War II.

With her flying personnel the *Ark*'s total complement was 1,575 She had twenty cooks and six months' supplies.

She carried sixty aircraft: five squadrons, composed of Blackburn Skuas and Fairey Swordfish. The Skuas were two-seater fighter dive-bombers with a speed of 200 m.p.h., armed with four .303 front guns and one rear gun; when not on fighter duty they could carry a 500-lb. bomb-load. Later these were replaced by Fairey Fulmars, with eight guns fixed in the wings to fire forward and a higher speed; like the Skuas, they carried a pilot and an air-gunner.

The Swordfish, which the *Ark Royal* carried throughout her career, was a torpedo-spotter-reconnaissance biplane, with a single engine, a fixed undercarriage, and an open cockpit. When used for attack it carried one 18-inch torpedo or a 1,500-lb. bomb-load. Its defensive armament consisted of a fixed gun in front and a free gun in rear. It carried a crew of three: pilot, observer, and air-gunner.

The Swordfish satisfied all the requirements of a carrier borne aircraft of those early days. It had a low landing speed, folding wings, rugged construction and could carry a good weapon load. It proved to be, in the early stages of the War, one of the most successful aircraft ever produced. By those who flew them they were affectionately known as 'String-bags', from the bits of wood, canvas, wire and other 'bits and pieces' which held them together in the air. Although sadly slow, they were excellent torpedo aircraft and good bombers capable of taking and meting out a lot of punishment.

In the early months of 1939, the crew of *Ark Royal* began to find their feet and work as a team. All this took time and was not achieved without hard work and much frustration. Few people who have not lived and worked in the close knit community of a steel

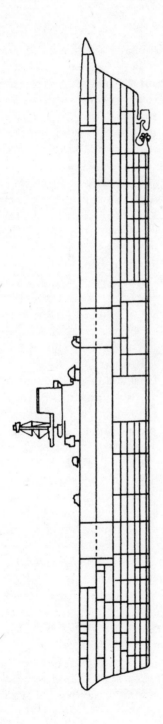
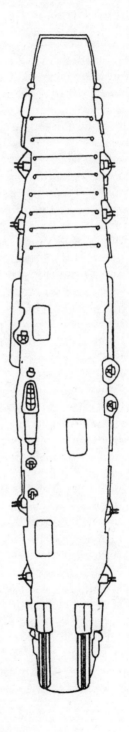

Ark Royal III; elevation and plan view of flight deck

village of 2,000 men, can appreciate the problems of learning to live and work together in harmony and efficiency. It takes patience, experience, knowledge and above all – sound leadership. *Ark* had men with all those qualities and they were to prove their worth in the months that lay ahead – but that was in the future and at the moment they had other things on their minds – like home, families and festivities – a few more days' leave for it was Boxing Day 1938 and *Ark* was alongside Asia pontoon in Portsmouth Harbour.

Ark's aircraft squadrons were working up at their own air stations ashore prior to their first embarkation sometime in January. They would be going in the ship on her first shake-down cruise in the Mediterranean before joining the Home Fleet at the end of the Spring. When they finally landed on for the first time on 12th January 1939, the ship had done all it could to prepare for their arrival, but her aircraft – the ship's main armament – was already sadly obsolete and totally unsuited to the work they would be called upon to do. The ghost of *Ark Royal* II and her seaplanes of 1915 lived on, and a new generation of pilots and observers would reap a bitter harvest from past indifference, mismanagement and plain incompetence – the neglected years from 1918 to 1937.

The Naval Wing of the Royal Flying Corps was established in 1912 and two years later, as a separate entity became the Royal Naval Air Service. As already mentioned earlier, the First World War stimulated a rapid expansion and pioneered many of the basic carrier operations, and provided much needed bombardment spotting and reconnaissance for the Fleet. Finally, on 2nd August 1917 Squadron Commander Dunning, DSC, RNAS, made history by landing a Sopwith Pup on the flight deck of HMS *Furious*. Tragically he was drowned in a third attempt a few days later, but he paved the way for carrier progress and development which would form the backbone of the Fleet Air Arm for over a decade.

On 1st April 1918 when the Royal Naval Air Service was amalgamated with the Royal Flying Corps to form the Royal Air Force the Admiralty surrendered the entire resources of the RNAS. Fortunately, the Admiralty persisted with its policy of building carriers and converting ships of the Fleet to carry aircraft, but deprived of the RNAS, it soon ran into serious equipment and manning problems. In April 1924 a special Arm of the Royal Air Force was formed. Known as the Fleet Air Arm, it was composed of RAF and Naval Officers, but all the maintenance personnel were

RAF. Units came under the operational and disciplinary control of the Navy when embarked, but reverted to RAF administration as soon as they went ashore. This ill-conceived and unworkable practice was doomed to failure from the start and naval aviation was the loser – handicapped, restricted, ill-equipped and frustrated by the policies and machinations of dual control.

It is not necessary to elaborate further, suffice it to say that in 1939 the Fleet Air Arm was ill prepared for modern war and though the Admiralty had regained control in 1937, upon the recommendation of Sir Thomas Inskip, two years could not repair or rectify the damage. Though some RAF other ranks were allowed to transfer to the RN either permanently or on five years loan, the responsibility for the training of pilots and the procurement of aircraft was retained by the RAF. But when War came, by far the most serious deficiency in the new Fleet Air Arm was its lack of modern aircraft.

One section of the Admiralty escaped the strangling effect of joint administration and though, to some extent, it shared in the legacy of those years of neglect, indecision and maladministration, the carrier design and construction department provided the spur for a belated war-time expansion.

By 1930 the Navy had six carriers of which one, the *Hermes*, had been built as a carrier from the start. Under the Washington Treaty of 1922, Great Britain and the United States were allowed a total carrier tonnage of 135,000. Our existing six carriers; *Argus, Eagle, Hermes, Furious, Glorious* and *Courageous* already combined to use up roughly 115,000 of the total tonnage allowed and now, only 20,000 tons was available for carrier building. But in fact the stringent economic policies of the British Government further restricted a carrier building programme and until 1935, new carriers for the Navy were mere plans on a board and dreams in the Admiralty. Drawing on the experiences of the First World War, the enthusiastic carrier design and construction section of the Construction Branch at the Admiralty was able to experiment and develop with a relatively free hand and, by the early 1930s, they had produced an excellent design of a ship, the fore-runner to the present day fleet carrier.

The experience with *Hermes* 'the only British vessel that has hitherto been designed from the start expressly as an aircraft carrier', as her designer, Sir Eustace d'Cyncourt stated at a meeting of the Institute of Naval Architects, showed that she was too small. He went on to add:

In this case I was instructed to combine, in as small and economic ship as possible, all the requirements of an efficient aircraft carrier, and the *Hermes*, of 10,000 tons, with a length of six hundred feet, was the result.

Although she proved to be an efficient aircraft carrier, yet she suffered from the disadvantage of not having the length and size of the larger ships, and I am personally of the opinion that a bigger vessel, of a length of not less than six hundred and fifty to seven hundred feet, should be aimed at.

The bigger ship certainly makes a steadier platform than the smaller one, and the pitching in the larger ships is of less amplitude and less angle than in the shorter vessel, and this helps the operation of flying on and off . . .

Certainly that was the opinion of the Admiralty Staff in 1934, who outlined a preliminary Staff Requirement for a new carrier in 1935 and gave the eager design section their long awaited chance. Their first demands for a flight deck some nine hundred feet long were out of the question within the limitations of 20,000 tons, but if the Board agreed to a reduction of one hundred feet, then a very good compromise could be effected and still within the restrictions imposed by the Treaty regulations. The final sketch design was given Board of Admiralty approval on 21st June 1934 and a new *Ark Royal* was conceived.

The first aircraft to land on the flight deck of the *Ark Royal* were the Swordfish of 820 Squadron, led by Lieutenant-Commander A.C.G. Ermen, RN, which flew off from Southampton on 12th January 1939, after the ship had completed her trials.

Sub-Lieutenant 'Mac' Mackinnon was one of the young pilots of 821 Squadron who sailed with *Ark* to the Mediterranean. He recalls:

We were the Air Group from *Courageous* and very excited at the prospect of going to *Ark*. We took off from Eastleigh and headed for the ship. I always remember my first sight – she was a very big ship for those days and the comfort!! As a twenty-two year old, I was in the lap of luxury with my own cabin and all the comforts of home. My bunk folded back to make a settee and there was even room for my record player.

With all her aircraft safely aboard, *Ark* turned down the channel and proceeded on her maiden cruise to the Mediterranean. 'Mac' Mackinnon continues:

On the way out to Malta, she carried out full power trials – the Carrier rattled along at well over 30 knots for what seemed like hours on end, but it was all very impressive. Her entry into Valetta Harbour at Malta created almost as much stir as the first motor-car that appeared in the streets of London. Officers from the aircraft-carrier *Glorious* flocked on board to examine her new contrivances with expert eyes. Others made scathing references to her 'great ugly snout' and drew caustic comparisons between her well-found cabins and their own Spartan quarters.

At Alexandria she continued with her night and day flying training, alternately carrying out mock torpedo and bombing attacks with HMS *Glorious*. Mackinnon remembers that:

We even disembarked for a spell under canvas at Aboukir Bay and then went back aboard for more work up flying. Tragically the *Glorious* lost two aircraft in night operations, and though we spent hours helping in the search for the crews, they were never found. All too soon it was time to depart from the warmth and sunshine and head back to the U.K. and home waters.

Perhaps the thing I remember most clearly of all was the spirit – *Ark* was a happy ship, you could tell that immediately you got on board. Even a minor disaster such as the fire on the way home after we left Lisbon, didn't spoil the spirit and determination of the ship's company to make her the best. Apparently someone was cleaning an aircraft or something in the hanger with petrol, while someone else was working on an aircraft radio. The result was a bad fire and a hangar full of aircraft destroyed – I think we lost 8 aircraft completely burnt out.

In March of that year, *Ark* was back once more in Home Waters and in May four squadrons of her aircraft flew past in salute to King George VI and Queen Elizabeth as their Majesties sailed for Canada in RMS *Empress of Australia* and the start of the Royal Tour.

Throughout the Spring and Summer months she continued to exercise and prepare for a war that seemed so inevitable. Mac Mackinnon left in July to undergo a minor op and was posted back to Eastleigh.

In spite of the fact that Eastleigh was the place chosen for the testing and flying of a new aeroplane called the Spitfire and a chap called Geoffrey Quill was in the Mess, I was sorry to leave the *Ark*.

The maiden cruise and her short work-up left the *Ark Royal* with her character still unformed. With so large a complement the ship had been slow to shake down. She had been regarded as a figure of fun rather than as a dazzling debutante and had not had time to acquire that personality which was to prove so outstanding throughout her war career: perhaps because many of her flying personnel had as yet little experience of service at sea and it took time for squadrons straight from shore-training to identify themselves with the ship.

The aircraft-carrier was still the Cinderella of the Navy, and the capabilities of a 'floating aerodrome' were not generally appreciated; many thought that naval aircraft must be restricted to scouting and reconnaissance. The airmen themselves knew better and awaited their opportunity to prove themselves.

It was not long in coming.

On 24th August 1939 the British Home Fleet sailed for its War Stations. Admiral Sir Charles Forbes in the *Nelson* had a formidable array of ships under his command. These included four battleships, three battle-cruisers, two aircraft carriers *Ark Royal* and *Furious*, five cruisers and three flotillas of destroyers. While the world speculated on the possibilities of averting war, the Home Fleet sailed northwards to patrol the waters between the Shetlands and Norway.

In the preceding week another force of ships had slipped quietly out of their bases and home ports. This time they were Germans – eighteen U-boats, two pocket battleships and two fast supply vessels – heading for their pre-arranged waiting positions and with orders to follow routes to avoid any possibility of chance detections.

On 1st September, *Ark Royal* launched one of her Swordfish on a routine reconnaissance sortie. There was nothing unusual except that the visibility was very bad and the crew had to fly low to keep out of the low cloud; to be able to see the mountains, coastline and fjords of Norway and report anything of note back to the ship. Unfortunately the crew had to make a forced landing in a Norwegian fjord. The aircraft sank and though the crew paddled safely ashore in their rubber dinghy, they were not overjoyed at their immediate prospects for the future. Happily for them, they were near a

Norwegian airfield and far from being interned, the sympathetic Norwegian Air Force hurriedly flew the survivors by seaplane to Bergen, and they were able to catch a ship to England a few hours before the declaration of war.

Shortly after eleven o'clock on 3rd September, while the *Ark Royal* was still on patrol with the Home Fleet, the Flag-Lieutenant, Lieutenant Charles Coke, received through the pneumatic tube which connected the main Wireless Telegraph Office with the bridge a sealed envelope addressed to the Vice-Admiral, marked 'Urgent Priority'. It contained a pink signal slip on which were written the two words, 'Total Germany', the Admiralty cipher message sent to every ship of the Royal Navy on the outbreak of war.

The Flag-Lieutenant took the signal to Vice-Admiral L.V. Wells, CB, DSO, Vice Admiral Aircraft Carriers, who was on the flight deck. At the time the ship was busy operating aircraft, and it was not until an hour later that the Boatswain's Mate went to the microphone below the bridge and shouted 'D'ye hear there?' – the preliminary call for all announcements. Captain Power followed him.

'This is the Captain speaking', he said, 'I have just received the signal "Commence hostilities against Germany".'

In his first naval order of the war and issued on 31st August 1939, Hitler stated: 'In its warfare on Merchant Shipping the Navy is to concentrate against England'. Just three days later and the night that war was declared, the Donaldson liner *Athenia*, sailed unescorted from Liverpool to Montreal, was torpedoed 200 miles west of the Hebrides and sank with the loss of over 100 lives. In his over enthusiasm Lieutenant Lemp, the commanding officer of *U-30*[1], had signalled the start of four years of unrestricted war at sea – a mistake which even the Germans had been at pains to avoid.

The main body of the Home Fleet cruised in thick fog, off the Orkneys until the morning of 6th September, when they returned to Scapa Flow. There they refuelled and the next day, Admiral Forbes sailed again with *Nelson, Rodney, Repulse, Ark Royal, Aurora, Sheffield* and ten destroyers to patrol the Norwegian coast and search for enemy shipping.

[1] Lieutenant Lemp was severely reprimanded on his return home. The Germans had intended to observe the Hague convention and had given their U-boat Commanders strict instructions. Lemp was transferred to *U-110*, sunk by our forces in May 1941.

The German U-boats, already at their war stations before war was declared, had sunk a number of vessels in the approaches to the Irish Sea and English Channel. Now ships were beginning to seek mutual protection and sail in convoy, whilst patrolling units of the Navy settled down into a steady routine and attempted to counter the threat.

In a bold, calculated risk Mr. Churchill decided to use his few priceless carriers to flush out the enemy U-boats and give much needed protection to the unarmed and vulnerable merchantmen:

> In order to bridge the gap of two or three weeks between the outbreak of war and the completion of new auxiliary anti-U-boat flotillas, we had decided to use the aircraft carriers with some freedom in helping to bring in the unarmed, unorganised and unconvoyed traffic which was then approaching our shores in large numbers. This was a risk which it was right to run.[1]

On September 9th, the *Courageous* and *Hermes* were sent to the western approaches and the *Ark Royal* to the north-west of Ireland. Each carrier was supported by her own escort of attendant anti-submarine destroyers and for the first few days, everything was quiet and then it happened.

On the morning of the 14th, the SS *Fanad Head* sent out an SOS reporting that she was being attacked by a U-boat, and that she had been torpedoed in a position some two hundred miles to the south-west. The *Ark* increased speed, altered course to close the *Fanad Head*'s reported position and hurriedly ranged a striking force of three Skuas on deck.

At 14.40, the Captain of *U-39* Lieutenant Commander Glattes looked through his periscope and saw the enormous, black shape of *Ark Royal* steaming into wind and launching aircraft. Unable to believe his good fortune he fired off a salvo of three torpedoes with magnetic pistols and went deep.

At that very moment Lieutenant Vincent Jones who was standing on the quarterdeck, saw the nose and wake of a torpedo rushing straight at the ship. He raced to the nearest telephone to raise the alarm and was given the wrong number. Fortunately Leading signalman J.E. Hall was on watch on the bridge and had also seen

---

[1]   *The Second World War*, Cassell & Co. Ltd.

the ominous tracks. His warning cry of 'Torpedo on the port bow' caused the Officer of the Watch Lieutenant Rodd to put the helm hard over to port and thus avoid the torpedoes.

The magnetic pistol torpedoes were meant to pass close under *Ark* and detonate as soon as her mass provided sufficient magnetic influence. Unhappily for Glattes and the *U-39*, two of the torpedoes passed astern and one actually detonated in the wake. The enormous column of water caused by the exploding warhead alerted the destroyer escorts *Faulknor, Foxhound* and *Firedrake* and immediately they moved in for a counter attack.

As *Ark* steamed on and out of danger, the destroyers gained sonar contact and commenced a depth charge attack. The first pattern of depth-charges jumped the U-boat's engines off their beds; the second blew her to the surface in a sinking condition. When she broke surface she was identified as *U-39*.

The destroyers opened fire, then ceased as men began to appear on deck. The whole of the submarine's company, including her captain – forty-three in all – abandoned ship and were taken on board HMS *Faulknor*. They appeared to be relieved when they found they were not to be shot, and were strangely young. The Captain, Lieutenant-Commander Glattes, was only twenty three and several of the crew were mere lads of sixteen and seventeen.

A few minutes later *U-39* went down in a torrent of foam and bubbles to become the first submarine to be sunk in World War II. Meanwhile away to the south-west, the three Skuas had found the abandoned *Fanad Head* about a hundred miles away. She was lying stopped, with her passengers and crew in several lifeboats in the calm sea around her.

The U-boat was on the surface and trying to sink her with gunfire. She was in the middle of a patch of oil some 50 feet in diameter and on the arrival of the Skuas, so rapid was her crash-dive that she left two of her gun crew treading water in the oily patch of sea. The three aircraft dived into the attack and released their bombs, but so low went two of the Skuas in their enthusiasm to gain a kill, that the blast from their bombs shattered their tailplanes, killing the air gunners and causing them to crash into the sea. With great good luck the two pilots survived to watch the surviving aircraft climb away and orbit the area.

Twenty minutes later the submarine (subsequently identified as *U-30*) reappeared on the *Fanad Head's* starboard quarter with her conning-tower above water. The surviving pilot dived again from 2,500 feet, firing his front gun and expending 1,150 rounds in a single burst. The U-boat submerged once more and now short of fuel, the Skua returned to the ship alone.

Ark now sent six of her Swordfish to the area to renew the attack. The *Fanad Head*, still afloat, but listing to port was a sorry sight. As they prepared to attack, a torpedo struck the vessel amidships and with her back broken, she settled with her bow and stern rising skywards, before sliding beneath the calm waters to leave only the lifeboats and an ever widening circle of flotsam to mark her grave. One of the Swordfish observers remarked afterwards: 'It was a moving sight to see this small cargo vessel slowly covered by the calm sea.'

All six Swordfish attacked the vague shape of the submerged U-boat with bombs, which fell so close that the crews of the Swordfish were convinced that they had sunk her, but later evidence showed that she returned to Germany after landing one of her wounded men in Iceland. With her she took the crews of the two crashed Skuas, the *Ark Royal*'s first casualties, and the first naval airmen to be made prisoners of war.

The following letter written from a German prisoner of war camp on 2nd November 1939 gives a graphic description of the fateful Skua attack from *Ark Royal* by Lieutenant G.B.K. Griffiths, RM, pilot of one of the Skuas from *Ark Royal* and taken prisoner by the German submarine.

2nd Nov. 1939.

c/o Agence de prisonniers de
   guerre,
Palais du conseil general
Rouge Croix,
Geneva, Switzerland.

Lt. G.B.K. Griffiths, R.M.,
English Prisoner of War,
OFLAG IX A,
GERMANY.

Dear —
   I am writing from our prison camp in Germany, to which we were moved nearly two weeks ago. I was taken prisoner on the 14th September 1939 whilst on a bombing raid. I went out in my machine to look for a submarine which was supposed to have sunk one of our merchant ships about 500 miles out from Ireland in the North Atlantic. Three machines went out, and I searched for the

sub., but failed to find it, and started back to the ship. My observer, a Chief Petty Officer, suddenly shouted to me: 'There's a merchant ship on the horizon, let's look at it.'

Well it was about 20 miles away, but away we went. When we were almost on it my chap said: 'Go low so that I can see its name'. So down I went to sea level, and slowed down. Suddenly just as I got alongside the ship, I spotted the sub. alongside the far side of the ship! Up I went, but the sub. had already got half submerged, leaving me no time to get to a safe height to bomb from. So I took a chance and bombed from a low height in order to hit. My first bomb missed by about 20 feet, and my next blew me up with the blast! I hit the sea at 200 m.p.h. at a steep dive and went straight down without stopping. I tried to get out of the cockpit but was jammed in with a stuck roof. When I was almost out of breath, I managed to break free; and came to the surface. My observer was killed at once, for I never saw him again. I looked for him, but with no luck. I then found that I was nearly a mile away from the merchant ship, in very cold water, with flying clothes on, and not a little knocked about. Somehow I got there, and clambered aboard the merchant ship. On board were some of the submarine's crew who were collecting the ship's papers when I had arrived. On board was also one of my squadron, who had done almost the same thing as I had. A few minutes later up came the submarine, and we were taken prisoners, and the ship was torpedoed almost at once, and once more we were submerged. We also had to swim to the sub!

Well, we spent a fortnight on that sub., before finally returning to Germany on 27th September. We were then lodged at the local Naval jail for a fortnight, followed by a fortnight with Poles, and then moved to this place.

I wrote home as soon as I could, and have since written again, but although that was over four weeks ago, I have not heard from any of them, although it may be here any day. English RAF prisoners have slowly joined us, and now we are 1 Navy and 1 RM, and ten RAF Officers, and quite a few French also. This place is high up in the hills, and is a very old castle surrounded by a moat, and some 'obstacles'.

In the centre is a courtyard where we take our exercise, or walk around the walls of the moat, on the inside. The moat is inhabited by 3 wild boars, and is a most unsafe place indeed.

Well, that is all the local news I am able to tell you. I expect that I shan't leave this place until the war ends, whenever that may be.

The directions given by the Swordfish observers enabled the destroyers to pick up the passengers and crew of the *Fanad Head* the same evening. The *Ark* returned to harbour on 17th and received a visit from Mr. Winston Churchill, but on September 19th, came the tragic and chilling news that the carrier *Courageous* had been sunk. She had been turning into wind to operate aircraft near the Bristol Channel, when Lieutenant Commander Shuhart in *U-29* managed to fire a salvo of torpedoes and score the vital hit. The *Courageous* capsized soon after she was hit and 518 of her company of 1,260 lost their lives. The news that the *U-27* had been sunk by the destroyers *Fortune* and *Forester* off the Butt of Lewis three days later did little to bring consolation nor lessen the blow.

On the morning of 26th September 1939, three British warships, *Nelson*, *Rodney* and *Ark Royal* were escorting a damaged submarine HMS *Spearfish* from the Norwegian Coast and steaming behind their destroyer escort. Just before 1100, two of *Ark Royal's* Swordfish reconnaissance aircraft flying a patrol over the ships, reported three large Dornier 18 flying-boats shadowing the Force some ten miles away to the south-east. It was a bright morning, with high, puffy white clouds etched against a clear blue sky, and a fresh breeze ruffled the sea and flecked the waves with streaky white crests.

Immediately this report reached the *Ark Royal* the 'Squealers' sounded and the command 'Hands to action stations' was piped over the ship's main broadcast. As the ratings doubled to their positions, nine Blackburn Skuas, waiting fuelled and armed in the hangars below, were brought up in the lifts and ranged on the flight deck.

By the time the pilots had received their briefing and reached their aircraft the engines had been started up and were ticking over. The fitters left the cockpits; the pilots and the air-gunners climbed in and *Ark* turned into wind. From the bridge, Commander Flying waved his green flag, the Flight Deck Officer repeated the signal and Lieutenant Commander A.T. Kindersley roared down the deck, to be followed seconds later by number two and then number three.

The three Dorniers kept very low on the water and with their dark blue and green camouflage, they were difficult targets to pick up. At last they were detected and made off, pursued by the Skuas. A sub flight of 800 Squadron led by Lieutenant Finch-Noyes fired all their ammunition at one of the shadowers, who succeeded in evading the hail of bullets by making very tight turns at sea level, before using his superior speed to escape with his companion. The third Dornier was not so lucky. He was attacked by Lieutenant B.S. McEwen, RN, who with his air-gunner, Acting Petty Officer B.M. Seymour, had the distinction of destroying the first enemy aircraft to be brought down by any arm in World War II. The Dornier force-landed in the sea and after one of the crew was seen waving his white overalls, the destroyer HMS *Somali* rescued the crew of four and then sank the flying-boat with gunfire.

The Commander-in-Chief Home Fleet, signalled his con-gratulations and there was great jubilation in the *Ark*, but the excitement for the day was not yet over. Though the shadowers had been driven off, they had obviously reported the whereabouts of the Fleet, and strong enemy reaction was bound to follow. The incredible, almost unbelievable truth is that the C-in-C recalled all the aircraft, ordered them to be struck down in the hangar with their fuel tanks drained, to reduce the risk of fire. The carrier was then ordered to fall in line behind the battleships and fire its anti-aircraft guns at the attacking bombers.

Flight Magazine of 22nd November 1957, reporting a lecture by Rear-Admiral D.R.F. Campbell at the Royal Aeronautical Society, Brough Branch, at Hull on 13th November 1957 makes the following interesting quote:

> Asked when it was that the Royal Navy had changed its mind and had begun to believe in aviation, the lecturer referred to the *Ark Royal* episode of September 1939 and of the frustration of *Ark*'s Squadrons. The change in attitude came, Admiral Campbell suggested, when the bombs began to fall.

The surviving shadowers had reported the position of the Force. At 2.20 that afternoon, half an hour after the last Skua had landed on, five twin-engined Heinkel 111's approached under the cover of cloud at a height of 6,000 feet. Under intense AA fire four of them jettisoned their bombs, but the fifth dived steeply upon the *Ark Royal* from stern to bow, released a 2,000-lb bomb and roared away in a climbing turn.

The officers on the bridge, with upturned faces, watched the bomb come wobbling down from 1,500 feet above the ship. One of them thought it looked like an Austin Seven. To another it looked more like a London bus. The Captain gave an order to alter course, and as the *Ark Royal* turned away to starboard the bomb exploded in the sea 30 yards from her port bow.

A solid wall of water rose as high as the flight deck and cascaded over the fore-end. The *Ark* lifted her bow and seemed to shake herself, then plunged down again, took a list of five degrees to starboard, and righted herself a moment later as she turned back upon her course. The only damage in the ship was some broken crockery.

The Heinkel turned and then flew back over the flight deck, blazing away with his machine guns before sheering off and climbing away. To the pilot of the enemy aircraft *Ark* must have looked fairly badly hit. With the enormous cascade of water pouring over the flight deck, the list and soot, loosened in the uptakes hissing and gushing out of the funnel in ominous black clouds, Lieutenant Adolf Francke was fairly sure he had scored a direct hit. On his return, Francke reported that he had dive-bombed an aircraft-carrier in the North Sea. He believed that his bomb had scored a direct hit, but he was not certain, and made no claim to have sunk the ship. The German Ministry of Propaganda made it for him. Next morning the newspapers throughout the Reich proclaimed the sinking of the *Ark Royal* in enormous headlines, some of them printed in red. Highly-coloured pictures of the *Ark*'s end appeared in the magazines.

At 1730 next day Hamburg Radio announced: 'We have an important communication for listeners. Where is the *Ark Royal*? She was hit in a German attack on September 26 at 3.00 p.m. Where is the *Ark Royal*? Britons ask your Admiralty!' Field-Marshal Goering sent Francke a telegram of congratulation, decorated him with the Iron Cross, and promoted him to the rank of *Oberleutnant.* Before long Dr. Goebbels's Ministry published an illustrated children's booklet *How I sank the Ark Royal*, purporting to have been written by Francke.

It seems that the German claims did not deceive Francke's brother officers. They knew that he was wearing a decoration he had not earned, and he soon became the laughing-stock of the Luftwaffe. This ridicule preyed upon his mind until he felt that the only way to save the honour of his family was to take his own life. An American journalist, Mr. William Bayles, to whom he confided his troubles in Berlin, suggested that if he chose to denounce the Ministry of

Propaganda suicide would become unnecessary.

Meanwhile the German broadcasting stations continued to ask, 'Where is the *Ark Royal*?' and the irritating, sneering voice of the infamous 'Lord Haw-Haw', the Irishman William Joyce kept up the radio propaganda in spite of the British Admiralty's repeated denials that she had been damaged. On the Sunday after her return to Scapa Captain Alan Kirk, USN, the United States Naval Attaché, attended divine service on board and wrote an official report of his visit which was made public, but still Lord Haw-Haw asked, 'Where is *Ark Royal*?'

The question was hailed with derision by the ship's company, who roared in answer, 'We're here!'

The officers sent Oberleutnant Francke an invitation to become an honorary member of their Mess, addressed c/o A. Hitler, Esq., Berchtesgaden. But the German people believed the story implicitly. Months afterwards, when the *Ark Royal* was in Rio, the German colony protested that she must be another ship of the same name.

Quite what happened to the unfortunate Francke is a bit of a mystery. It appears that there were two pilots named Francke. One was test pilot for Heinkels, Karl Francke, who ultimately became a Director of the Company after the War. But of the other, Adolf Francke, there is little really known. The Ministry of Defence (Air) are unable to confirm the truth of the suicide story, but Kenneth Poolman in his book on *Ark Royal*, says that Francke was in fact dissuaded from committing suicide but was killed later in the war on the Eastern Front.

The *Ark* had achieved in just one month of war, through the German propaganda machine, a reputation and fame that has been almost unrivalled in naval history. If they really believed her sunk, then during the next two years both the Germans and the Italians were to have good cause to know that the *Ark Royal* was still upon the face of the waters, for, in the words of Zechariah, she passed through the sea with affliction. Her fighters were to shoot down or damage over 100 enemy aircraft, and to protect many a convoy in the Atlantic and the Mediterranean, while her torpedo-bombers were to bring havoc to the aerodromes of Sardinia, to wound the Italian fleet, and – in the words of the First Lord of the Admiralty – 'to encompass the destruction of the *Bismarck*'.

CHAPTER 4

The Graf Spee

When the *Ark Royal* put to sea at short notice at 1800 on 2nd October, 1939, from Loch Ewe, in company with the battle-cruiser *Renown*, no one on board but Vice-Admiral Wells and Captain Power had any inkling of her destination. All that the ship's company knew was that the *Renown* and the *Ark Royal*, with a screen of four destroyers, were to be known as Force K and that they were steering south. It was not until they were well out to sea that Captain Power told them that the first port they would sight would probably be Freetown, Sierra Leone.

It was the beginning of a long and eventful partnership between the two ships. Each had her own function. That of the *Ark Royal* was to operate in areas which could not be reached by shore-based aircraft; that of the *Renown* to give the carrier the protection of her guns, and to complete the work the aircraft had begun.

Officially Force K's mission was Trade Protection and Ocean Search in the South Atlantic, where a surface raider, at first believed to be the pocket-battleship *Admiral Scheer*, had broken out and was attacking merchant shipping.

On the previous day, 1st October, the Booth liner *Clement* en route from Pernambuco to Bahia had been intercepted and sunk by a German warship – believed at the time to be the *Admiral Scheer*. Six days later, *Ark Royal* was in the tropics and up to 10th October, four more ships were sunk on the trade routes from the Cape. The Force reached Freetown on 12th October. By then both officers and ratings were making do with any cool clothes they could find, for there had been no time to buy or obtain tropical rig before sailing. The Officer of the Guard, coming on board the *Ark Royal* in immaculate whites, was astonished to find the Paymaster-Commander on the quarter-deck in drill shorts, an aertex vest, and carrying an umbrella.

Having refuelled at Freetown, Force K left the destroyer screen and sailed on to the southward, for a sweep towards St. Helena.

From that time onwards the *Ark*'s Swordfish were airborne constantly. For hour after hour, day after day, her aircraft ranged out over the vast, lonely wastes of the South Atlantic Ocean. Eyes straining and searching for a small dot or a tell-tale wisp of smoke on the empty limitless horizon.

An aircraft flying over the South Atlantic is the most solitary object in the world. It ranges the sky as lonely as a cloud, beyond the view of its fellows or its parent ship. Hour after hour would go by without the sight of so much as a soap-box, yet each member of the crew had to keep constantly alert. In fair weather there would be little diversion beyond a spouting whale or an occasional flurry of flying-fish. In foul weather – and with tropical storms flying conditions were often terrible – the crews faced the perils of the air and sea, dependent upon their single engine or, if that were to fail, upon their rubber dinghy. Week after week they 'flogged' huge areas of salt water, morning and afternoon, straining their eyes for the raider which never came within their range.

Early in November, however, a Swordfish sighted a prize at last – the German steamer *Uhenfels* of 7,500 tons. When intercepted she was found to have on board, besides a general cargo of hides, nuts and copra, a consignment of opium valued at £250,000. Force K took her in to Freetown.

On the following day the Commander-in-Chief, South Atlantic, received a report that the raider had worked round the Cape of Good Hope into the Indian Ocean. This information was confirmed by the news that SS *Africa Shell* had been sunk in the Mozambique Channel. Force K accordingly sailed on 18th November to patrol a line south of the Cape, to intercept the raider in case she should try to double back into the Atlantic.

From intelligence reports, it now seemed that in fact two pocket battleships were operating in the Atlantic, the *Scheer* and the *Deutschland*.

On 23rd November, the armed merchant cruiser *Rawalpindi* was sunk while escorting a convoy between Iceland and the Faeroes. Her attacker was assumed to be the *Deutschland*. Again the attacker vanished and there was silence.

The weather was so bad that from 27th November to 2nd December there was only one day on which it was possible to operate aircraft, and since it seemed unlikely that the patrol line could extend far enough to the southward to intercept a raider bent on evasion, the Force continued to patrol where they were.

On 2nd December, they had a stroke of luck. A South African bomber reported the German liner *Watussi* south of Cape Point and by the time Force K arrived, she had scuttled herself and was on fire. After being sent to the bottom by *Renown*, they received news of another attack by the surface raider.

The SS *Doric Star* sent out an SOS reporting that she was being attacked in a position between the Cape and Freetown, just south of St. Helena. It looked as though once more, the elusive enemy had slipped through the net, to resume his profitable trade in his old hunting grounds of the South Atlantic.

Before Force K left to sweep towards the enemy position, the Admiral decided to put into Capetown to give a few hours' precious leave and to refuel his ships.

The *Ark Royal*'s entry into Capetown harbour caused great excitement, for it was her first public appearance since the Germans had claimed to have sunk her. The South Africans showed their feelings by their hospitality. Every officer and rating who went ashore received an invitation to one private house or another.

Twenty-four hours later, the ships sailed once more and headed for a position in the middle of the South Atlantic, from where they could proceed to Freetown, Rio or the Falkland Islands should the enemy choose to show himself again and the situation develop.

Three thousand miles away, Commodore Harwood's Force G comprising the heavy cruisers HMS *Exeter* and HMS *Cumberland* and the light cruisers HMS *Ajax* and HMNZS *Achilles* were patrolling between Rio and the River Plate, keeping a weather eye open for any German shipping using neutral South American ports, and who might be tempted to head for home. In early December, *Exeter* and *Cumberland* were at Port Stanley in the Falkland Islands, *Ajax* was on passage from the Falklands to the estuary of the Plate while *Achilles* patrolled off Rio.

The sinking of the *Doric Star* prompted Commodore Harwood to concentrate his forces and by 1800 on 12th December, three of his four ships were off the entrance to the Plate. He reasoned that the raider – tempted by the rich pickings off the South American Coast – would head their way and could make the River Plate area by 13th December. In the event he was absolutely right. Just twenty-four hours after their arrival, at eight minutes past six on the morning of

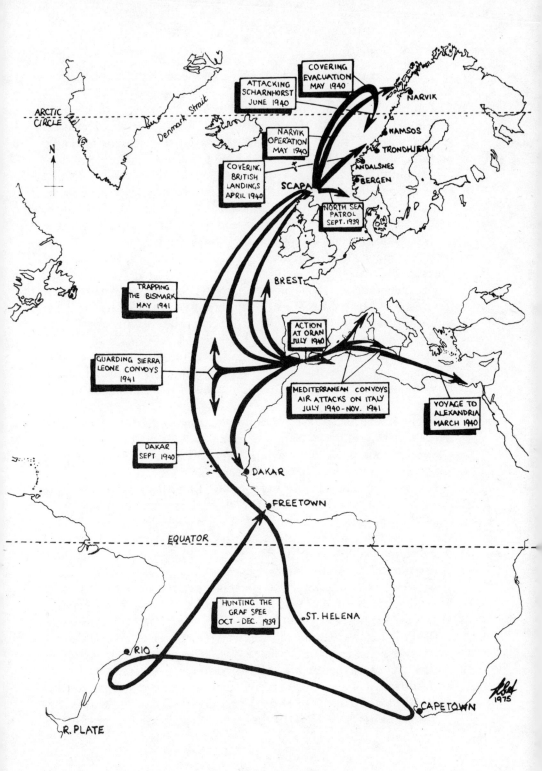

ARCTIC
CIRCLE

N

Denmark Strait

COVERING
EVACUATION
MAY 1940

NARVIK

ATTACKING
SCHARNHORST
JUNE 1940

NAMSOS

NARVIK
OPERATION
MAY 1940

TRONDHJEM

ANDALSNES

COVERING
BRITISH
LANDINGS
APRIL 1940

BERGEN

SCAPA

NORTH SEA
PATROL
SEPT. 1939

BREST

TRAPPING
THE BISMARK
MAY 1941

ACTION
AT ORAN
JULY 1940

GUARDING SIERRA
LEONE CONVOYS
1941

MEDITERRANEAN CONVOYS
AIR ATTACKS ON ITALY
JULY 1940 - NOV. 1941

VOYAGE TO
ALEXANDRIA
MARCH 1940

DAKAR
SEPT. 1940

DAKAR

FREETOWN

EQUATOR

HUNTING THE
GRAF SPEE
OCT - DEC. 1939

ST. HELENA

RIO

CAPETOWN

R. PLATE

1975

the 13th, *Ajax* reported smoke to the north-west. Eight minutes later *Exeter* signalled:

'I think it's a pocket battleship.'

The pocket battleship (or *Panzerschiffe*) *Graf Spee* was the ideal surface raider. Heavily armed with six Krupp 11-inch guns capable of hurling a 670-lb shell some 30,000 yards, and a secondary armament of eight 5.9 inch guns, six 4.1 inch anti-aircraft guns and eight 21-inch torpedo-tubes, she was a formidable adversary. Diesel engines developing 54,000 h.p. gave the ship a speed of 26 knots, while at her economical cruising speed of 15 knots she had a radius of action of around 10,000 miles. She carried a seaplane for reconnaissance and 4-inch armour on her sides as protection against the torpedo.

An ingenious product of Germany's re-armament programme designed to beat the Treaty limitations, the German pocket battleship *Graf Spee* (Kapitan zur See Hans Langsdorff) left Wilhelmshaven on 23rd August 1939, and for nearly four months ranged across the Atlantic and Indian Oceans, sinking nine ships in positions as far apart as Pernambuco (*Clement*, sunk on 30th September) to the Mozambique Channel (*Africa Shell*, sunk on 5th November).

In the long search for their elusive quarry, *Ark Royal*'s Swordfish had flown literally thousands of miles, while incredibly the nine Swordfish squadrons in the five carriers had searched something like six million square miles of ocean.

In fact, *Graf Spee* was short of fuel and Langsdorff elected to go to the Plate to refuel. Here he hoped to rendezvous with his support ship, the SS *Tacoma*, which under the guise of a genuine merchant ship, was berthed and waiting at the neutral Uruguayan port of Montevideo. At dawn on 13th December, *Graf Spee* sighted *Exeter* and closed her at full speed, believing her to be part of a convoy escort.

At 0617, that morning, the *Graf Spee* opened up with her main armament at a range of nearly ten miles, to start what history now knows as 'the Battle of the River Plate'. Although it was three to one, with the 6-inch armament of the two cruisers *Ajax* and *Achilles* and the 8-inch armament in the case of *Exeter*, they were outranged by the superior guns of the enemy ship. Nevertheless, the cruisers replied and started to close the range, using their speed advantage and splitting into two units to divide the enemy fire.

Two minutes later at 0619 the *Exeter*'s 8-inch proved so effective, that the *Graf Spee* immediately concentrated the fire of all her 11-inch guns on her, leaving the *Ajax* and *Achilles* disengaged. *Ajax* carried two Seafox seaplanes, and one was catapulted off at 0637, piloted by Lieutenant E.D.G. Lewin, RN with Lieutenant R.E.N. Kearney, RN as his observer, to act as spotting aircraft for the cruisers.

By the time the smaller cruisers had closed to the maximum range of their 6-inch guns, *Exeter*, who had borne the brunt of the enemy's fire, was already heavily hit. For the next fifteen minutes, the savage action raged and *Exeter* became very badly damaged. Two out of three of her turrets were knocked out; everyone on the bridge except Captain F.S. Bell, RN was either killed or wounded; fire was raging between decks and steering could only be carried out from right aft. Though the ship was down by the bows with a seven degree list, she continued at full speed to close the enemy, bravely and unhesitatingly firing her one remaining turret. Later the observer in *Ajax*'s Seafox reported how at one moment, 'She completely disappeared in smoke and flame and it was feared that she was gone.'

Lieutenant Commander R.E. Washbourn, RN, in the *Achilles* says of the action:

> I can remember feeling a quite illogical resentment every time he put his great eleven-inch cannon on us, when I saw those damn pieces belching their unpleasantnesses at myself, and I can remember feeling unspeakably grateful to poor old *Exeter* every time I saw them blazing in her direction.

He went on to add:

> . . . It was a plain straightforward scrap, with none of the 'hit and run' tactics which the Yellow Press credited us with. We hammered away for an hour and a half, and then hauled off under smoke. I must admit to a certain feeling of being baulked of my prey when we were ordered to turn away because the last twenty minutes at really effective range had been most enjoyable.[1]

With *Exeter* badly damaged, the situation was fairly critical, though the *Graf Spee* outwardly undamaged, had also taken heavy

[1] *The Official History of the War at Sea,* HMSO.

punishment. At 0640, she had had enough and turned to the westward under cover of a smoke screen. It now developed into a chase, though the *Exeter* with her last turret out of action due to flooding, was forced to leave it to the two small cruisers to maintain contact and limp along behind.

Lieutenant Commander Washbourn continues:

We shadowed all day. Once or twice we ventured a bit too close and he swung round and let us have it, but he was out of our range and we didn't reply.

The *Graf Spee* was unable to shake off the two cruisers, who with their superior speed, were able to follow like a couple of snapping hounds in her wake and just out of range of her guns. Shortly after midnight, she entered Montevideo and sought temporary refuge in a neutral port. It was 14th December 1939.

At this time, *Ark Royal* and *Renown* were still some 2,000 miles to the north-east. They had been steaming at sea for two weeks and though they could just reach the Plate by the 17th, fuel would be low and if the *Graf Spee* decided to make a break for it, then every ton of oil would count in any subsequent chase. Admiral Wells decided to risk losing twelve hours and top up in Rio. Force K made what must be one of the shortest visits to South America by any foreign warship, securing on the morning of 17th December and sailing again that afternoon.

Their visit created enormous interest, for rumour of *Ark Royal*'s sinking had even reached South America. German propaganda had been very effective, but now the people of Rio had proof of the German lies and as one of the newspapers neatly put it the following day ... 'Rio de Janeiro has been visited by the world's largest submarine!'

Though they were given a warm welcome by an enthusiastic Brazilian crowd, no one was allowed to land. Near the ship was a large Neon sign advertising beer, and during the *Ark*'s brief stay in harbour the flight deck was crowded with sailors licking their lips and pawing the ground: even Tantalus was only denied water. But every hour counted. By six o'clock that evening the *Ark Royal* had refuelled and sailed for the Plate at 25 knots; the *Renown* followed four hours later.

A small crowd on the quay gave three cheers as *Ark Royal* and

Renown slipped away on the evening of the 17th and headed south once more for the Plate and *Graf Spee*. At the same time 1,200 miles to the south in the harbour at Montevideo, the final act in the incredible drama of the *Graf Spee* was about to begin.

Everyone in the Force was expecting the *Graf Spee* to put to sea again. The Swordfish crews were looking forward to showing what they could do with their torpedoes after their long search. But shortly before midnight a signal told them that, rather than fight, the Germans had scuttled their ship outside Montevideo harbour. The long hunt was over and the Swordfish had been baulked of their prey.

At about 1730, the *Graf Spee* weighed anchor and with battle ensigns flying on both masts she steamed through the breakwater followed by her supply ship *Tacoma*. Outside and cruising off the mouth of the Plate, were the two British cruisers *Ajax* and *Achilles* now joined by HMS *Cumberland*. Thousands of spectators thronged to the waterfront at Montevideo to watch. *Ajax* catapulted her aircraft once more and the British ships went to action stations. Slowly the German pocket battleship edged out and when she was about 6 miles south-west of Montevideo, she turned to the west in shallow water and stopped. A bustle of boat activity surrounded the pocket battleship and went to and fro to the *Tacoma*.

A few minutes before sunset and with the brilliant orb of the sun exactly behind her as though resting on the water, a great pall of smoke rose into the air – a blinding flash and then seconds later, the boom of a tremendous explosion. The time was 2054 and *Graf Spee* had blown herself up. In the words of Commodore Harwood:

> It was now dark, and she was ablaze from end to end, flames reaching almost as high as the top of the control tower, a magnificent and most cheering sight.

Although *Ark* played no part in the victory over the *Graf Spee*, the fact that Force K was in the area had an important influence on Captain Langsdorff's fateful decision.

On 15th December the gunnery officer of the *Graf Spee* informed Captain Langsdorff that he could see the masts of *Renown* from the pocket battleship's control tower. Langsdorff automatically concluded that both *Ark Royal* and the battlecruiser were at the mouth of the Plate and waiting for him to come out. He managed to obtain a seventy-two hour extension for his ship to remain in the neutral harbour. In his cable to Germany, Captain Langsdorff reported:

> Strategic position off Montevideo: Besides the cruisers and destroyers, *Ark Royal* and *Renown*. Close blockade at night. Escape into open sea and break through to home waters impossible.

Ark and *Renown* were not there and *Graf Spee*'s gunnery officer must have mistakenly identified the masts of *Cumberland* for those of the battlecruiser.

The Germans had had a taste of action and the damage inflicted by the British cruisers would take at least fourteen days to put right. Time was not on his side; at 8 p.m. on the 17th, the *Graf Spee*'s extension was due to expire.

Though skilful British propaganda had greatly magnified the strength of the force blockading Montevideo and the approaches to the Plate, Langsdorff – who shot himself after the scuttling in his room at the Naval Arsenal, Buenos Aires – had known that *Ark* and *Renown* were in the area, and he had no desire to take on Force K.

Mr. Churchill was now able to tell the First Sea Lord:

'Now that the South Atlantic is practically clear except for the *Altmark*, it seems of high importance to bring home the *Renown* and *Ark Royal* together with at least one of the 8-inch cruisers. This will give us more easement in convoy work and enable refits and leave to be accomplished . . .'

An unsuccessful attempt was made to find *Graf Spee*'s supply ship *Altmark*, but as Force K moved slowly towards Freetown, they wondered about the future and Christmas and news from home.

During the hunt for the *Graf Spee* the *Ark Royal* crossed the Equator several times, but owing to the exigencies of war Father Neptune's ritual passed almost unobserved at sea. On one occasion when the ship was in Freetown, however, tradition was allowed to have its way. Neptune, represented by a stout cook, accompanied by his minions carrying barber's chair and gigantic wooden razor and buckets of lather, set up his court on the flight deck and laid hands upon all who had not crossed the Line before the hunt began.

It so happened that the Captain had never been initiated. He appeared on deck in a shirt and a pair of shorts. He was lathered, shaved and ducked with the rest.

It is doubtful whether a Commanding Officer in any other navy in the world could thus join in the rough-and-tumble of the Lower Deck. The incident, seemingly trivial, had its significance, for it was one which ratings do not forget. It set the seal on the *Ark* as a happy ship, and so she remained until the end.

It is not easy to say what makes a happy ship. Comfortable quarters are not necessarily the cause. Big ships are more comfortable than small ones, and the *Ark* was more comfortable than most, but ratings commonly prefer to serve in destroyers rather than in battlecruisers. A ship is made happy by the men in her, but the lead must come from the top: from the Captain, perhaps even more from the Commander. During the long zig-zags in the South Atlantic the officers and ratings of the *Ark Royal* had learned to work together and to play together. Seamen and airmen had shaken down and had become a team.

'It was the mucking-in spirit,' said one of the Petty Officers. 'There wasn't a lot of bull. And we liked being told what was going on.'

As time went by the ship's company was to know many changes, and two Commanding Officers were to follow Captain Power. But the spirit of the *Ark* did not change, and the Chaplain, whose finger was on the pulse of the Lower Deck, said that the only moans he ever heard were from men who were to be transferred to another ship.

There was a happy Christmas jollification in which all joined when, her long search over, the *Ark Royal* reached Freetown on 27th December. Presents were distributed on the quarter-deck by a Captain of Royal Marines, disguised as Father Christmas, but wearing a very small bowler hat.

The ship's company had earned their leave and it was a welcome break. During the chase of the *Graf Spee* the *Ark Royal* had steamed 75,000 miles and her aircraft had flown nearly 5,000,000. Between 18th November and 27th December she had spent only thirty-six hours in harbour, with steam on her main engines all that time. The endurance of the Swordfish crews had been tested and their experience tempered. The ordeal of the Skua crews was close at hand.

Now it was February and time to go home. En route, *Ark Royal's* Swordfish participated in a search for enemy blockade-runners off the coast of Spain, and successfully found five out of six German merchant ships attempting to reach Germany. So serious did the Germans now regard the threat of this one ship, that the U-boat

High Command laid a trap with *U-39, U-29* and *U-56* as the carrier returned through the Bay of Biscay.

Again she eluded the submarines and her luck held. In his speech of 18th December 1939, Mr. Winston Churchill had warned of the 'rough and violent times that lay ahead'. *Ark* was now ready for them and her testing time was just around the corner.

CHAPTER 5

Northern Waters

The *Ark Royal* returned to England to refit on 16th February 1940, and secured alongside the South Railway Jetty, while the ship's company went on leave – the first they had had since the outbreak of war.

On 22nd March she sailed for the Mediterranean with three squadrons of Swordfish on board to work up night flying over the desert, and arrived at Alexandria in company with HMS *Glorious*. For a week her aircraft crews carried out intensive training ashore. Then, on 10th April, the day after Germany invaded Norway, the *Ark Royal* and the *Glorious* were recalled at best possible speed to Gibraltar, where they were ordered to rejoin the Home Fleet.

On the morning of 7th April, RAF reconnaissance aircraft sighted a large group of German warships some 85 miles to the SSW of Kristiansand. It was obvious that a major operation was underway, though it was not until late on the 8th, that it became clear that the Germans were heading for Narvik and Trondheim. The Invasion of Norway would start the next day – 9th April 1940.

At about this time and on the morning of 8th April, the small destroyer *Glowworm* was off the Norwegian Coast in the vicinity of Trondheim, when she sighted some heavy units of the German Navy supported by destroyers. In fact she had become detached from a group of British ships laying a minefield in Norwegian waters in the early hours, and had stumbled across the German heavy cruiser *Hipper* and her escorts – part of the invasion covering force. She made her sighting report and against hopeless odds, increased to full speed to attack.

It was not until after the war was over that the full story of this tragic and gallant fight came out. From the German account, the *Glowworm* steamed straight at the enemy and in spite of being shot to pieces, actually rammed the *Hipper*, tearing a gash 100 feet long in the cruiser's side. There were few survivors and her Commanding Officer, Lieutenant Commander Broadmead-Roope, RN, was posthumously awarded the Victoria Cross.

After picking up stores at Scapa Flow, the British Force, comprising the carriers *Ark Royal* and *Glorious*, the cruisers *Berwick* and *Curlew* and five destroyers, sailed for Norway in the early morning of 23rd April and arrived to relieve the carrier *Furious* on station off Trondheim, on the 24th. The *Ark* carried 28 Skuas and Rocs and *Glorious* 6 Skuas and 18 Gladiators, but perhaps the most welcome addition to the force was the cruiser *Curlew*. She was one of the first ships to be fitted with radar and was able to give warning of approaching enemy aircraft at ranges out to 60 or 70 miles.

Initially the German successes were rapid and almost complete. Within the space of twelve hours the Germans had occupied Oslo, the capital and all the principal ports and airfields. Though in the first few days of the invasion, the German units were small in numbers, they were well equipped, determined and were able to rely on complete and paralysing air superiority.

In the fourteen days or so before the arrival of *Ark* and *Glorious*, small counter-attacks were made by Allied troops. Attempted landings from the sea proved abortive in the face of German air-power, and attempts to weaken the Luftwaffe by RAF long range bombing attacks on their airfields proved almost useless.

In desperation, the cruiser *Suffolk* was sent to bombard Sola airfield with the promise that she would receive RAF Blenheim fighter cover. None turned up and *Suffolk* who was subjected to heavy and accurate Luftwaffe air attacks for many hours, limped back to Scapa with her quarter-deck awash and almost under water.

It provided costly evidence, if indeed it were still needed, of relying on shore-based aircraft to provide support at sea, and when none was available, of trusting in the effectiveness of AA firepower alone. That the lessons were still unheeded was even more tragically demonstrated by the loss of the *Prince of Wales* and *Repulse* some twenty months later, and the success of two German capital ships, heavily screened by fighters, who were to brave the might of the air forces in the United Kingdom within twenty miles of its shores and escape unscathed.

The main object of the carrier force was to 'protect the naval ships and convoys, to give cover to the troops at the landing places, and to attack the German-occupied air bases in Norway'. Swordfish and

The last voyage of the Fanad Head

Fanad Head, a large cargo ship, left Montreal 2nd September 1939 en route for Belfast. A German submarine intervened and the passengers arrived eventually in a Scottish fishing port by courtesy of a British destroyer. *(Right)* 14th September, three hundred miles from Ireland, passengers assemble on deck with life-jackets, as German submarine closes from the stern and orders ship to heave to.

(Left) German submarine fires shell, *Fanad Head* stops and crew prepare to lower lifeboats. Fortunately for survivors *Ark Royal* heard SOS and launched six Swordfish to hunt and kill enemy submarine. The picture *(right)* shows survivors waving to one of the venerable biplanes as she orbits the lifeboat. *Fanad Head* sank 35 minutes after being torpedoed and nearly 8 hours after she was abandoned. Survivors were picked up by HMS *Tartar*.

9th July 1940. Forty SM 79 bombers attacked Force H in three waves dropping over 100 bombs. *Ark Royal*'s Skuas shot down one, damaged two others and forced the remainder to jettison their bombs and turn away. Picture shows *Resolution* and *Hood* taken from the *Ark Royal*.

Action off Cape Spartivento 27th November 1940. Savoia 79s repeatedly bomb Force H. At 1645 they attacked with great determination and at one time *Ark Royal* disappeared from the Force's sight behind a great wall of water flung into the air by no less than thirty bombs falling round her. She came out undamaged, 'with all her guns blazing like a great angry bee'.

Two of the many misses on HMS *Ark Royal*.

Her luck runs out. *(Top)* HMS *Ark Royal* listing heavily to starboard thirty minutes after she had been struck by a torpedo fired by *U-81* at 1541 on 13th November 1941. The destroyer *Legion* stands by. *(Right)* An hour after the attack. Ship's company struggle to keep steam as HMS *Ark Royal* makes for Gibraltar 40 miles away with the aid of tugs. The coast of Spain is in the background.

The last of the survivors slide down to the destroyer *Laforey* before *Ark Royal* finally sinks at 0613 on 14th November.

Ark Royal IV and Britain's last strike carrier proudly displays symbol of Fleet Air Arm past, present and hopefully future FLY NAVY.

Skuas were limited in performance and speed, and it was not a carrier's proper role to operate against shore-based aircraft, but the Admiralty accepted the risk, since the Royal Air Force had no aerodromes in Norway and the distances were too great to send any but long-range fighters from the United Kingdom. Not many of these were available and they could spend at the most one hour in the combat area, allowing for the transit time there and back.

From the outset of the campaign, therefore, both the *Ark Royal* and the *Glorious* were faced with grave hazards. They had to operate within hostile aircraft range of the coast, and between them they had only four squadrons of fighters, against the latest enemy types, which were faster and more powerful. These intensive operations were possible only for four or five days at a time, after which, having stirred up the enemy on the mainland, the carriers would, as Admiral Wells put it, 'retire into the long grass'.

Between 24th and 28th April the *Ark Royal* gave fighter protection over the Namsos and Andalsnes areas, where British forces had landed to attack Trondheim from the north and south. The Skuas flew to the limit of their endurance, fighting many gallant combats, sometimes against odds of six to one. Outnumbered and outdistanced though they were, they established moral ascendancy over the enemy and shot down at least twenty German aircraft, damaging twenty more. The German pilots soon learned to respect them, and in the later combats used their superior speed and climb and evade the Skuas by taking refuge in the clouds.

Glorious's principal mission was to launch the 18 Gladiators of 263 Squadron, RAF and fly them ashore to Lake Lesjashon and return to Scapa for another load. In the event, the RAF planes were unable to ease the burden thrust on the Fleet Air Arm, since they were all unserviceable or out of action within forty-eight hours.

On 27th April five Skuas attacked two Junkers 88s which were dive-bombing a convoy entering harbour. Both turned away with their engines on fire, losing height. The Skuas then attacked a number of Heinkel 111s, two of which made off in flames. Having driven off two Dornier 17s, they engaged fifteen more Heinkels which were approaching in ragged formation, severely damaging one. By this time the Skuas had expended their ammunition, but rather than abandon the convoy they started dummy attacks on the enemy aircraft, putting them to fight and making them jettison their bombs.

During this period only one Skua was shot down in battle. Eight others were lost because they flew to the limit of their endurance and then didn't have enough fuel to rejoin the ship.

Swordfish were not designed for raids on heavily-defended land positions, but while the Skuas were attacking German shipping and float-planes in Trondheim harbour, the *Ark*'s faithful 'String-bags' bombed Vaernes aerodrome near by, destroying hangars and many buildings. The raid was made in daylight, at 6,000 feet, and one of the pilots described the flak as 'so close that you could smell it', but in spite of that, they only lost one Skua shot down.

Like the Skuas, the Swordfish had no rest. Day after day they went ranging up and down unimaginably lovely fjords looking for targets, embarrassed by the permanent escort of Heinkels and Junkers overhead. On one occasion a Swordfish was chased by a Heinkel 111, another by a Junkers 88, but he escaped by skilfully outflying the enemy and coming down almost to water level on the edge of a fjord and then heading out to sea.

During this hectic period, many of *Ark*'s aircrews got back to the ship after hair-raising exploits. Captain Partridge, RM, Commanding Officer 801, on patrol over the Andalsnes area, shot down a Heinkel 111, got hit himself and had to crash land on a road within a mile or so of his victim. Together with his Observer Lieutenant Bostok, RN, he made for a small house nearby.

The house was empty but a few minutes later, the three men of the Heinkel walked in. After a fairly strained night, the five men were found next morning by a Norwegian ski patrol and knowing neither English nor German, they had a few awkward moments dissuading their 'saviours' from shooting everyone present. One of the Germans produced a revolver and was promptly shot and the other two taken prisoner.

Eventually after borrowing skis which neither of them had ever used before, the British pilot and observer reached safety on the coast some fifty miles away. This was not uncommon, for many of the *Ark*'s air crew returned to the ship only after forced landings on frozen lakes, in snowdrifts, or in the sea. Sometimes ships that were close at hand gave prompt assistance. Sometimes the crews reached safety after trudging many miles over mountains and through deep snow, fed, clothed, hidden and guided (more than once through the enemy lines) by friendly Norwegians.

Another Skua pilot, Midshipman Gallagher flying alone, found himself separated from his section after air combat. Shortage of petrol compelled him to land on a frozen lake alongside a damaged RAF Gladiator, but he was advised to leave at once owing to the presence of German aircraft and the anticipation of a fresh attack. He filled up with petrol from the wrecked Gladiator, borrowed a Norwegian school atlas, and after flying unaided across 350 miles of sea made a good landfall in the Shetlands, where he refuelled and then joined the naval air station, Hatston.

Ark Royal replenished on 28th April and in the few short days of combat, the Skuas and Gladiators from the carriers had accounted for nearly forty enemy aircraft destroyed or damaged, for the loss of only one Skua in combat.

Although a carrier's aircraft have the advantage in mobility over those of the RAF, they have no secure base and may be more vulnerable in their hangars than in the air. When the crews returned to the ship, cold and tired out, they were often heavily bombed. During the campaign the *Ark Royal* became the 'Aunt Sally' of the Luftwaffe. Once she was attacked almost continuously for twelve hours by Heinkels and Junkers, which scored ten near misses but no hits.

At dawn of 1st May, the Skuas were launched to give fighter cover to the ships evacuating troops from Andalsnes. At 0750 an enormous column of water erupted from the sea about 40 yards from *Ark*'s starboard quarter, followed by yet another a little way further off. A Ju 88 had slipped in unobserved, dived straight out of the early morning sun dropped two bombs and made off low across the water. *Ark*, a sitting target, had been missed yet again and still her luck held!

At 1525 there was another high level attack by five bombers, followed twenty minutes later by another three. This time a 'stick' fell just ahead and deluged the ship in spray. A pause until 1827 provided a welcome relief, but then they came again. At 1830, a large formation of twelve Ju 87s and five Heinkel 111ks closed the force and for the next few minutes, bombs rained down as every available gun opened up and the fighters weaved and twisted in an effort to counter the onslaught.

All through the long day, the Luftwaffe had sent in aircraft against the two carriers and miraculously, not one ship had been hit. They had had their share of luck, but the risks were becoming unacceptable. The cover that the carriers could provide did not justify the possible loss of one or both ships and since the evacuation of the troops from Namsos was almost complete, it was decided to withdraw the carriers.

Ark anchored in Scapa on the morning of 3rd May and Captain A.J. Power left the ship. He was relieved by a new Commanding Officer, Captain C.S. Holland, but in his twenty-one months, the personality of 'A.J.P.' as he was known, had welded the new *Ark* into a happy, efficient fighting machine, and a ship that Captain Holland would be proud to command.

By this time, the British forces had been withdrawn from the areas to the north and south of Trondheim, and the Germans held the port itself. But if Narvik to the north could be recaptured, then the enemy would be contained and valuable breathing space achieved. Off Narvik, lie the Lofoten Islands, separated from the coast line by the Great Vestfjord, from whose northern coast the Ofotfjord runs eastward to the town and port of Narvik itself. Allied forces were in possession of the southern shore of Ofotfjord and the Narvik area and were desperately trying to consolidate their position in spite of increasing enemy opposition.

The *Ark*, with the battleship *Valiant*, the cruiser *Curlew* and six destroyers sailed for the Norwegian coast again on 4th May with orders to give air protection to our troops in the area of Narvik until shore-based RAF fighters could be provided. Great efforts were being made to prepare two airfields at Bardufoss and on Skaanland, but the RAF would not be able to fly in for at least a fortnight.

She cruised about 100 miles from the coast, and for the next fortnight was almost continuously in action. There was no night and so flying began at midnight and went on until 11 p.m. Fog and low cloud hampered the fighters, and sometimes the swell was so deep that the motion on the ship made flying operations impossible. The requests for protection were numerous and insistent, but the distances were such that it was impossible to maintain patrols over all the areas at once unless the carrier operated close inshore, and this exposed her to unacceptable risks.

Meanwhile the Swordfish were busily photographing the area around Narvik in an attempt to assist the Army, whose maps were inadequate, of very small scale and doubtful accuracy. During one of these sorties, a Swordfish flown by Lieutenant H. de G. Hunter, RN, was jumped by three German Heinkels. He managed to escape by putting his 'String-bag' into a near vertical dive and then flying up a very narrow valley. His telegraphist and gunner, Leading Airman Bennett, emptied his machine gun at the enemy during their vertical and very rapid descent, but complained afterwards 'that he couldn't see the result'.

As they were returning to *Ark Royal*, the observer, Lieutenant Dayrell, tapped out a very typical and brief naval signal: '*Swordfish 4F to Ark Royal* Delayed by 3 Heinkels.'

The Luftwaffe reaction to *Ark*'s presence off the Norwegian coast was predictable and not long in coming. They used the much faster Heinkel MK Vs, which could outpace the slower Fleet Air Arm Skuas. The only advantage to *Ark* was that at the moment, the German aircraft had to operate from Trondheim over 300 miles away to the south, and they couldn't spend much time over the ships.

The Skua pilots fought many combats, but found that the enemy aircraft now showed more spirit when attacked and were better handled; the improved performance of the Heinkels of Mark V type enabled them to avoid battle unless surprised. Constant cloud favoured evasion, so that there were fewer successful engagements than off Trondheim, for the Skuas lacked the speed to press their attacks home.

'The performance of the aircraft crews was nevertheless as fine as ever,' wrote Vice-Admiral Wells, and when forwarding this report the Commander-in-Chief, Home Fleet, observed:

> Our fleet aircraft are out-classed in speed and maoenoeuvrability, and it is only the courage and determination of our pilots and crews that have prevented the enemy from inflicting far more serious damage.

One day five Heinkels took advantage of their superior speed and engaged the Skuas on patrol over the Fleet anchorage at 18,000 feet. After a determined dogfight, during which the Skuas attacked both head-on and from astern, one Heinkel was set on fire. The leading pilot, Lieutenant W.P. Lucy, DSO, RN, with Lieutenant M.C.E. Hanson, RN, as his observer, then dived after two other Heinkels which had hurtled down to water level. He went in close to attack, fired a burst, then banked away: one Heinkel's port engine was seen to be smoking.

Then Lieutenant Lucy's aircraft appeared to explode about 50 feet above the surface and crashed into the sea. One of his section orbitted over the scene and directed a destroyer to the spot. His body was found, but there was no sign of his observer. Lieutenant Lucy had distinguished himself many times in the campaign, both in bombing raids and air combats; in his last fight he had broken up the attack by his resolute leadership and had caused the surviving aircraft to jettison their bombs and make good a hasty escape.

The last section on this patrol sighted four Junkers 88s dive-bombing. Two Skuas followed one of them down in its dive and attacked as it pulled out, putting both the Junkers' engines out of action. It crashed into the sea and the crew of five swam ashore; as one of the Skuas dived to make observations, the Germans fired at it with their revolvers.

Meanwhile the Swordfish were also in constant action, taking photographs of enemy positions, patrolling over the Fleet, and bombing shore objectives, notably railway communications.

On 9th May six Swordfish attacked the railway line east of Narvik which came up from the German held part of Norway. On this particular day it was blowing half a gale and the wind was so strong, that it took the slow old bi-planes over two hours to reach their target area. In spite of being late, it was a comforting sight to find a fighter patrol of Skuas from *Ark Royal* still overhead. Under their protective umbrella, the striking force split up into two sub-flights of three Swordfish each and proceeding independently to their allotted targets.

One bombed the Nordalshoen Viaduct near the Swedish border, scoring two magnificent hits in the centre of the track, and placing a salvo in the mouth of the tunnel. The second sub-flight overturned a train in Hunddallen railway station and inflicted heavy damage on the railway sidings. During the attack, two Swordfish were hit by anti-aircraft fire; one of them so repeatedly that its port mainplane 'looked like a cheese-grater', but both managed to stagger back to the ship and land on. One of the supporting Skuas force-landed over Rombaks fjord, but the crew walked across country through the German lines to the coast, where they were taken aboard a destroyer and eventually returned to *Ark*.

During this phase of the campaign the *Ark Royal*'s Skuas destroyed or damaged six enemy aircraft, and probably nine more, with the loss of nine Skuas (including one crash on deck) and five Swordfish; casualties to the crew were two killed and two slightly wounded.

On 25th May the *Ark Royal* left the Norwegian coast for Scapa. British troops captured Narvik on the 29th, and, having destroyed the facilities of the port so that the export of iron-ore would be impossible for some time, prepared to evacuate northern Norway.

Meanwhile, the two carriers *Glorious* and *Furious* arrived off the Norwegian coast on 18th May with their precious cargoes of replacement aircraft. This time they brought out more RAF Gladiators and new Hurricanes to be flown ashore and operated from Bardufoss. Even the cruiser catapult aircraft were called in to perform reconnaissance and liaison duties, and one Squadron, 701, consisting of six Walrus amphibious aircraft, gave sterling service right up to the moment of final evacuation.

The new Hurricane fighters did a marvellous job and within two weeks, had accounted for no less than forty-eight enemy bombers destroyed. But it was too late to do any lasting good, and the end was near for the Allies and Norway.

After a short spell, refuelling, replenishing with stores, taking on replacement aircraft and more ammunition, *Ark* once more headed for Norway. On June 2nd she accompanied a convoy of four liners bound for Narvik to evacuate the troops. For the next few days, her aircraft operated 'round the clock', covering the merchant ships carrying out the evacuation and watching the Germans advancing from Bodö.

The evacuation of Norway was planned to take place between 4th and 8th June. On 4th June another mass exodus had been completed some hundreds of miles to the south at a place called Dunkirk. Three hundred and thirty-three thousand men had been safely evacuated from France to England and as Mr. Churchill, now the Prime Minister, said in his famous broadcast to announce the success of the Dunkirk operation: 'We will fight on! If necessary, alone.'

Fifteen thousand men sailed for England in six troopships on the morning of June 7th. The only escort available was the old converted seaplane carrier *Vindictive*, but they managed to reach England without incident. By the afternoon of the same day a second troopship convoy of seven merchantmen carrying about nine thousand men was ready and assembled at the rendezvous, to leave with *Ark* and the cruisers *Southampton* and *Coventry* and eight destroyers on the morning of the 9th.

Among the last to leave were the surviving RAF Gladiator and Hurricanes from Bardufoss. All landed safely back aboard *Glorious*, despite the fact that they were flown by RAF pilots who had never deck-landed in their lives before. But even more remarkable was the fact that the aircraft had no hooks and were not equipped for deck landing. In his despatch, 'Norway Campaign, 1940', the British Naval C-in-C, Admiral of the Fleet the Earl of Cork and Orrery, wrote of No. 46 Squadron RAF, 'The courageous action of the pilots in volunteering to fly their machines onto the flying deck of *Glorious*, and of Group-Captain Moore in allowing it to be done, resulted in all eight (hurricanes) being got safely away . . .'

It is now known that the Germans were unaware that Norway was being evacuated, but they had contingency plans in hand to attack Allied forces off the Norwegian Coast. On the morning of 4th June, the *Scharnhorst* and *Gneisenau*, with the heavy cruiser *Hipper*, and four destroyers left Kiel with orders to attack warships, transports and bases in the Harstad area and the Ofotfjord. By 7th June, the German force commanded by Admiral Marschall was in approximately the same latitude as Harstad, though many miles to the seaward and west of the British base.

On the morning of the 8th, the three large German warships intercepted and sank the *Oil Pioneer* and her escorting trawler *Juniper*, both homeward bound from Tromso. Later they found the 20,000 ton troopship *Orama* and the hospital ship *Atlantis*. By 1100, the troopship *Orama*, fortunately returning to England empty – except for 100 German prisoners of war – had been sent to the bottom, and the hospital ship allowed to proceed on her way. The following day *Hipper* and four destroyers were detached, through shortage of fuel, to proceed to Trondheim and replenish. Meanwhile Admiral Marschall in the *Scharnhorst* and accompanied by *Gneisenau*, decided to seek out and destroy the British ships now known to be evacuating from Norway.

Ark Royal and *Glorious* were still in company on the morning of June 8th, but *Glorious* was now running short of fuel, so after successfully recovering the RAF Hurricanes and Gladiators, she was ordered to proceed independently. Accompanied by an escort of two destroyers, *Acasta* and *Ardent*, the carrier turned south and headed for home waters.

Three important factors contributed to the disaster that was about to overtake the unfortunate *Glorious* and her escorts. Firstly the prevailing wind was from the north and since she was steaming southwards for England, it meant that she would have to turn on a reciprocal course if she wished to operate aircraft. Secondly, her deck was cluttered with RAF Hurricanes and Gladiators, which couldn't be operated at sea and of her own aircraft only one Swordfish was serviceable. And lastly, she was very short of fuel, so apart from the fact that she could ill afford either the time and extra fuel that flying operations would consume, it appears that all her boilers were not connected in an effort to reduce fuel consumption.

At 1545 that afternoon, she sighted the upper works of the two German capital ships looming over the horizon to the north-west. Forty five minutes later it was apparent that the range was closing and the enemy opened fire at 28,000 yards. The only hope was to reduce the enemy's speed and fly off a striking force of every available Swordfish armed with torpedoes. Perhaps they should have had a striking force of aircraft ready, since rumours of German ships in the area were known to the Admiralty, though records now prove that Admiral Marschall's force was never sighted until it intercepted and sank the luckless *Oil Pioneer*. In any event, Captain D'Oly-Hughes and the crew of *Glorious* now made desperate efforts to range a few aircraft armed with torpedoes, while the two destroyers gallantly tried to shield and hide the carrier with smoke-screens astern.

As usual, the German gunnery was deadly accurate and one of the first salvoes hit the hangar, started a serious fire and prevented any chance of flying off an aircraft strike. At 1700, more hits completely wrecked the island structure and twenty minutes later, she was a blazing, helpless shambles, lying stopped in the water. The *Ardent* closed the enemy ships and fired two four-tube salvoes of torpedoes, before she too was shot to pieces and sunk. At 1740, *Glorious* listing over to starboard, finally rolled over and sank leaving *Acasta* alone and only 13,000 yards from the German heavy guns.

Still this gallant little ship fought on against hopeless odds. Driving at the enemy and under cover of her own smoke screen, she fired four torpedoes at *Scharnhorst* and registered a hit abaft the after turret, which caused heavy casualties and put two of her three boiler rooms out of action. At 1803 however, with her machinery smashed and a heavy list to port, the brave *Acasta* finally went down with her colours still flying, and leaving the German sailors deeply moved by her incredible courage and bravery.

1,515 officers and men had perished in the three ships, but their efforts had not been in vain. The action and the damage to *Scharnhorst* caused the German Admiral to return to Trondheim, to replenish and replace *Scharnhorst* with the *Hipper*, before resuming his hunt for likely targets off the Norwegian coast. Valuable days had been won and time was all important. For *Ark Royal* and the convoy, the German decision to return to Trondheim was a lucky stroke of fate, for they had been ordered to follow the same route home as *Glorious* and her escorts.

Although subjected to a number of air attacks en route, they all reached the safety of their home ports without loss. The evacuation was nearly complete, but there must have been many a man listening to the jubilant German broadcast reporting the sinking of *Glorious*, who had cause to reflect on their luck and to remember the name of one little ship, who by her own sacrifice, had given them the chance to escape – *Acasta*![1]

On 10th June RAF reconnaissance found the German force at Trondheim and two days later, Commander in Chief Home Fleet, Admiral Forbes in the battleship *Rodney*, with *Ark Royal, Renown* and escorting destroyers, sailed once more from Scapa to Trondheim to avenge *Glorious*. The *Ark* had been ordered to prepare every available aircraft for a strike the next day – the morning of the 13th.

Trondheim lies snugly tucked away in a deep fjord some fifty miles from the coast. The Skuas had a distance of some 160 miles to fly, and because of the perpetual daylight and the distance they had to fly overland, the chance of a surprise attack was almost an impossibility. The aircrews in *Ark Royal* were under no illusions. The odds were stacked against them, but most had had friends in *Glorious* and there was a score to settle. The German ships were anchored within a few miles of an airfield, the fjord was well protected with AA guns and the only chance of a surprise attack seemed to rest with the Met. man. Perhaps the weather would give them the cover and the one chance they so desperately needed.

The original plan had called for torpedo attacks by the Swordfish as well as dive-bombing by the Skuas, but the weather conditions caused them to change their minds. In the clear weather, without the advantage of cloud cover, the Swordfish wouldn't stand a chance. At 2245, the Skuas of 800 and 801 were ranged and armed with one

---

[1]   Only one able seaman survived from *Acasta* and was picked up by the German ships, though a Norwegian ship picked up thirty-eight survivors from *Glorious* and *Ardent* three days later.

500-lb. armoured piercing bomb each, and just after midnight they took off. The early morning sky was clear except for some scattered light cloud, and it was estimated later that watchers on the coast gave the alarm twenty minutes before the striking force arrived over the target, by which time the enemy fighters were airborne and the anti-aircraft gunners were waiting for them.

On approaching Trondheim at 11,500 feet they sighted the *Scharnhorst*, with two cruisers and four destroyers, lying at anchor off the town. They had been briefed that RAF Beaufort bombers would attack the nearby Vaernes airfield to prevent the defending fighters from getting airborne, while a second force of RAF Blenheim fighters would provide long-range fighter cover to the Skuas during the attack. Actually, they saw smoke rising from Vaernes but the enemy were up in strength and they found themselves heavily engaged by Messerschmitt 109 and 110 fighters. As for the Blenheim fighter cover, either they didn't arrive or were completely ineffective. They met with intense and accurate anti-aircraft fire from the ships and shore batteries, and were thus forced to take violent evasive action and attack as best they could.

Lieutenant Commander J. Casson, RN, who was leading the first Squadron of 801 Skuas, carried out a shallow dive and attacked the *Scharnhorst* from bow to stern at 3,000 feet. The last section of his Squadron went in at deck level from the opposite direction and reported a near miss some 15 feet from the enemy's stern.

The second Squadron, 800, led by Captain R.T. Partridge, DSO, RM, pressed home their attacks with equal determination from 7,000 feet. They were set on by the defending Messerschmitts just as they started their dives, but though they twisted and turned as they hurtled down, the pilots reported a near miss on the ship's port quarter and two vivid flashes abaft the funnel.

After releasing their bombs, pilots roared away at deck level trying to escape from the murderous barrage of the AA guns and the deadly cannon fire of the defending fighters. One of the pilots, streaking across the fjord at wave top height, nearly collided with a German float-plane. 'I was so close', he said afterwards, 'that all I could do was wave my hand!'

From this abortive sortie eight of the fifteen attacking Skuas were shot down and failed to return, and though several near misses were reported, only one bomb found its mark and that failed to explode. Those who did survive, escaped by flying at deck level in the rising mist that came up as the morning wore on, and headed as fast as possible for the open sea and *Ark*.

That is, all except one. Sub-Lieutenant (A) G.W. Brokenska, DSC, RN, who circled round the whole area, twice, and risking both the fighters and the flak, 'to see if he could help any of his comrades in trouble'.

The evening before the raid some of the aircrews had gathered round the Wardroom piano for a sing-song, but that night there was no singing and little laughter in the Wardroom or on the Mess Decks of *Ark Royal*. The claim of one, or possibly two hits on the *Scharnhorst* was a sad and mournful compensation for the loss of sixteen of their friends. The hangar looked strangely emptied and was the heaviest loss the *Ark* had known, or was to know, in a single operation.

That same day, the ship's company learned that the evacuation of Norway was complete and that their own operations off that inhospitable coast were at an end. It was a sad voyage home. They wanted a rest and a break. The ship was overdue for a refit, so it was a relief when the Captain told them that the *Ark* would be going into drydock at Greenock and the men would get some leave.

CHAPTER 6

War in the Mediterranean

On the day that *Ark* reached Scapa, prior to her sailing for her refit and much needed leave for the ship's company, the news on the war front seemed to have gone from bad to worse. The situation on the home front in Europe had been deteriorating rapidly, when on June 10th the Italians entered the war on the side of Germany. The Regia Aeronautica at once launched into the attack and on 11th June, carried out a heavy attack on Malta.

In the early hours of Friday, 14th June, the advance German troops entered Paris and three days later, Marshal Petain, who succeeded M. Paul Reynaud as Prime Minister of France on 16th June, announced that he had been in communication with Herr Hitler with a view to concluding an honourable peace. On the one o'clock news on Monday, 17th June, *Ark Royal*, the Fleet and the rest of the British Isles heard the worst. France had laid down her arms and England now stood alone.

The future of the French Fleet was causing Mr. Churchill and the British Government grave anxiety. Clause 8 of the Articles of the Armistice submitted by the German and Italian Governments to the French stated:

> The French Fleet, except that part left free for the safeguard of French interests in the Colonial Empire, shall be collected in ports to be specified, demobilised and disarmed under German or Italian control. The German Government solemnly declare that they have no intention of using for their own purposes during the War the French Fleet stationed in ports under German control except those units necessary for coast surveillance and mine-sweeping. Except for that part (to be determined) of the fleet destined for protection of Colonial interests, all ships outside French territorial waters must be recalled to France.

The French Fleet was a strong one and in the Mediterranean, more than a match for the Italians. With certain re-inforcements from the British, such as aircraft carriers, it would assure the Allies of maritime supremacy in the whole of the Mediterranean area. But if it were not merely lost to Britain, but added to the Italian fleet and to such units as the Germans possessed in the area, then the combined balance of sea power would shift into the Axis favour and present serious problems.

The French Admiral of the Fleet Jean Darlan had told Churchill at a meeting on 11th June, that there was no question of the French Fleet being handed over to the Germans: 'It would be contrary to our traditions and our honour.'

The new French Government under Petain were determined never to surrender the Fleet, and orders were issued for all ships that could steam to proceed to French harbours in Africa. 'Those ships remaining in French metropolitan waters and could not move, will be destroyed by their crews, rather than fall into German hands.' As the days dragged by and the entreaties of the British Government failed to move the French, it became clear that Darlan was determined that his beloved Fleet should remain French, under the French flag or cease to exist.

In the Prime Minister's own words he stated:

'At all costs, at all risks, in one way or another, we must make sure that the Navy of France did not fall into the wrong hands, and then perhaps bring us and others to ruin.'

The War Cabinet never hesitated. Those Ministers who, the week before, had given their whole hearts to France and offered common nationhood resolved that all necessary measures should be taken. This was a hateful decision, the most unnatural and painful in which I have ever been concerned.

The *Ark* was ordered to leave Scapa on 17th June and next day, she cleared Hoxa Boom and picking up her destroyer escort, turned to the west and then south into the Atlantic. Unknown to them, they were sailing to take part in one of the most tragic and controversial episodes in World War II – Operation Catapult scheduled for 3rd July.

France's two new battle-cruisers, the *Strasbourg* and the *Dunkerque*, were lying with two battleships, several light cruisers, destroyers and submarines at Oran and its adjacent military port of Mers-el-Kebir on the Moroccan coast. It became essential to ascertain the attitude of the French Commander-in-Chief, Admiral Gensoul, and to use all possible diplomatic persuasion to prevent the force under his command from falling under German control.

For this delicate mission the Admiralty selected the Commanding Officer of the *Ark Royal*, Captain C.S. Holland, who until the outbreak of war had been Naval Attaché at the British Embassy in Paris and subsequently Liaison Officer to Admiral Darlan. Captain Holland had been on friendly terms with Admiral Gensoul: they had last met some months previously in Toulon, when the Admiral had given a luncheon party in Captain Holland's honour.

Ark secured alongside the dockyard wall at Gibraltar on 23rd June, to make good her defects, carry out much needed maintenance and above all, give her crew some shore leave. In the following ten days or so, they all quietly waited for news, praying that commonsense and diplomacy would win the day. On the 26th, they sailed out with *Hood* to intercept the 35,000-ton French battleship *Richelieu* reported to be off the West African coast, but she met the British cruiser *Dorsetshire* and put into Dakar, so they returned once more to Gibraltar to await developments.

On 2nd July the battleship *Valiant* arrived from England and the same day, Vice-Admiral Sir James Somerville hoisted his flag in the *Hood* to form Force H. At 1600, he sailed in *Hood*, with the battleships *Valiant* and *Resolution, Ark Royal*, the cruisers *Arethusa* and *Enterprise* and eleven destroyers. They turned to the east and into the Mediterranean at 1700 and headed for Oran 195 nautical miles away.

Admiral Somerville had discussed the whole operation with Captain Holland and his other senior officers and then signalled Admiralty:

> After talk with Holland and others, Vice-Admiral Force H is impressed with their view that the use of force should be avoided at all costs. Holland considers offensive action on our part would alienate all French wherever they are.

The reply came back that same evening:

> Firm intention of HM Government that if any French will not

accept any of your alternatives they must be destroyed.

That evening Mr. Churchill requested the Admiralty to send the following message to Admiral Somerville:

> You are charged with one of the most disagreeable and difficult tasks that a British Admiral has ever been faced with, but we have complete confidence in you and rely on you to carry it out relentlessly.

At 0135 on the morning of 3rd July, Somerville received another Admiralty message which stated, that although no time limit had been set for the acceptance of the British demands, it was very important that the operation be completed during daylight hours on the 3rd. At first light the British Force H arrived off Oran and the ultimatum issued.

Briefly the main options offered to the French Admiral Gensoul were either to join the British Fleet, or to sail under British supervision to a British port. The crews would then be repatriated to France and the ships impounded and returned to the French Navy after the War. Failing French acceptance of either of these proposals, the Admiral was to sail his ships to the French West Indies, or to scuttle them within six hours.

Finally, if all these terms were unacceptable, then the British Government would accept the demilitarization of the ships in their present berths, so long as the measures were effectively carried out.

If the French Admiral was not able to accept any of the above terms, then Admiral Somerville and Force H had orders to use 'whatever force might be necessary to prevent the French ships falling into the hands of the enemy'.

Captain Holland had been sent on ahead in the destroyer *Foxhound*, to discuss the British proposals with Admiral Gensoul. He arrived at the anti-submarine boom defence net at the entrance to Oran harbour at 0705, just five minutes after Admiral Somerville had signalled to the French Admiral Gensoul:

> I am sending Captain Holland to confer with you. The Royal Navy hopes that the proposals made will allow the valiant and glorious French Navy to range itself at our side. In this case your ships will remain in your hands and no one need have any fear for

the future. The British Fleet is lying off Oran to welcome you.

The choice of emissary was perfect. Captain Holland was well known, respected and liked by Admiral Gensoul, but the French authorities refused to allow *Foxhound* to enter harbour. Instead he had to proceed by motor launch and then the French Admiral refused to see him. For most of the day, the French Admiral studied the British demands and signalled his own French Admiralty, seeking instructions and hoping to gain time.

Meanwhile, Admiral Darlan had ordered all available French units in the area to close Oran and help keep the French Fleet bottled up. Admiral Somerville, realising that his own ships would soon be at grave risk from submarines or other French warships, issued his final signal:

If one of British proposals is not accepted by 1730 B.S.T. – I repeat 1730 B.S.T. – I will have to sink your ships.

As the minutes ticked by the French Admiral finally agreed to see Captain Holland, but it was already too late. At 1753 Force H opened fire on the French ships. The bombardment lasted for ten minutes with the *Ark Royal*'s Swordfish spotting for the Force. Five others, with an escort of Skuas, dropped mines at the entrance to Mers-el-Kebir harbour. The battleship *Bretagne* and two destroyers were sunk; the *Dunkerque* was damaged and ran ashore.

Shortly before this melancholy action (as Mr. Churchill described it) began, the *Strasbourg*, with a screen of six destroyers, broke out of the harbour at dusk, and in a feat of fine seamanship, eluded Force H and made off at full speed to the eastward.

Six Swordfish from the *Ark Royal* were sent in pursuit, and though their bombs straddled the *Strasbourg*, no hits were obtained. On the return passage two aircraft force-landed in the sea through lack of fuel and the crews were picked up by the destroyer *Wrestler*. At 2000 a second striking force of Swordfish, armed with torpedoes, was flown off. They sighted the *Strasbourg* steaming at 28 knots three miles off the African coast, making clouds of black smoke. She opened on them with accurate anti-aircraft fire, as they swung down to the surface, and, working round in a wide sweep, flew ahead of her. They flew up and down the shore a hundred feet above the water, keeping her in sight and waiting until sunset, when the target would be silhouetted against the sunset. Twenty minutes after the sun had finally disappeared they went in to attack, keeping low against the loom of the land.

This was the first time that the *Ark Royal*'s aircraft had attacked a capital ship at sea with torpedoes, and the pilots, still unaware that they could penetrate the destroyer screen, dropped their torpedoes outside it. So far as they could observe, in the twilight and through the pall of smoke, they scored only one hit. That did not stop the *Strasbourg* and she disappeared into the gathering darkness.

Next day reconnaissance over Oran harbour showed that the *Dunkerque*, although grounded, was not permanently out of action. As an alternative to further bombardment two squadrons of Swordfish were ordered to attack her with torpedoes.

The aircraft took off in the dark from the Flight deck of *Ark Royal* at 0515 on 6th July and arrived off the harbour just as the sun rose. As soon as the first watery rays of the sun sparkled on the *Dunkerque* above the haze that clung to the water, the Swordfish commenced their attack. Going into a shallow dive from 7,000 feet in line astern, they flew low over the breakwater and straight at the target from up sun. The six torpedoes headed towards the ship and seconds later, enormous geysers and muffled explosions told them that no less than four had found the target.

They reformed over the harbour and met the second and third waves preparing to go in. The first attack had been very effective and had achieved complete surprise with no opposition, but the second and third groups met with a very stiff reception. Nevertheless, all the aircraft returned safely, although one Swordfish had a very large hole in the fuselage where an unexploded shell had passed up through the floor, missed the rear gunner and ripped out the gun and support.

The incidents at Oran and the painful memories that they revive, are related and require mention only because they were significant to the history of *Ark Royal* and the Fleet Air Arm. In the first place, the pursuit of the *Strasbourg* proved that aircraft could successfully attack a fast moving ship with torpedoes.

Secondly and perhaps most important, the total immobilisation of the *Dunkerque* proved that when the target was a ship in harbour, an aerial attack with torpedoes was more economical than a fleet bombardment and far more effective. The Swordfish had done what the Fleet's 15-inch shells had failed to do, they had put *Dunkerque* out of action for a very long time. The aerial torpedo had shown itself to be more deadly than even the bomb, for it was able to open up the side of a heavily armoured ship where she was most vulnerable – below the water-line.

Lastly, the successful operation by *Ark*'s aircraft at Oran ended once and for all, the arguments and discussions as to whether or not night carrier-borne attacks were possible. The take-off in the darkness had ensured surprise, even though the actual attack had been made at sunrise. It convinced everybody that torpedo-carrying aircraft were a most potent force at night.

From *Ark*'s point of view, both actions helped her squadrons to perfect the technique of the night attack, and in this, they felt that they had made history. The had regained much of the confidence lost after the abortive raid against the *Scharnhorst* a month earlier, although their sense of achievement lost much of its savour because it had been won against former Allies, of whose capabilities they had formed a high opinion earlier in the war.

Three days later, *Ark* was at sea again and this time she was taking on the Italians. After a short forty-eight hour spell in Gibraltar, where she was able to repair a troublesome and very leaky propeller stern gland, she sailed with Force H on 8th July. Up until the entry of Italy into the war, things had been very quiet in the Mediterranean theatre with all its shores either in Neutral or Allied hands. Now the situation had changed almost overnight and the enemy were astride our east-west supply route stretching from the Canal to Gibraltar. Heavily outnumbered on land and in the air, our forces would become increasingly dependent on just three main bases – at Alexandria, Malta and Gibraltar.

The Italian Fleet, consisting of two 'Cavour' class battleships, seven 8-inch gun cruisers, twelve 6-inch gun cruisers, fifty fleet destroyers and no less than 106 submarines, were disposed in three main ports of Taranto, Naples and Augusta. In addition they had two modern 'Littorio' class battleships and two more 'Cavour' class battleships nearing completion and almost ready for service. Supported from the air by the powerful Regia Aeronautica, the Italians were nicely placed in the centre of the Mediterranean, to attack our supply lines and challenge any British moves to enforce our maritime supremacy.

To counter this threat, the British Mediterranean Fleet under Admiral A.B. Cunningham comprised four battleships, the old aircraft carrier *Eagle*, eight 6-inch gun cruisers, twenty destroyers and twelve submarines. These were all based at Alexandria, while at the other end of the Mediterranean nearly 2,000 miles away at Gibraltar, was Admiral Somerville's newly formed Force H.

On 7th July, the Mediterranean Fleet sailed west from Alexandria, to cover two convoys leaving the battered Island of Malta with evacuee women and children and supplies for the Egyptian base. A day later Force H left Gibraltar to probe Italian defences and carry out diversionary attacks, but after their baptism of fire from high level Italian bombers, who seemed to drop scores of bombs with a singular lack of success, they were recalled to Gibraltar. A slight brush with the British Mediterranean Fleet resulted in the Italians turning away at speed and thereafter, showing little stomach for venturing into the Mare Nostrum.

While covering convoy movements in the western Mediterranean on the afternoon of 9th July, a section of Skuas on patrol, led by Lieutenant R.M. Smeeton, RN, sighted an Italian aircraft fine on their starboard bow, at 12,000 feet and three miles away. The section went into line astern and altered course to close. The Italian immediately turned, but the Skuas chased him for half an hour, and gained slowly until they were within 800 yards, when they identified the aircraft as a Cant 506 float-plane. Lieutenant Smeeton fired three short bursts in the hope of slowing it down, then the remaining Skua's took up the attack and forced it down to the sea.

During the afternoon forty Savoia SM 79 bombers attacked Force H in three waves, dropping over 100 bombs. The *Ark Royal*'s Skuas shot down one and damaged two others, forcing the remainder to drop their bombs and turn away.

As far as *Ark Royal* was concerned, the Italian Air Force reported that they had scored direct hits with their bombs and inflicted heavy damage. An official Italian communique stated that, 'the aircraft carrier *Ark Royal* was squarely hit on its deck by two large bombs. This has been ascertained by photographs taken after the action'.

A broadcast on 13th July alleged that both *Hood* and *Ark Royal* were out of action. This was followed up the next day by details of hits on a turret and main gun-control position of the *Hood*, 'taking about twenty days to repair', and on the superstructure and flight-deck of *Ark Royal*, where seven aircraft were alleged to have been destroyed. Later it was reported that she had entered Gibraltar for repairs and men were 'working on the *Hood* day and night'.

On July 24th, the old carrier *Argus* sailed from the United Kingdom with a cargo of twelve Hurricanes for the beleagured island of Malta. Throughout July, the situation on the Fortress Island had steadily deteriorated until at the end of the month, only one Hurricane and two Gladiators were left serviceable for defence. Force H was ordered to escort *Argus* as far as Cape Bon, from where she would be able to fly the Hurricanes off to Malta, designated Operation Hurry, while from the other end of the Mediterranean Admiral Cunningham and the Mediterranean Fleet would attempt diversionary tactics.

Both forces sailed from their respective ends of the Mediterranean on 31st July, and at dawn the next day the two battleships and old carrier *Eagle* of Admiral Somerville was steaming towards Sardinia. Shadowing aircraft had picked up Force H on the first evening they sailed, but had escaped before they could be intercepted. Obviously the enemy would know they were at sea and would be planning some sort of reception fairly soon. In spite of a few false alarms early in the morning of 1st August, the day seemed very quiet and peaceful as the *Hood, Ark Royal, Valiant, Resolution*, the cruisers *Arethusa* and *Enterprise*, ten destroyers and *Argus* steamed on towards Cape Bon.

At 1750 that evening and without any warning, Italian high level bombers came in three waves and for the next ten minutes, with much noise, flash and smoke, proceeded to drop a large number of bombs around Force H. It did no damage and after the Italians had lost a shadowing aircraft to *Ark*'s patrolling Skuas, Day One of Operation Hurry was over. While the rest of the Force H steamed on towards Cape Bon, *Ark Royal, Hood, Enterprise* and four destroyers turned north and headed for the Island of Sardinia.

At 0215 on the morning of 2nd August, aircrews of 810,818 and 820 Squadrons of Swordfish were piped to man aircraft. Twelve of the aircraft carried bombs, but three were armed with 'Cucumbers' (Mines) to be laid in Cagliari harbour. It was to be the first attack on Italian soil and before the raid, the Flag Officer Force H made the following signal to *Ark Royal*: 'The object of this operation is to test the quality of the ice-cream.'

The target was Cagliari, on the southern coast of Sardinia, and at 0230 the first aircraft roared down the flight-deck. Unfortunately the fifth Swordfish in the deck park veered to starboard as he gathered speed, struck the forward pom-pom mounting and crashed over the side. In spite of a search, the crew were lost, though by 0315 all the remaining aircraft had taken off without incident and were heading towards the coast some sixty miles away.

It was a fine night, with no cloud, but a strong head-wind reduced the aircraft's speed of approach to about sixty knots. Owing to the intense darkness, the aircrews found it very difficult to recognise or identify the coastline, and the bombing force at first mistook Cape Spartivento, the eastern horn of the bay, for Cape Carbonara. They then had to fly all the way back along the coastline in the increasing light, and soon realised that what had been planned as a 'dawn attack', would now be a daylight raid.

Meanwhile the three minelaying aircraft led by Lieutenant Robert N. Everett, RN, had also lost their way and finally found themselves over the mountains. Eventually they reached Cagliari and were heavily engaged by the defensive coastal batteries. One was even firing 6-inch shells and hoping that the splashes would swamp the attackers and knock them into the sea. As the bombing force crept back along the coast, they saw the gunfire being directed at the minelaying aircraft, and the eleven surviving Swordfish dived to attack.

Led by Lieutenant Commander G.B. Hodgkinson, RN, the dive-bombing Swordfish struck Elmas aerodrome on the outskirts of Cagliari. In the face of intense anti-aircraft fire, they went into line astern and attacked hangars, buildings and aircraft on the ground. In about sixty seconds the whole attack was over. There was virtually no reaction from the defending fighter aircraft and though they were airborne, only one made an attack on the last Swordfish which suffered no damage. In fact, the fighter's presence was rather welcome to the Swordfish crews, for the Italian gunners, who had been putting up a fierce barrage at short range, were compelled to cease fire to avoid hitting their own aircraft. After expending its ammunition the fighter flew alongside the Swordfish so that its rear gun could not bear. The Swordfish observer (a midshipman) drew his revolver and engaged the fighter with that. The Italian turned away and did not renew the attack.

The raid was extremely successful. The bombs wrecked four hangars, set the aerodrome buildings on fire, and destroyed two large aircraft on the sea wall and two float planes at moorings, damaging others. One Swordfish was lost. The pilot, his engine hit, made a forced landing on the enemy's airfield in the middle of the battle and the crew were taken prisoner.

The remainder of the striking force returned to the ship independently, with one observer slightly wounded. The Skuas provided cover for the returning Swordfish and shot down one Cant 501 shadowing aircraft. The Swordfish had 150 miles to fly and the last did not land on until after seven o'clock having been over four and a half hours in the air. Three reached the ship with less than five gallons of petrol in their tanks.

While the attack was going on, *Argus* flew off her twelve Hurricanes from a position off Cape Bon and to the west of Sicily, well within range of Malta. With two Skuas to lead and provide navigational assistance to the Hurricanes, all the aircraft arrived safely in Malta, to complete Operation Hurry – the first aircraft ferry operation of its kind – and the pattern for many such future reinforcement operations.

The rest of August was spent in the Atlantic, patrolling and guarding against a possible breakout by the French battleship *Richelieu* from Dakar. Apparently no one appreciated or thought to tell *Ark*, that a strike by *Hermes* aircraft on 8th July had disabled the French ship.

At the end of the month, on 2nd and 3rd September, the Swordfish made two further attacks on the airfield at Cagliari, led by Lieutenant-Commander Mervyn Johnstone, RN. The attacks on the Sardinian airfield of Elmas, were intended as a diversionary measure to cover the passage of the new carrier *Illustrious* through the Sicilian Narrows en route to join the Mediterranean Fleet.

In the first (officially known as 'Operation Smash') the striking force established their position by dropping parachute flares, although these soon became unnecessary, for the airfield was lighted by huge quantities of 'flaming onions' which the Italian gunners shot into the sky. Hits were observed on the barracks and on the aircraft dispersed round the field, and one wing of the military headquarters was destroyed. As the Swordfish dived to make their attacks, the pilots reported that they could see plenty of damage from the attack a month earlier. Three hangars were still in ruins, although a fourth was in the process of being rebuilt, and numerous buildings were burnt out or destroyed.

The weather was unfavourable for the raid on the following morning (Operation Grab), the night having been dark and hazy. When the striking force approached Cagliari the valleys were filled with mist and low clouds. For forty-five minutes the observers dropped flares in the hope of identifying their targets, but without success. Four aircraft attacked the searchlights and put one out of action. Two dropped their bombs on what they took to be a flare-path for night landings: seen from the sky it glowed like a gigantic gas-fire. The remainder jettisoned their bombs into the sea.

The striking force returned safely to the ship to find that one of *Ark*'s cats had given birth to a couple of kittens. Not surprisingly, they were christened 'Smash and Grab' – the Cagliari twins.

After a short stay at Gibraltar, Force H was off to sea on the evening of 6th September heading southwards for Freetown, Sierra Leone. On 30th August, Force M had sailed from the UK with Vice Admiral J.H.D. Cunningham in the cruiser *Devonshire*, the cruiser *Fiji*, seven destroyers, three Free French sloops and six troops transports carrying a total of 7,000 Free French and British Troops. General de Gaulle's headquarters in London had received messages of support and sympathy from Frenchmen in Dakar and Senegal and it was firmly believed that any Free French force arriving there would meet with little or no resistance. It was code-named Operation Menace. However, the success of any operation to land and win over French West Africa would depend to a large extent, on the accuracy of General de Gaulle's information. After the fiasco of Oran, the stakes were high, but in the words of Churchill: 'Dakar was a prize, rallying the French Colonial Empire or greater.'

In company with Force M, the *Ark Royal* sailed from Freetown on 21st September with twenty Free French flying personnel on board and two French Luciole training aircraft. At daylight on the 23rd, when approaching Dakar, she flew off three Swordfish and the two Lucioles. One Swordfish acted as a guide, the remaining two carried three Free French officers as passengers.

The mission of these officers was to announce the arrival of General de Gaulle's force. Like all their comrades, they were fairly optimistic as to the result, and at first it seemed that their optimism was to be justified. The Swordfish and the Lucioles were allowed to land without opposition. The Lucioles taxied to the hangars, and the Swordfish, having disembarked their passengers, then returned to the ship.

Later in the morning, however, the situation deteriorated. The Dakar French fired on General de Gaulle's emissaries, who were approaching the town, unarmed, in a motor-launch flying a flag of truce, and two were seriously wounded. Reconnaissance aircraft from the *Ark Royal*, taking photographs and dropping leaflets, were also fired on by the French battleship *Richelieu*, and others were attacked by French fighters. When General de Gaulle tried to land his troops peacefully from three French ships the shore batteries opened fire, to prevent them getting ashore.

As the day wore on the attitude of the Dakar French became even more hostile, and Force M, which was standing by to support General de Gaulle, was attacked by gunfire, submarines and aircraft. But General de Gaulle, being unwilling that his troops should be led against their fellow countrymen and should shed French blood, requested that the action should not be continued, and accordingly Force M was ordered to withdraw on 25th September.

In the words of the official history of the War: 'So ended in total failure an amphibious expedition on which considerable hopes had been based.' That night, Force M headed back to Freetown and anchored three days later. The fiasco and embarrassment of yet another operation designed to win over the French to the Allied cause was summed up by a disgusted pilot aboard *Ark Royal* who said: 'Operation Menace, I call it Operation Muddle.'

After the Dakar debacle, in which she had lost a total of nine aircraft through enemy action, *Ark Royal* returned at last to the United Kingdom for a short refit. In thirteen months plus since the beginning of the war, she had steamed over 103,000 miles and had steam on the main engines for 301 days. It was time to have a rest! As she came alongside the jetty at Gladstone Dock, officials poured on board to plan her maintenance and organise the refit, which would last a little over two weeks.

When she returned to Gibraltar at the beginning of November, her fighter strength was augmented considerably by the replacement of 808 Squadron's Fulmars for the obsolescent Skuas of 803 Squadron. On 9th November, her Swordfish delivered yet another raid on Cagliari. Hangars and a factory were successfully hit, in spite of what one pilot called 'all sorts of fanciful disruptions'. He was referring to the fact that the Italians had increased their anti-aircraft defences and when *Ark*'s aircraft went in, they came under very intense AA fire from more than one hundred guns. The new Fairey Fulmar was soon to prove its worth, claiming a Savoia 79 shadower on the 8th followed by two more aircraft on the 9th.

Two days later, at 2040 on 11th November 1940, twelve Swordfish took off from *Illustrious* led by Lieutenant Commander Williamson. Forty five minutes later a second wave of eight Swordfish got airborne. Striking Taranto naval base at a range of 170 miles and for the loss of only two aircraft, these venerable old aircraft achieved in minutes more damage to the Italian fleet than had been inflicted at Jutland. As the last aircraft headed back to *Illustrious*, they left behind the 23,600 ton battleship *Cavour* so badly damaged that she would later have to be beached; the battleship *Duilio* also badly hit and beached; the battleship *Italia* down at the bows and gushing oil; the cruiser *Trento* bombed and out of commission; the 35,000 ton new battleship *Littorio* hit by three torpedoes and out of commission for six months; two destroyers damaged, two supply ships sunk, the Taranto seaplane base knocked out and the oil storage depot virtually burned to the ground.

In one shatteringly effective blow, a score of Swordfish aircraft had reduced the strength of the Italian Fleet by half, and *Cavour* took no further part in the War. 'It is hoped that this victory will be considered a suitable reward to those whose work and faith in the Fleet Air Arm made it possible,' wrote Captain Boyd of the *Illustrious* some time later, and in a classic understatement when *Illustrious* rejoined the Mediterranean Fleet the next morning:

From Commander in Chief to Illustrious:
    Manoeuvre well executed.

As a direct result of the sensational victory at Taranto, it was decided that it would be comparatively safe to send a convoy through the Mediterranean from west to east, comprising two transports for Malta and one for Alexandria. It was the first time for months that even fast merchantmen had attempted to brave the Narrows and they arrived to pass through the Straits of Gibraltar during the night of 24th November.

Force H comprising *Renown, Ark Royal, Sheffield, Despatch* and nine destroyers, together with a close escort force of corvettes, was to escort the three merchantmen to a position to the south of Sardinia, to be met by *Ramillies, Newcastle, Berwick, Coventry*, and five destroyers of the Mediterranean Fleet. When they had completed the dangerous passage of the Narrows under cover of darkness, Force H, with *Ramillies, Newcastle* and *Berwick* would turn back for Gibraltar.

Just before sunrise at 0630 on the morning of 27th November, a reconnaissance aircraft from Malta reported sighting a force of battleships, cruisers and destroyers near Cape Spartivento, off the southern tip of Sardinia. A little later, the sighting was confirmed by a Swordfish reconnaissance search-plane from *Ark Royal*, who reported no less than two battleships, six cruisers and sixteen destroyers. Another Swordfish was sent out to relieve the shadowing aircraft and dodging from cloud to cloud at 2,000 feet, he managed to keep about three miles from the enemy fleet and report their every movement. At 1130, Force H turned towards the enemy with battle ensigns flying and guardrails down and stowed for action. It seemed that at long last, an uneventful convoy trip was to be transformed into the long-awaited engagement with the Italian Navy.

Ark Royal launched a striking force of eleven Swordfish of 810 Squadron in an effort to slow the enemy down. Armed with torpedoes and led by Lieutenant Commander Mervyn Johnstone, RN, they lumbered off the flight deck and staggered into the Mediterranean sky. It was one of those clear, brittle Mediterranean days: the sun shining in a cloudless sky, the sea as smooth as a piece of satin. The striking force had as little cover as a battalion marching across a meadow.

After flying for twenty minutes they sighted the Italian cruisers steaming in two columns, then, 25 miles to the eastward, the two battleships, screened by seven destroyers. It was now 1220, and the cruisers were being engaged by the advanced units of Force H. At 1240 the Swordfish dived to attack the battleships out of the sun and as they went down, the cruisers to the westward opened fire in short bursts, as though to warn the battleships of their danger.

Selecting as the target the leading battleship, the *Vittorio Veneto*, one of the new and powerful 'Littorio' class, the striking force pressed through a formidable anti-aircraft barrage and dropped their torpedoes inside the destroyer screen, at a range of 700 yards. The leader found himself too close to the *Vittorio Veneto*, so he banked hard to port and fired at her consort, one of the 'Cavour' class.

A great column of brown smoke and water rose above the *Vittorio Veneto* as she was hit abaft the after funnel. Seconds later there was another explosion astern, and a third ahead of the second ship. As the striking force pulled away, the air-gunners opened fire on the bridges of the battleships and the destroyers.

In the meantime and without waiting for the slower battleships, the enemy cruisers were retiring towards the shelter of the Sardinian coast at high speed, and although the *Renown* did her utmost to close and bring the battleships to action, the attack by the Swordfish had not reduced their speed sufficiently to enable her to come within effective range. They too, withdrew at maximum speed towards Sardinia, and soon after one o'clock Force H was compelled to abandon the chase.

An hour later a second striking force of nine Swordfish, led by Lieutenant-Commander J.A. Stewart-Moore, RN, was again flown off in pursuit. They sighted three of the cruisers first, then the battleships, to the southward of Cape Carbonara. Monserrato aerodrome in Sardinia was now only forty miles away, and as the enemy already had fighters in the air, an immediate assault was essential.

The enemy cruisers were closer and offered a better target, so forming up in line astern, the Swordfish went in. As they closed their targets and were committed to the torpedo drop, the enemy ships took avoiding action and turned away to starboard. Two of them were not quite quick enough however, for there was an explosion underneath one of the rearmost cruisers followed almost immediately by an enormous geyser of water which 'rose high as her bridge'. The Swordfish also claimed a hit on the leading cruiser and reported her slowed down.

The enemy put up what might have been an effective barrage, but it was too late to cause any serious damage to the striking force. The Italian gunners fired in every direction, regardless of danger to their own ships, so that salvoes from close-range weapons were bursting alongside their own cruisers. Two Swordfish were hit, but not seriously, and all got back to the ship in formation and landed on safely.

Later in the day seven Skuas, led by Lieutenant R.M. Smeeton, RN, were flown off to search for and to bomb the damaged cruiser. They failed to find her, but sighted three of the 'Condiottiere' class, steering north in line ahead. A thin layer of cloud enabled the Skuas to achieve complete surprise; the cruisers took no avoiding action and did not open fire until the attack was over. But in spite of this however, the bombs failed to find their marks, and only near misses were claimed. For compensation, the Skuas suffered no casualties and shot down an RO 43 float-plane on their passage back to the ship.

During the afternoon squadrons of Savoia 79s repeatedly bombed Force H. The *Ark Royal*, always an irresistible target, was operating three miles from the main Force and attracted most of the attention.

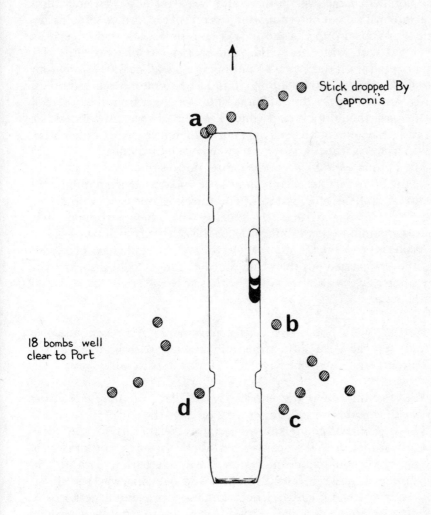

Stick dropped By
Caproni's

a

b

18 bombs well
clear to Port

d

c

a. Just below corner of flight deck (2)
b. Failed to explode
c. 20 to 30 yards off
d. Immediately below "7" director, (10 yards)

TCSA ♦ 1975

Bombing attack on Ark Royal *III, 27th November 1940*

The bombers came over in wave after wave for about an hour, and attacking with great determination. As one of the ratings said, 'Every time the Wops dropped a stick it was a straddle.' The flight deck was drenched with water from the near misses. At one time the *Ark* disappeared from the Force's sight behind a wall of water flung into the air by thirty bombs falling round her, some no more than 20 yards from her side. Admiral Somerville, watching from the bridge of the *Renown*, thought she had gone. Then he saw the fore-end of her flight deck emerge, and she came out undamaged, 'with all her guns blazing, like a great angry bee'. *Ark*'s luck was still holding!

The Fulmars and Skuas of the fighter patrols did particularly well, breaking up numerous enemy air attacks and destroying a number of enemy aircraft. A lone Skua hurled himself at one formation of five SM 79s (Savoias) with such ferocity, that they jettisoned their bombs and made off at full throttle for the safety of Sardinia.

As one report of the time stated, 'those were the gala days of battle'. But the *Ark* carried out the tiring routine of the Mediterranean war, day after day, week after week, with seldom a break for essential maintenance!

> At sea with Force H covering movements. Air reconnaissance and search. Anti-submarine and fighter patrols maintained. Fulmars shot down one Savoia 79 shadowing aircraft.

Thus would run many entries in the diary of *Ark Royal*'s war service during this period, and it went on until the end of the year.

The war in the Mediterranean certainly took a turn for the worse in the last month of the year – December 1940. The withdrawal of the battered remnants of the Italian Battle Fleet from Taranto and the dispersal between Spezia, Naples and Messina was one thing, but the transfer of the experienced and battleproven Fliegerkorps X bombers and fighters of the German Air Force from Norway to Sicily was quite another. The year 1941 was ushered in with a full gale and on 2nd January, the Chief of Staff of the Italian Air Force broadcast an official message of welcome to the Luftwaffe. Force H and *Ark* were to escort yet another convoy to Malta, now reduced to four merchant ships plus warship reinforcements for the Mediterranean Fleet.

Somerville's force continued eastward guarding its precious cargo of merchant ships, and by 0930 on 9th January all ships were intact and some 120 miles south-west of Sardinia. Unfortunately the weather was clear and the ships would be easy to find, especially as the *Clan Cummings*, one of the convoy persisted in belching out an enormous pillar of smoke, as Admiral Somerville remarked, 'As if leading the Exodus out of Egypt'. Fortunately nothing happened! However, at 1320, *Sheffield* detected contacts on her radar at a range of 40 miles and minutes later, ten Italian SM 79s came over the force and carried out a high level bombing attack. Lieutenant Commander R.C. Tillard, RN and Commanding Officer of 808 Squadron of Fulmars, send two sections of waiting fighters into the attack, while he went after two detached aircraft. At first he thought that they might be fighters and he could keep them busy, while his squadron waded into the attacking bombers. As he closed however, he identified them as SM 79s and they jettisoned their bomb load as he approached. He dived into the attack:

> Coming up astern of the rear bomber from a range of 450 yards and closing to about 260 yards. The guns were firing all the time and eventually they produced the effect. The Savoia caught fire and then exploded.

One of the crew baled out by parachute and was rescued by *Foxhound*, but now it was the turn of the the second enemy aircraft. Closing at a range of less than 170 yards, Tillard opened fire and again set the enemy aircraft alight. This time the enemy ditched in the sea and its crew of two were picked up by HMS *Forester*. Both bombers fell into the sea within sight of HMS *Malaya* which caused them great delight, because she had been very narrowly missed by the bombs dropped from the rest of the enemy formation. For the destruction of two enemy aircraft, the Fulmar had expended just 320 rounds of ammunition per gun.

Later three CR 42s were engaged by *Ark*'s Skuas without success, and at nightfall, Force H turned back once more towards Gibraltar, while the convoy escorted by *Gloucester, Southampton* and some destroyers headed for the Narrows and its rendezvous with the Mediterranean Fleet 100 miles West of Malta. The next day, 10th January, within 60 miles of the Island of Malta at about 1330, a very strong force of JU 88s and 87s attacked them. Within minutes, the principal target, the aircraft carrier *Illustrious* had received hits by six 500-kg armour piercing bombs, was seriously on fire, had half her guns out of action, her steering gear was out of action and she had heavy casualties. Miraculously she reached Malta under her own power and eventually sailed for America and lengthy repairs.

On her return to Gibraltar, *Ark* remained in harbour for sixteen days to make good the host of defects which had built up over the months of continuous operating. After a two day shake down at sea on completion of her mini refit, she sailed once more with Force H for an attack on the Italian mainland. The arrival of the Luftwaffe had not only bolstered a somewhat flagging Italian morale, but with over 250 German aircraft now operating from airfields in Sicily, they had altered the strategic balance of power in the Central Mediterranean. Malta was under constant bombardment and with the difficulty of running in convoys of supply ships, it was in danger of becoming almost blockaded. Force H needed to strike back and Genoa, the great seaport and manufacturing centre was selected.

It was a daring plan, for the naval ships would be exposing themselves to attack from the enemy air forces operating from Sardinia, and the important Italian naval base of Spezia was less than 50 miles away. Lastly, Genoa was at least 700 miles from Gibraltar and surprise would be almost impossible to achieve. With a neutral, though decidedly unfriendly Spain just across the water from Gibraltar, the Germans would know the minute our forces sailed. As a subsidiary operation, *Ark*'s Swordfish were to carry out a torpedo attack on the San Chiara Ula Dam on Lake Tirso, Sardinia.

This important dam fed a hydro electric plant, which supplied one third of Sardinia's power requirements.

It was pitch black, very cold with a strong gusty wind blowing, as the flight deck party struggled to range the strike aircraft on *Ark*'s heaving deck. Armourers loaded the torpedoes and just before 0600, eight Swordfish of 810 Squadron took off from a position 60 miles west of Cape Mannu. By the time they reached the Sardinian coast it was raining hard, with showers of hail and clouds from 1,500 to 5,000 feet. Eventually ice began to form on the aircraft and conditions became so bad, that they turned out to sea and decided to wait for daylight. One of the Swordfish became thoroughly lost in the cloud cover and unable to find the rest of his squadron, returned to the carrier alone.

As soon as the light improved, the other seven aircraft flew inland again, over the mountains, to make individual approaches to the target. The Lake itself is some 1,200 feet above sea level, so with the

Sea Vixen, all weather fighter of 890 Squadron landing aboard HMS *Ark Royal*.

Phantom of 892 Squadron on *Ark Royal*'s catapult due to be launched on exercise Sally Forth 1973, with the guided missile cruiser HMS *Fife* and the plane guard Helo in the background.

Phantom of 892 Squadron about to land aboard *Ark Royal* IV, July 1974.

Buccaneer S Mark II of 809 Squadron taking off from the port angle catapult. Launching catapult strop drops clear and hopefully is caught and retained by Van Zelm bridle arresting gear, designed to catch the very expensive wire bridles after each catapult shot.

Home to mother. A Phantom F 4K returns to land aboard *Ark Royal* after a two inch rocket firing sortie. Rocket pods can be seen under each wing.

HMS *Ark Royal* cross-operating with the USS *Forrestal* of the American 6th Fleet during exercises in the Mediterranean in the winter of 1972.

cloud base at around an average of 1,500 feet and severe icing conditions in cloud, the Swordfish pilots had very little air space to play with. In addition, the debriefing reports stated that 'the ground defences were unusually alert, and all the aircraft came under heavy fire, which grew more intense as they reached the dam'. Perhaps somebody had been indiscreet and talked too much in Gibraltar before the Force sailed! As the ice built up, two aircraft became sluggish and overloaded and so were forced to jettison their torpedoes; another was shot down and the pilot and observer taken prisoner, but four made it to the target and completed their attacks.

The most successful drop was made by sub-Lieutenant (A) R.S. Charlier, RN, who flew at 50 feet and followed a valley all the way from the coast. He was so low that he was not fired on until he had made his attack, then he released his torpedo, banked sharply away and went out at ground level. The last pilot flew over the dam at sixty feet after his drop, machine gunning the defenders and trying to make them keep their heads down, but he was not able to see any of the results of the attack. In fact, no explosions were observed and it was feared that all four torpedoes either failed or stuck in the mud and silt accumulated on the face of the dam. It was a shame that a combination of bad weather, lack of local knowledge and the failure of the weapons should have contrived to rob this brave and hazardous operation of success.

A week later, the Swordfish took part in a more successful, though no less hazardous operation while Force H was engaged in the bombardment of Genoa. At 0505 on the morning of 9th February, *Ark Royal*, detached from the main force and screened by three destroyers, flew off a striking force of fourteen Swordfish to attack the Azienda oil refinery in Leghorn, and one of the largest plants in Italy. Armed with a mixture of bombs and incendiaries, they were followed shortly after by four more Swordfish carrying mines to block the harbour of Spezia.

The moon had set and it was still very dark when the aircraft made their landfall some forty-five minutes later, but they were too far to the north, so banking round to starboard they continued to climb and head for Leghorn. Eleven aircraft went into their dives from 9,000 feet, dropping the 250-lb. bombs and following them with the incendiaries. There were a number of explosions and fires, but the aircrews could not be certain of the extent of the damage. One thing was certain, the enemy had been caught completely by surprise, and scarcely a gun opened up until six minutes after the attack had begun. As the Swordfish came out of the attacking run they flew through a balloon barrage, and one of the aircraft was thought to have collided with a balloon or cable and crashed. In any event, one aircraft failed to return from the mission and it was later learned that the crew of three had been buried by the Italians with full military honours.

The other three aircraft lost the leader and made for the airfield and railway junction at Pisa – the alternative target. Again they reported damage and one pilot – wrong as it later turned out – considered that they might have straightened the Leaning Tower. Meanwhile the mine-laying sub-flight of four aircraft approached the shore where Byron and Trelawney had once made a funeral pyre for Shelley, made gliding approaches over the town of Spezia, and laid their 'cucumbers' in the western channel and harbour entrances.

As the aircraft were circling to land on, *Renown, Malaya, Sheffield* and their escorting destroyers were preparing to bombard Genoa with their heavy guns. Spotting aircraft were airborne from the ships as well as three Swordfish from *Ark* and a fighter protection umbrella of Fulmars.

> The scene off Genoa immediately before opening fire was almost dramatic in its contrasts [wrote Admiral Somerville]. A fine, calm morning, the foreshore hidden from view by haze above which the mountains stood out, turning from grey to rose with the rising sun – nothing to break the peace and silence of the Sunday morning until *Renown* fired her first salvo. In spite of what the Italians may have to say, the bombardment must have had a shattering effect on the morale of the people of Genoa, as it would on the people of any other town whose defenders had been so criminally negligent in the performance of their duty.

For half an hour the ships pounded the Ansaldo works, marshalling yards, docks and installations. The spotting aircraft could see fires and explosions, though smoke did tend to make things difficult towards the end. Lieutenant V.N. Graves, RN, earned high praise for the accuracy and precision of his spotting reports. The information which he relayed to the ships below was superb. In the words of the official report 'they contributed materially to the success of the operation, although observation was made difficult by two changes of targets to widely-separated areas and by clouds of smoke from the explosions and the burning oil tanks.'

The withdrawal was expected to receive heavy retaliation from the air, but apart from the odd scare and the inevitable shadower, the return passage was uneventful and the ships of Force H arrived at Gibraltar on 11th February without incident.

During the rest of February and March *Ark Royal* and Force H spent much of their time in the Eastern Altantic, escorting the slow, ponderous outward and homeward bound Sierra Leone Convoys. The German surface raiders *Scharnhorst, Gneisenau* and *Hipper* were reported at various times to have left their base at Brest, for yet another sortie against our lightly protected convoys, and Force H were the only cover force available. *Ark*'s aircraft spent hundreds of hours and covered thousands of miles in a vain search for the elusive raiders, but they were unlucky except for one brief sighting late on 20th March.

Renown and *Ark* had just left a particularly slow convoy en route for Sierra Leone at seven knots, and after nine days of boring, tiring and routine escort duty with her aircraft covering nearly three quarters of a million square miles of empty ocean, *Ark* and the battleship headed almost thankfully back to Gibraltar. The convoy and her new escort were barely over the horizon, when a signal was received ordering the two ships to head north and search for a surface raider supply ship, *Antarktis*, which had sailed from Vigo some thirty-six hours before. They also received a list of Allied merchantmen captured or sunk by the enemy surface raiders in their recent operations some four days earlier. In all probability, the captured ships would be making for German occupied ports in the Bay of Biscay area, so *Ark Royal* flew off her Swordfish aircraft in yet another far ranging search of the ocean.

This time luck attended their efforts and three of the four captured merchantmen were sighted by the reconnaissance planes. With prize crews aboard, the ships were heading for enemy ports, but more important, Somerville realised that the German battle-cruisers might still be in the vicinity. The first ship was a captured British tanker, *Bianca*, sighted some sixty miles away, but as soon as *Renown* came over the horizon, the Germans scuttled the ship and both the German prize crew and the British merchant seamen took to the boats. At 1147, another captured tanker was spotted making for the French coast.

This time it was the *San Casimiro* and to attract the attention of any searching plane, the ship's baker had contrived to write the letters 'SOS' in flour on the after part of the deck. As the Swordfish approached the observer saw another member of the crew waving a swastika from one of the portholes. In spite of signalling a message to the ship in International Code; 'Do not lower boats', and re-inforced by a few bursts from the air-gunners .303 machine gun, the vessel was hastily abandoned and the scuttling charges fired. Again, the British crew were rescued and the Germans taken prisoner by *Renown*.

By the time *Renown* had finished picking up the merchant ship survivors, it was getting late and although *Ark Royal* flew off more searches, time was running out and the weather deteriorating. The *Scharnhorst* and *Gneisenau* were steering north-east to Brest at a speed of 20 knots when at 1730, a Fulmar of 808 Squadron, piloted by the Commanding Officer Lieutenant Commander Tillard, caught a brief glimpse of the two ships. They were at the extreme range of the crew's visibility of about 8 miles, but there was no doubt that they were the ships that Force H were seeking.

Three factors then conspired to prevent *Ark Royal* from launching what could have been a very effective strike, and either to severely damage or sink the enemy, or at least slow them down enough to allow the battleships to be brought into gun action. Firstly the Fulmar's radio went unserviceable and they were prevented from sending their initial enemy sighting report back to *Ark* and *Renown*. They had to make a visual report by lamp to the nearest ship 110 miles away to the south, and this lost precious time and was not relayed to Admiral Somerville until 1815 – 45 minutes after the initial sighting. Secondly, the enemy had altered course to the north when sighted by the Fulmar, and the Admiral guessed wrongly that the two German warships were heading for Iceland. This meant that the subsequent searches in the worsening visibility were made too far to the north. And lastly, it was nearly dark when the strike of torpedo-armed Swordfish were ready to go. With only one hour of daylight left and at least a two hour flight to the last known position of the enemy ships, followed – if they found them – by a night attack, the chances of success were very remote. The Admiral looked at the low cloud and bad visibility and considered the risks too high. *Ark*'s crew were now trained and efficient, but they were too valuable to hazard on such a venture. He did send another search aircraft out in an effort to find and shadow the German ships, but it was unsuccessful and returned long after dark.

With one short break for refuelling at Gibraltar, Force H spent the period until 1st April patrolling the sea areas to the westward from Ushant to Lisbon. It was rough, cold, miserable and fruitless, but the aircrews learned to operate from the wildly pitching deck and after the relative calm of the Mediterranean seas, this was a very new and sometimes, exciting experience. Most aviators accustomed to landing on acres of smooth and stationary tarmac, will appreciate the problems of 'plonking' an aircraft down on 800 feet of metal, which one minute is level with you, the next minute has dropped 30 feet down and sometimes pitched even 30 feet up!!

As one eager young lady remarked to her over-attentive escort; at a ship's cocktail party in Gibraltar, 'I don't know how you do it, Charles, it must require a lot of luck!'

'No', he replied disarmingly, 'Just sheer nerve, judgement and skill!' He was a supply officer!

In early April, the situation in the Mediterranean was extremely serious. On the 6th the Germans invaded Greece and Yugoslavia, Rommel's offensive in North Africa was advancing eastwards with great success and Malta, still under almost continuous air attack, was running dangerously short of fighter aircraft. *Ark* had delivered 12 replacement Hurricanes on 3rd April, but they were being used up at an alarming rate and without more aircraft, the situation could become critical.

On April 19th Captain L.E.H. Maund relieved Captain Holland as the new Commanding Officer of *Ark* and on the 24th, she sailed once more for Malta with 23 Hurricanes aboard. The old *Argus* was too small, too slow and her flight deck too short. The few Hurricanes that she could carry had to fly off with a reduced fuel load, thus restricting the range rom Malta. With the intelligence network operating from Gibraltar and Spain, the enemy knew within hours when the next consignment was due and their intelligence experts could then make a fair assessment of the probable flying off point. Now that Fliegerkorps X was operating in the area, the risks to *Argus* were very considerable and Admiral Somerville decided that *Ark* would be used instead.

807 Fulmar Squadron had arrived in the aircraft carrier *Furious* to relieve 800 squadron of Skuas in *Ark*, which had been in the ship since the outbreak of war. Also with *Furious* came four new ASV

radar-fitted Swordfish for 825 Sqaudron, now, at last, they would have a much better search capability.

As the Force headed east once again they were told that the weather at Malta was clamped and unsuitable and that the flying off would have to be delayed 24 hours. On the 27th, after a long and anxious wait, three flights of aircraft each led by a Fulmar flew off successfully. They arrived at their destination without incident, and once more provided the beleagured island with timely, but temporary relief.

One of her more important missions at this time was to support a vital convoy of tanks through the Mediterranean to Egypt. General Wavell commanding the British Forces in North Africa was being steadily pushed back by Rommel's forces. Tobruk was besieged and even the vital Suez Canal was threatened. Everywhere it seemed, the Germans were on the offensive and scoring notable successes. Operation Tiger was a bold attempt to reinforce the British Army in the desert with much needed tanks. They had plenty of drivers and crews, but the tanks had been knocked out and there was a critical shortage. Five fast merchantmen were to carry 307 tanks right through the Mediterranean and under the noses of the Luftwaffe, now firmly based in Sicily and Sardinia though no one thought it would be easy.

On 5th May, Force H reinforced by the cruiser *Fiji* sailed out of Gibraltar, but instead of heading east, they turned west and disappeared over the horizon. To the ever watchful eyes ashore, they hoped that it would be reported to Berlin as yet another Atlantic patrol. Well out of sight of land, they met up with the precious convoy and the battleship *Queen Elizabeth* and the cruisers *Naiad* and *Phoebe* – reinforcements for the Mediterranean Fleet.

The whole force passed through the Straits of Gibraltar in darkness and proceeded towards the Sicilian Narrows. Nobody in the convoy or the escorting ships doubted the reception they would get once the enemy detected them. Equally, they realised the vital importance of the tanks that particular ships carried. 'The convoy must go through,' emphasised Flag Officer, Force H. His famous signal and part of the message sent to all ships prior to sailing.

On May 8th the new radar-equipped Swordfish searched out to a range of 140 miles ahead of the force, but nothing was sighted. It was overcast and raining and good concealment for the ships, who were now approaching the narrowing area of sea between Sardinia and

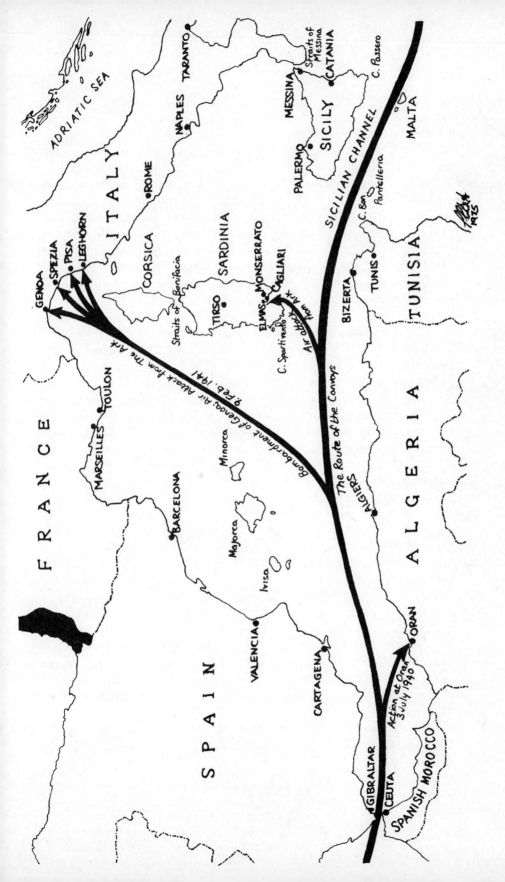

the Coast of Tunisia near Bone. At 1115, an enemy signal was intercepted and showed that the force had been sighted, and minutes later the shadowing aircraft was spotted and engaged. It was a float-plane and after turning away, he managed to escape in the clouds, but Somerville now knew that the enemy would be coming in force.

The passage of the convoys lasted several days, and the pattern was always the same. On the second day Italian reconnaissance aircraft would make their appearance and the Fulmars (which by that time had replaced all the Skua squadrons) went out to intercept as many as possible before they could send back information. The third day was always the most critical of all. The surviving Italian shadowers would report the position of the Force and the convoy early in the morning, and a couple of hours later the high-level bombing attacks would begin, often synchronised with torpedo attacks. These would last continually throughout the day.

Although the *Ark Royal* remained as close to the main force as possible during such operations, she had to some extent to work independently in order to have freedom of movement for operating her aircraft; for making the best use of her guns, and for manoeuvring to avoid torpedo attacks. When the day was calm and there was little or no wind, she would have to proceed at a very high speed to achieve the necessary wind over the deck to operate aircraft. The 'command' on board would pray for a breeze ahead. When the wind shifted, she had the choice of flying off her aircraft down wind, or of heading into wind with the risk of becoming separated from the Force and the protection it gave her. Once when she was compelled to accept the first alternative, there was barely enough wind to enable the Fulmars to clear the sea as they left the bows of the ship.

During the critical hours she always had to keep as many fighters over the convoy as possible, directing them on to the incoming enemy formations. On one passage sixteen Fulmars were kept in the air for over four hours after the first enemy bombers had been sighted: some of the pilots had to make four sorties in one day. It was always a race to fly off the aircraft, to land on those which had been damaged in combat, or were short of fuel and ammunition, strike them down to the hangars, refuel and re-arm them, bring them back to the flight deck, and then, the pilots and observers fed and a little rested, would fly them off again.

All this could be done only when the guns and the manoeuvres of the ship would allow. A bombing attack had to be engaged by the ship's armament on the most favourable bearing, which was seldom in the direction of the wind, and even if it had been, the blast from the guns would have prevented the aircraft from being flown off or landed on. Sometimes it was possible for the ship to turn into the wind to take on a fighter which needed an emergency landing, but one at least was compelled to come down in the sea while the *Ark*'s guns were firing, the crew being rescued by a destroyer.

The Italian torpedo-aircraft would attack most gallantly, particularly in the beginning of the operations, flying in tight formation and coming in among the ships only a few feet from the surface of the sea. Their losses were consequently very heavy: during one attack they lost eighteen out of thirty-six aircraft by action of the Fulmars and by gunfire of the Fleet. Italian fighters, Fiat CR 42s, accompanied the bombing formations, and although they usually kept beyond range of the warships' guns, their superior speed accounted for several of the *Ark*'s Fulmars.

Each passage provided its peculiar excitements, but one day's engagements are typical of many. The *Ark Royal* started the day of 8th May with twelve Fulmars. Combats soon reduced the number serviceable to seven, then to five. But by rapid re-equipment and repair the carrier maintained a permanent patrol throughout the day. There were times when no more than two aircraft were over the Fleet, but whenever a raid appeared to be impending every fighter that could be made fit for service was sent into the sky.

The ship's company had been at action stations since dawn and at 1345, eight torpedo-dropping planes approached making straight for *Ark* and *Renown*. Escorted by·CR 42 fighters, they flew in low over the water and escaped detection on the radar screens. Eventually they were sighted visually by the screening destroyers and came under such intense AA fire, that they were forced to drop their torpedoes outside the screen. Fortunately both capital ships were able to take evasive action and the torpedoes missed. The Fulmar fighters dived on the escorting CR 42 fighters and early in the action *Ark Royal* lost a gallant pilot and observer who had been together in many a combat and had both won the Distinguished Service Cross: Lieutenant-Commander R.C. Tillard, RN, and Lieutenant M.F. Somerville, RN. Seeing three CR 42s 200 feet below, Lieutenant-Commander Tillard turned towards them for a head-on attack. The Fulmar broke away to port in a vertical dive, flattened out at 500 feet, and was not seen again.

Three of the torpedo-droppers were splashed by the Fleet's gunfire
and at least one CR 42 was damaged by the fighters. In the short lull
which followed, another small formation of SM 79s was driven off
and one bomber shot down, for the loss of one Fulmar whose pilot
and observer were both picked up.

From 1620 the Italian attacks seemed to follow one another almost
without a break, though the main onslaught of the day came shortly
after 1900. The official report says that 'The sky was bright and
clear, but a great black cloud, rising from sea level to 9,000 feet, was
closing in from the northward.' Darkness would bring a much
needed respite from the incessant attacks, but at that moment
reported contacts away to the north. Hostile aircraft from Sicily were
sighted approaching over the top of the cloud to attack the convoy.
This time they were not the familiar SM 79s or CR 42s, they were
twenty-eight Junkers 87s and six Messerschmitt 110s in three
separate formations.

By this time *Ark* had only seven Fulmars fit to fly. Three Fulmars
were already airborne over the ships and heading for the enemy
formations, and two sections of two aircraft each were on deck as
standby. The trouble was that there was very little natural wind and
it would take time for the carrier to build up speed and get enough
wind over the deck to launch. It was a desperate situation with the
enemy bombers and fighters drawing closer every second, and the
carrier seeming to take minutes to wind on the speed. As soon as
they achieved the minimum wind speed over the deck, Commander
(Flying) gave the order to launch and the first of the standby
Fulmars raced down the deck. It seemed to everyone watching that
the aircraft was anything but airborne when it reached the bows and
'ran out of deck'. Somehow, it sank out of sight, staggered along –
probably on its own ground cushion – a few feet above the water, and
slowly climbed away. 'The other three launches were just as hairy',
(dangerous) remarked one of the aircrew later.

Ark's fighters were divided into three sections of three, two and two
aircraft respectively and outnumbered though they were, they went
straight for the enemy formations. In the few hectic minutes that
followed, the defending fighters shot down one bomber, damaged
several others including at least one of the Me 110s and scattered
the rest. In one never to be forgotten action, a screening destroyer
watched a solitary Fulmar repeatedly attacking a large group of
enemy aircraft. Eventually he managed to break up the formation and

forced them to retire. Soon all cohesion in the attack disappeared. Aircraft jettisoned their bombs and dived to gain the safety of the clouds. Ships' companies could see the splashes of the jettisoned bombs as they fell into the sea miles to the northward, and the enemy retired without a single bomber having broken through to make his attack.

The day ended with a most determined torpedo attack on *Ark Royal* and *Renown* by three SM 79s flying low over the water on the Carrier's port quarter. A section of two Fulmars (Lieutenant R.C. Hay, RM, and Lieutenant Guthrie, RNVR) was flown off, but they were unable to prevent two of the aircraft from closing. In spite of intense anti-aircraft fire from nearly every gun in the Fleet, the two Italians pressed on in close formation and displayed great gallantry as they loosed off the torpedoes and turned away. Fortunately *Ark* managed to turn to port under full helm, and two of them passed within 50 yards down the starboard side.

As a result of the day's attacks seven enemy aircraft were destroyed, anti-aircraft fire accounting for four and the fighters for three. The enemy obtained no hits, either by bomb or by torpedo, and there were no casualties in the ships. Two Fulmars were lost, but the crew of one was saved.

When every combat was a gallant and resourceful action, and when the hazards of the day were shared by all, it may seem invidious to mention individual exploits. But a few may be described as representative of all these operations. There was Lieutenant (A) R.E. Gardner, RNVR, leader of blue one section which carried out four fighter patrols on 8th May, and in three of them he was in action. He took every opportunity of engaging the enemy, and during the day shot down one Junkers 87 and helped three other pilots to destroy a Savoia 79, firing the last burst before it broke up; he damaged, even if he did not destroy, two more. After his last engagement, and when his aircraft was severely damaged and the windscreen shattered, his one anxiety was to get airborne again as quickly as possible.

The observers played their part as well as the pilots. Leading Airman Ralph N. Orme, who was only nineteen and had never been in combat against enemy fighters before, kept his pilot supplied with accurate information during an attack on several Fiat CR 42 fighters, even after the Fulmar had been knocked out of control by their gunfire. Having exhausted every alternative method of warding off stern attacks, he finally used wads of paper which he hurled at the attackers, twice causing an enemy fighter to cease fire and break away.

Another rating observer who showed a fine example was Petty Officer Airman Leslie G.J. Howard. He was severely wounded in an engagement with CR 42s, but continued to pass information of their movements to his pilot until they had been shaken off. When the pilot reported Howard's wound and asked permission to bring him back to the ship, Howard insisted that he was fit to carry on and begged the pilot to continue the engagement.

This was the last engagement of a very tiring busy day. As darkness fell the convoy reached the entrance to the Skerki Channel and proceeded on their way undamaged, escorted by the warships who were due to join the Mediterranean Fleet. *Renown*, *Ark* and *Sheffield* turned to west and increasing speed to 25 knots, headed proudly for Gibraltar. As the ships neared their familiar 'Rock', Flag Officer Force H, received the following signal from the Flag Officer, Gibraltar:

'Small round object sighted 180 degrees 5 miles from Europa Point. Probably mine.'

From Flag Officer Force H:

'Certainly not mine.'

On the morning of 21st May in Company with *Furious* and her usual Force H, the two carriers launched forty-eight Hurricanes for Malta. After a few mishaps with the Fulmar leaders, forty-seven aircraft finally reached their destination and landed safely. The missing hurricane had mysteriously dived into the sea off Cape Bon, and no reason could be found for its loss. It is perhaps worth mentioning that these reinforcement flights were made in aircraft which had come straight from a factory – often crated – on a long journey by land, sea, and air to arrive on some carrier's flight deck. They were then taken to a launch point – up to 450 miles from their destination – and the pilots flew off a short deck, mostly for the first time, on their lonely and very long flight over the sea. It speaks highly of the courage of the RAF ferry pilots and one wonders that there weren't more losses.

In spite of the success of this operation, Somerville had misgivings about continuing the operations in their present form. As a glance at the map will show, a convoy for Malta from Gibraltar, sailed for much of its journey flanked by enemy held territory. With the information passed to them as soon as our ships left Gibraltar and noting that the carriers had land-based fighters on board, it was not difficult to work out the approximate position and time of launch of the carriers and their planes. The future pattern of operations would need review and alteration.

Force H returned to Gibraltar for a short respite before yet another foray into the Eastern Mediterranean. The news of the war in general still made pretty sombre reading, but away to the north some two and a half thousand miles, another event stole the headlines and would soon involve *Ark Royal* and Force H. On the evening of 22nd May, Commander-in-Chief Home Fleet received confirmation from a naval reconnaissance aircraft flown from Hatston to Bergen, that the German Battleship *Bismarck* and cruiser *Prinz Eugen* had sailed for the Atlantic. The Home Fleet sailed and Force H waited expectantly. At 0050 on the morning of 24th May, a signal from Admiralty read:

> Proceed as soon as ready to join (Convoy) after daylight May 26th. Should reconnaissance today indicate one or both German battle cruisers have left Brest, it will be necessary to alter these instructions.

Two hours later, Admiral Somerville in the battleship *Renown*, *Ark Royal*, *Sheffield* and six destroyers were leaving Algeciras Bay and turning west into the Atlantic.

CHAPTER 7

The Sinking of the Bismarck

At 1500 on 20th May, two large German warships escorted by six destroyers were sighted steaming out of the Great Belt and into the Kattegat. Their course led them northwards, then went through the Skaggerak north of the Jutland Peninsula and finally, north once more to a quiet fjord near Bergen to refuel on 21st May. One of those German ships was the *Bismarck* and the other the *Prinz Eugen*.

The Washington Treaty of 1921 was a specific attempt to limit the allied nations on owning a battle fleet of more than a specified tonnage. It placed an embargo on all parties to the treaty from building any battleship for the next ten years, and after that, their size was to be limited to a maximum of 35,000 tons. Germany was not even considered capable of constructing such a vessel and thus, was not a party to the Treaty.

Hitler and his naval advisers of the Third Reich devised a ship building programme aimed at giving Germany a strong navy, and restoring once more her influence and maritime supremacy. The programme included a strong submarine fleet, destroyers, heavy cruisers and four giant battleships. Eventually, only two of the battleships were completed. Fortunately for the Allies, the remaining two to be named the *Grosse Deutschland* and the *Friedrich der Grosse* never got beyond the drawing board stage.

The first to be completed was the *Bismarck*, followed by her sister ship *Tirpitz* shortly afterwards. The fourth *Bismarck* was by far the biggest warship ever built in Germany. Laid down in the Blohm and Voss shipyard in Hamburg in 1936, she was not launched until 14th February 1939. She was given out to be a battleship of 35,000 tons standard displacement – that is exclusive of fuel and reserve feed water for her boilers – but she was actually 50,900 tons fully loaded. This monster battleship was 791 feet long at the waterline, had a beam of 118 feet and a draught of 28 feet. Her impressive armament boasted eight 15-inch guns, twelve 5.9-inch guns and sixteen 4.1 inch anti-aircraft guns as well as a profusion of smaller AA weapons.

The day of the launching ceremony was St. Valentine's Day, though this choice of date probably had little or no significance in the Nazi calendar. Hitler himself was present to witness his new, giant warship slide gracefully into the river, to the accompaniment of brass bands, wild cheering and Nazi flags fluttering in the breeze. After fitting out, she steamed to the Baltic for her trials; and by the spring of 1941 she was lying at Gdynia – awaiting orders from the German Naval High Command.

The battle cruisers *Scharnhorst* and *Gneisenau* had already sunk twenty-two allied merchant ships in the North Atlantic. Admiral Erich Raeder, the Commander-in-Chief of the German Navy, had been impressed with their success, but *Bismarck* would greatly strengthen and increase the effectiveness of their surface raiding force. At a meeting on 18th March 1941 presided over by Hitler, the German plans for *Bismarck* were formulated and a month later, approved.

Operation *Rheinuebung*, or Rhine Exercise, was simple; the *Bismarck* and *Prinz Eugen* were to proceed via the Belt and North Sea out into the North Atlantic. There they were to intercept and attack Allied shipping when opportunity offered, replenishing stores and ammunition as required from either a port on the west coast of France or suitably positioned tankers and supply ships. They would be supplied with intelligence information on our convoys by an elaborate special reconnaissance link between the raiders, U-boats and cunningly disguised merchant ships. The Germans had already sailed the support forces of two scout ships, two supply ships, five tankers and six submarines. Operation *Rheinuebung* differed from the earlier operations of the *Scharnhorst* and *Gneisenau* in one important respect; they had been restricted to attacking unescorted merchant shipping only, whereas the *Bismarck* group was ordered to attack all shipping including protected convoys, unless a 15-inch gun battleship was present.

Raeder appointed Vice-Admiral Guenther Luetjens to command the two raiders. He was a quiet, humourless and rather forbidding character, with a forceful character. His crew nicknamed him the 'Black Devil'; but to Raeder he was an effective leader, and that was what the surface raiding ships required. Luetjens realised that the most dangerous part of the operation would be getting out into the

Atlantic. To be unobserved was of paramount importance, and he could take one of four possible routes: to the north of Iceland through the Denmark Strait; between Iceland and the Faeroe Islands; the passage between the Faeroes and the Shetlands only one hundred and fifty miles wide or lastly, the narrow sixty mile gap between the Orkneys and the Shetlands. They opted for the Denmark Strait, which although patrolled by the British cruisers *Norfolk* and *Suffolk*, offered the best chance and in any case, *Scharnhorst* and *Gneisenau* had used it without being detected.

As the two German ships and their escorts headed for the first rendezvous in the Norwegian fjord of Korsfjord just to the south of Bergen on 20th May 1941, they were spotted by a party of people walking by the shore in Kristiansand's Vesterveien. They were Viggo Axelssen, a wealthy young ship's chandler, his friends Arne Usterud, solicitor, a photographer called Wintersborg and half a dozen others. The group stopped at a place called Runningen to admire the view, and on that calm, still evening, they could see far out to seaward beyond the Oksy lighthouse eight miles away. Suddenly they saw a group of ships steaming at high speed on the horizon. A closer look through Winterborg's old-fashioned spy-glass revealed two big camouflaged warships, with aircraft circling overhead and escort craft ahead, steaming at high speed towards the Norwegian Fjords.

Axelssen worked in the Norwegian resistance movement for the Oslo-Stavanger circuit, and late that evening the urgent coded message of twelve words was being transmitted to London. Operation *Rheinuebung* had been detected and reported – now it was up to the British authorities to act. The Admiralty sent an immediate signal to the Commander in Chief Home Fleet at Scapa.

The sighting and intelligence reports which reached Admiral Tovey on the 20th came as no surprise. Increased enemy reconnaissance flights in the Denmark Straights area had hinted at something about to happen, and had caused him to station cruiser patrols in both the channels between Greenland and Iceland and the Faeroes and Iceland.

On 21st May, Flying Officer M. Suckling was flying his reconnaissance Spitfire over the fjords to the South of Bergen, when he saw and photographed two large warships steaming in company. The destroyers had been sent back to their base, and after spending the day refuelling and preparing themselves for action, the *Bismarck* and *Prinz Eugen* headed quietly away for Iceland that evening.

The German Admiral was unaware that the two ships had been spotted and from his point of view, there was no reason to think otherwise. Late on the 21st, a force of Hudson and Whitley bombers from the RAF was sent to try to deal with the threat, but in the awful weather conditions over the Norwegian coast, only two aircraft got as far as Bergen and they could see nothing on a coast completely shrouded in fog.

The next day the weather was even worse with heavy rain, cloud down to 200 feet and a visibility of less than 1,000 yards, but a naval target-towing Maryland aircraft managed to take-off from Hatston in the Orkneys and head for Norway. Under appalling conditions the aircraft managed to search Korsfjord and confirm that the enemy had gone, and the vital information was passed via the Admiralty to an anxious and worried Commander-in-Chief.

The situation for the British Commander-in-Chief and the Admiralty was extremely serious. There were already ten British convoys at sea: an eleventh, carrying twenty thousand troops to Egypt, and guarded by a flotilla of destroyers and the First World War battle cruiser *Repulse* was about to depart. In every case the escorts and the convoys would be at the mercy of the superior fire power of the *Bismarck* and *Prinz Eugen*. They had to be found, and found quickly.

Tovey had two cruisers *Suffolk* and *Norfolk* under the command of Rear Admiral W.F. Wake-Walker, patrolling the Denmark Strait, and a further three deployed in a barrier between the Faeroes and Iceland. At Scapa Flow, he had his own flagship, the battleship *King George V*, the very new and unworked up carrier *Victorious* – reckoned to be about thirty per cent efficient and carrying nine Swordfish of Lieutenant Commander Esmonde's 825 Squadron, four cruisers and seven destroyers. With this force, he sailed out of Scapa on the evening of 22nd May and headed for Iceland.

The German Commander-in-Chief Admiral Raeder had decided to route his two ships through the Denmark Strait: Tovey guessed that that would be their most likely course of action. Accordingly, he had sailed his Atlantic covering force consisting of the battle cruisers *Hood* and *Prince of Wales* and six destroyers to intercept any attempted break through and act as 'long stops' from a position to the South of Iceland. Finally, there was always the back-up support of Force H, though admittedly they were some thousands of miles to the south at Gibraltar.

The armada of British ships was gathering from all directions, in an attempt to close a net round the two, dangerous enemy ships, although it would be many hours before they were in a position to pull the net tight.

Between Greenland and Iceland there is a dreary expanse of Arctic which is frozen and icebound for a considerable distance from the coast of Greenland. Known as the Denmark Strait, it is an inhospitable part of the world and is frequently shrouded in swirling banks of fog and mist. It was here on the evening of 23rd May that the cruisers *Norfolk* and *Suffolk* first sighted and reported the enemy warships as they skirted round the edge of the ice pack. Both ships had been fitted only recently with their new radar sets and were patrolling a clear channel some 10 miles wide extending from the ice pack to the North West to the edge of a thick fog bank nearer Iceland.

At 1922 on the evening of 23rd May Able Seaman Newell, a lookout aboard HMS *Suffolk* (Captain R.M. Ellis, RN) spotted *Bismarck* and *Prinz Eugen* emerging from a snow squall between *Suffolk* and the ice pack. They were at a point blank range of only seven miles and unmistakable, though the somewhat inappropriate remark of a midshipman on *Suffolk*'s bridge – '*Hood* and *Prince of Wales*, I suppose!' – subsequently became legendary. *Suffolk* sent out the first sighting report, but because of some fault in her transmission it was not received by Admiralty. An hour later hower, she was joined by *Norfolk* who at 2032 sent the signal. 'One battleship, one cruiser in sight.'

The eagerly awaited news was received by the Commander-in-Chief in *King George V* with *Victorious*; it was also received by the battle cruisers *Hood, Prince of Wales* and six destroyers pounding through heavy seas from a position south of Iceland to intercept. The chase was on, and the destroyers found the pace in the heavy seas a bit of a trial and started to lag. Eventually *Hood* had to signal to her escorts; 'If you are unable to maintain this speed I will have to go on without you. You should follow at your best speed.'

The two cruisers *Norfolk* and *Suffolk* continued to shadow their quarry at a respectful distance throughout the night, dodging in and out of the many rain and sleet squalls which gave them a very necessary degree of protection. All the time they tracked the two Germans on radar and passed situation reports back continuously. Between the first sighting at 1922 on the 23rd and 0538 next morning, *Suffolk* made thirty reports by signal.

As the Arctic twilight gave way to the watery Northern day, the *Bismarck* could be seen some 12 miles away to the south making about 27 knots on a south westerly course. At 0500 on the morning of 24th May while Commander-in-Chief and the *Victorious* group where still some 400 odd miles to the south-east, the two shadowing British cruisers sighted the *Hood* and *Prince of Wales*, who had maintained their high speed dash all through the night on a north-westerly course to intercept.

At 0544 *Hood* reported: 'One enemy battleship distant 14 miles.' 'Ye Gods! – what a size!' someone muttered on the bridge of the *Prince of Wales*, as the two groups headed towards each other and the range closed at an alarming speed. *Hood* opened fired on the enemy at 25,000 yards and the enemy quickly replied. The *Bismarck's* second or third salvo – and possible one also from *Prinz Eugen* – hit the *Hood* and started a fire amidships near the port after 4-inch gun. This fire spread quickly until the whole of the midships section of the *Hood* seemed to be in flames.

Lieutenant E. Knight, RNVR, was in the *Prince of Wales* and recalls[1]:

> I saw a great fire burning on the boat deck of the *Hood*. They would have a job to put that out. Then, as one looked ... the incredible happened: there had been that rushing sound which had ominously ceased, and then, as I looked a great spouting explosion issued from the centre of the *Hood*, enormous reaching tongues of pale red flame shot into the air, while dense clouds of whitish-yellow smoke burst upwards, gigantic pieces of brightly burning debris being hurled hundreds of feet in the air. I just did not believe what I saw – *Hood* had literally been blown to pieces, and just before she was totally enveloped in that ghastly pall of smoke, I noticed that she was firing her last salvo. When the smoke had cleared the *Hood* was no more; there was nothing to be .seen of her. It was fantastic, one just couldn't grasp it.

Just as the British ships were being turned to enable the after turrets to join in the engagement, the *Hood* was hit again and rent in two by a huge explosion between the after funnel and the mainmast.

[1]   *Official History of the War at Sea*, HMSO.

The forepart began to sink immediately bows up, while the after section remained shrouded in an enormous cloud of dense smoke. Three or four minutes later she had disappeared completely beneath the waves leaving only one midshipman and two ratings to survive from a ship's company of 95 officers and 1,324 men and a vast cloud of smoke drifting like a tombstone downwind to leeward.

The destroyer *Electra* (Commander C.W.May, RN) was one of the ships which went to pick up survivors and Lieutenant Commander T.J. Cain RN, describes the incident with startling clarity:

Where were the boats, the rafts, the floats? ... and the men, *where* were the men? I thought of how we'd last seen *Hood*; and I thought of her impressive company. Like a small army, they'd looked, as they mustered for divisions. Then I thought of my words to Doc ... 'We'll need everyone we've got to help the poor devils inboard.'

But almost immediately came another hail, and far over to starboard we saw three men – two of them swimming, one on a raft. But on the chilling waters around them, was no other sign of life ...

Chiefie exclaimed incredulously as we looked again, 'But there *must* be more of them – there can't be only *three* of them! Where the hell are all the others?'

The enemy now turned his undivided attention on to the *Prince of Wales*, but she was no match for the combined fire power and accuracy of the two German ships and when she was hit by four 15-inch shells, and three from *Prinz Eugen*'s 8-inch guns, it was decided to break off the engagement and retire under cover of a smoke screen. One 15-inch shell hit the bridge of the *Prince of Wales* and killed or wounded all the officers and men with the exception of the Captain and a signalman. It would seem from the later reports of the enemy survivors that the *Prince of Wales* had achieved two hits on the *Bismarck* before withdrawing from the action. One of her shells had in fact penetrated the enemy's starboard side under water and had flooded three sections, causing her to lose valuable fuel oil and contaminating other fuel with sea water.

In fact, we now know that at 0801 she made the following signal after the attack:

From *Bismarck*
1. Electrical engine-room No. 4 broken down.
2. Port boiler-room No. 2 is making water but can be held. Water in forecastle.
3. Maximum speed 28 knots.
4. Two enemy radar sets recognised.
5. Intention to put into St. Nazaire. No losses of personnel.

Thus ended the brief – and for us – the tragic engagement on the morning of 24th May 1941, but it was not without some compensation, for a little later on in the day a shadowing RAF Sunderland reported that the *Bismarck* was leaving a trail of oil in her wake and the two cruisers, still hanging on, but keeping out of harm's way, reported that she appeared to be damaged and had reduced speed.

The first round had gone clearly to the enemy and the action was being closely watched by an anxious Admiralty. The Commander in Chief Home Fleet, hurrying southwards decided that *Bismarck*'s speed must be further reduced if he was to be sure of catching her. At 1440, he detached Rear Admiral A.T.B. Curteis commanding the Second Cruiser Squadron, with *Galatea, Aurora, Keyna,* and *Hermione* and sent the following:

Take *Victorious* and cruisers to provide a screen for her under your orders and steer for nearest position within 100 miles of *Bismarck* and from there launch torpedo bomber attacks. *Victorious* is not to come under gunfire from enemy ships. As cruisers run short of fuel they are to be detached to Reykjavik. *Victorious* is to maintain contact as long as torpedo bomber and reconnaissance aircraft are available. *King George V* is altering course more to the southward.

As the day had worn on and the *Victorious* had battled her way at 30 knots to the north-west, the weather which had been bad to start with had worsened noticeably. The flight deck of the carrier presented a most forbidding picture as it pitched up and down in the angry seas, whipped up into a 32-foot swell by a howling wind from the north-west. In the high latitude of the Denmark Strait, sunset was not until an hour after midnight, so it was still daylight when at 2214, the first of nine Swordfish of 825 Squadron took off to avenge the *Hood*.

As soon as they were airborne the Swordfish disappeared into a rain squall and were lost to view, but without too much difficulty the squadron formed up and, flying through broken stratus at 1,500 feet, Lieutenant Commander (A) Eugene Esmonde with three Fulmars of 800Z Flight for escort and to act as shadowers, set course of 225 degrees and at a speed of 85 knots headed for *Bismarck*. The shadowing Fulmars were briefed to maintain contact at all costs so that if necessary, another strike could be flown off next day at dawn.

In the terrible weather conditions prevailing, a visual search for the enemy ships was like looking for the proverbial 'needle in a haystack', but the Swordfish of 825 Squadron had also been fitted with ASV radar – Air to Surface Vessel radar – a new innovation but with very limited range. At 2327, it was this device which gained a contact some sixteen miles ahead of the formation and *Bismarck* was sighted briefly through a gap in the clouds; only to be lost again seconds later. The Strike leader relocated the cruisers still shadowing, and the *Norfolk* directed the aircraft towards their target some fourteen miles ahead on the starboard bow.

At 2350 there was a further contact and Esmonde and his Squadron again broke cloud cover to investigate. This time it was the United States Coastguard cutter *Modoc*, lying stationary and peacefully pitching and rolling in the heavy Atlantic swell.

The *Bismarck*, who was then only six miles to the south, spotted the aircraft and they lost the vital element of surprise. When the Swordfish closed to deliver their torpedo attack, they were met by the enemy's short range AA armament which was 'very vigorous and accurate'.

In fact, so accurate was the *Bismarck*'s fire, that Esmonde's Swordfish was hit was a range of four miles form the enemy ships. One of the Swordfish lost contact in the dense cloud covering the ships, but the remaining eight aircraft pressed home their attack with dash and nerve.

At exactly midnight Esmonde led the first sub-flight of three heavily laden and lumbering Swordfish into a simultaneous attack. His starboard lower aileron was hit and he abandoned his original intention to attack from starboard, deciding to drop there and then, whilst he was still in a good position on the target's port beam. The *Bismarck* was steaming at high speed in a heavy sea and nicely silhouetted against the glow of the setting sun.

Three more Swordfish of the second sub-flight were led in by

Lieutenant P.D. Gick and, not satisfied with his first approach, he worked his way round to a better position, coming in to attack low down on the water on the enemy's port bow a minute after his leader. One aircraft came in from the starboard bow, whilst the last one took the long way round to attack from the starboard quarter. As the aircraft turned away, the air gunners sprayed the *Bismarck*'s superstructure and gun positions with .303 machine gun fire at almost point blank range. As one of the air gunners remarked later:

'It didn't sink the *Bismarck*, but it certainly kept their heads down and in any case, it relieved our feelings.'

A German account of the attack is summarised from an eye-witness report and states:

They came in flying low over the water, launched their torpedoes and zoomed away. Flak was pouring from every gun barrel but didn't seem to hit them. The first torpedo hissed past 150 yards in front of the *Bismarck*'s bow. The second did the same and the third. Helmsman Hansen was operating the pressbuttons of the steering gear as, time and time again, the *Bismarck* manoeuvred out of danger. She evaded a fifth and then a sixth, when yet another torpedo darted straight towards the ship. A few seconds later a tremendous shudder ran through the hull and a towering column of water rose at *Bismarck*'s side. The Nickel-chrome-steel armour plate of her ship's side survived the attack, but Bo'sun Heiners was flung against a bulkhead and did not – he died of severe internal injuries and was the first of over 2,000 deaths aboard the 'Pride of the German Navy'.

In fact one hit was confirmed by a shadowing Fulmar who, just after midnight, reported a 'great, black column of dense smoke rising from the starboard side', and also that 'the battleship's speed was reduced'.[1]

Sunset was at 0052, and the returning strike force had to make most of their journey back to *Victorious* in the dark. The homing beacon aboard the carrier had failed and Captain Bovell, risking the danger from enemy submarines, shone his searchlights on to the clouds vertically upwards to guide the aircraft, until ordered to put them out by Rear Admiral Curteis. Bovell then signalled the cruiser

---

[1]   *Struggle for the Sea*, Grand Admiral E. Raeder, William Kimber, 1958.

flagship using his brightest 20-inch signal projector! All nine Swordfish found the carrier and landed on safely, though two of the shadowing Fulmars were never seen again.

Just after the last aircraft had landed aboard *Victorious*, the two shadowing cruisers lost contact with *Bismarck* at 0306, and for the next thirty six hours a vast network of airborne and surface ship searches attempted to locate the elusive enemy ships. Just before the *Victorious* strike, at 2331 on the evening of 24th, Admiralty had signalled *Ark* and Force H: 'Steer so as to intercept *Bismarck* from southward. Enemy must be short of fuel and will have to make for an oiler. Her future movements may guide you to this oiler.'

As British forces combed the most likely routes open to the *Bismarck*, an official Admiralty communiqué told an anxiously waiting world the outcome of events so far:

> After the engagement yesterday in the North Atlantic, the enemy forces made every effort to shake off the pursuit. Later in the evening an attack by naval aircraft resulted in at least one torpedo hit on the enemy. Operations are still proceeding with the object of bringing the enemy forces to close action.

The *Bismarck* was obviously impressed by the fact that British radar had enabled the two cruisers to keep contact with her for a night and a day, in darkness and very bad weather. At 0401 on the morning of the 25th, she was obviously unaware that at last she had given them the slip.

> Enemy radar gear with a range of at least 35,000 metres interferes with operations in Atlantic to considerable extent. In Denmark Strait ships were located and enemy maintained contact. Not possible to shake off enemy despite favourable weather conditions. Will be unable to Oil unless succeed in shaking off enemy by superior speed . . .

It was only when Group West replied to *Bismarck* somewhat curtly at 0846, that they believed contact had been lost some six hours earlier, that Luetjens realised his luck and thereafter maintained a strict radio silence.

All through the 25th and 26th *Victorious* continued to fly off her Swordfish on anti-submarine patrols and air searches for *Bismarck*, but nothing was found. At 1625 on 25th Adolf Hitler sent a personal message to Admiral Luetjens offering, 'Best wishes on your birthday'. It was not acknowledged and still *Bismarck* kept silent, as she steamed at high speed for the safety of a French West Coast port. At 1924 the Admiralty told all ships that they considered the *Bismarck* was making for western France.

That night, Somerville in *Renown* with *Ark Royal* and *Sheffield* steamed northwards into an increasingly heavy sea and a rising wind. At 2115 they were forced to come down in speed to 23 knots, but by 0112 the next morning they were down to 17 knots. At dawn on 26th, *Ark* was taking it green over the front of the flight deck, some 62 feet above the water and the wind over the flight deck reached 50 knots.

At half past ten that morning, Flying Officer D.A. Briggs sighted *Bismarck* and the long and anxious search was over. He was flying a Catalina of 209 Squadron from Lough Erne, Ireland, on the southernmost of the Bay patrols, when he was engaged by heavy and accurate fire from the enemy ship. His report put *Bismarck* 690 miles to the west-north-west of Brest and gave the pursuers less than 24 hours in which to intercept, before she could reach friendly Luftwaffe protection and the sanctuary of port. Clearly Admiral Tovey would need to slow her down with yet another air strike, and the only carrier within striking distance was *Ark Royal* coming up from the south.

As luck would have it, *Ark* had launched a search of her own and her aircraft were covering the same area. At 1114 Swordfish 2H, piloted by Sub-Lieutenant (A) J.V. Hartley, with Observer Sub-Lieutenant P.R. Elias and Telegraphist Air Gunner Leading Airman N. Huxley saw a warship which they thought was a German cruiser. Seven minutes later Swordfish 2F (Lieutenant (A) J.R. Callander, Lieutenant P.B. Schondfeldt, Leading Airman R. Baker) joined 2H and identified *Bismarck*:

At 1154 *Bismarck* broke radio silence to report that she was being shadowed by an enemy 'Land plane'. Thereafter and until 2320 that night, *Ark*'s Swordfish working in pairs kept the *Bismarck* under continuous observation. The carrier herself came within range of the enemy at 1450 on the afternoon of 26th May and launched her first strike.

This was to provide a lesson that the Fleet Air Arm and the Royal Navy will never forget, for 11 torpedoes were released at a ship before the aircrew realised to their horror that their target was the cruiser *Sheffield*! Unfortunately Admiral Somerville failed to brief *Ark Royal* that he had ordered the cruiser *Sheffield* to close and shadow at 1315 that afternoon, and the aircrews had been told that only *Bismarck* was in the area.

Appreciating that it was a case of mistaken identity and to the eternal credit of Captain Larcom in the *Sheffield*, he ordered his guns to remain silent and on no account to fire. Then, quite calmly, he rang down to the engine room for full speed ahead and successfully dodged the torpedoes.

One pilot, recognising the *Sheffield* after he had dropped, made a signal to her, 'Sorry for the Kipper', but they were a very crestfallen band of men when they finally landed back aboard. Landing conditions had become even worse than before, and the Deck Control Officer had to attach a rope to his waist before he could stand, back to the wind, holding up the 'bats'. Three aircraft crashed on the flight deck as they came on, the rising stern smashing their undercarriages, and the wreckage had to be cleared away before the others could be taken on. Fortunately, there were no casualties to the crews.

By 1900 the second striking force had been ranged. It was led by Lieutenant-Commander T.P. Goode, RN, with Lieutenant E.S. Carver, RN, as his observer; Lieutenant-Commander J.A. Stewart-Moore, RN, was second-in-command and leader of the second wave. Leaders and crews realised the importance of their task. They, and they alone, could stop the *Bismarck* from reaching the safety of Brest, for it was certain that the Fleet could not possibly catch up if the Fleet Air Arm Swordfish did not slow the battleship down.

The *Ark Royal* turned into the wind. One can imagine that scene: the fifteen Swordfish ranged on the pitching flight deck, wing-tip to wing-tip; the tumultuous roar of the exhausts; the flurries of spray rattling on the fuselages; the ratings at the chocks bracing their bodies against the drive of the wind. Then the Flight Deck officer waving his green flag; the chocks being whipped away from the wheels and the first Swordfish moving forward, roaring along the deck and taking off into the gale.

At 1915 the *Ark* launched her second strike of fifteen Swordfish. Mostly they were the same aircraft, but this time the aircrew were determined to redeem themselves and there was no mistake. *Sheffield* was in radar contact with *Bismarck* and shadowing, so the strike of four Swordfish from 810 Squadron, four from 818 and seven from 820 headed for *Sheffield*, who half an hour later made contact and directed them to the target bearing 110°, range 12 miles.

Lieutenant-Commander Goode had planned a co-ordinated attack – the sub-flights coming in simultaneously from different angles, forcing the *Bismarck* to divide her fire and making it harder for her to evade torpedoes. With no sign of a break in the cloud cover – down to 2,000 feet – the chances of reforming were slender, so each flight was ordered to return independently.

Twelve minutes after leaving *Sheffield*, Goode estimated that they should be in a good position and started the dive. 'Visibility was limited – a matter of yards. I watched the Altimeter go back', reported Goode later. 'When we reached 2,000 feet I started to worry. At 1,500 feet I wondered whether to continue the dive. At 1,000 feet I felt sure something was wrong, but still we were completely enclosed by cloud. I held the formation in the dive, and at 700 feet only we broke cloud, just when I was running out of height.'

Goode found he was 4 miles ahead and to leeward of the target. A slow approach against the wind would be suicidal, so he re-entered the cloud and made his final dive on *Bismarck*'s port beam. Most of the striking force became split up in the thick blanket of cloud, and they went in to the attack as best they could; in pairs, threes, fives and even singly. The Commander-in-Chief stated afterwards that the attacks were pressed home 'with a gallantry and determination which cannot be praised too highly'.

The intensity and accuracy of the *Bismarck*'s anti-aircraft fire compelled some of the aircraft to turn away before they could drop their torpedoes, but they went in again with a second attack. Sub-Lieutenant (A) A.W. Duncan Beale, RN, having lost touch with his subflight in cloud, returned to the *Sheffield* to get a new range and bearing of the enemy, then flew back and by himself attacked *Bismarck* from ahead on the port bow. His observer, Sub-Lieutenant (A) Friend and TAG Leading Airman Pimlott, clinging on the sides of the open cockpit for dear life, as the aircraft corkscrewed and bucked to make its getaway. In spite of the very intense and accurate fire they saw an enormous column of smoke and water rise up the port side of *Bismarck*'s deck, which they were certain was a hit by their torpedo.

Five of the attacking Swordfish were hit by AA fire and one, flown by Sub-Lieutenant (A) Swanton, had no less than 175 holes in it.

Both Swanton and his TAG, Leading Airman J.R. Seager were wounded, but somehow the observer, Sub Lieutenant (A) G.A. Woods escaped unhurt. Swanton managed to get Swordfish 4C back on to *Ark's* deck in 'one' piece, but on closer inspection was found to be damaged beyond repair and ditched.

Such were the difficulties of observation that the leader of the striking force reported immediately after the attack, that he did not think the *Bismarck* had suffered any damage. But as the aircraft returned to the ship and the observers made their individual reports, it became clear that the results were more successful than he had supposed, and it was first established that the *Bismarck* had been hit on the port side, then on the starboard quarter. Later still a possible hit on the port quarter was reported. The damage was confirmed by a signal, received at 2300 that the ship had made two circles at slow speed and was staggering off to the north-north-west out of control.

These hits from the *Ark Royal's* aircraft put the *Bismarck's* steering gear out of action and reduced her speed, so that she was apparently unable to hold her course with the wind and sea astern.

'This was a result', wrote the Commander-in-Chief, 'which the *Ark Royal* and her aircraft crews had well earned and which ensured my being able to bring the *Bismarck* to action next morning'.

In *Bismarck*, Admiral Luetjens was beginning to feel a little more hopeful. Carrier planes had been shadowing all day, but the expected attack had not materialised. His most urgent concern was fuel and at 1903, he sent to Group West: 'Fuel situation urgent. When can I expect fuel.'

Fifty minutes later she had a far more urgent problem – *Ark's* planes were going in to attack. The rest of the drama is best told by *Bismarck's* signals sent to Group West in those last few fateful hours.

26th May	1954	Am being attack by carrier borne aircraft
	2015	Ship no longer manoeuvrable.
	2105	Approx. position 47° 40'N, 14° 50'W. Torpedo hit aft.
	2115	Torpedo hit amidships.
	2140	Ship no longer manoeuvrable. We fight to the last shell. Long live the Fuehrer.
	2325	Am surrounded by *Renown* and light forces.
	2359	Armament and engines still intact. Ship however cannot be steered with engines.

Ark Royal had an extraordinary piece of luck when she was launching aircraft earlier that evening: she passed right through the sights of U-566, a U-boat returning from a very successful patrol with no torpedoes left. Captain Wohlfahrt's diary reads:

26th May 1948. Alarm. A battleship of the King George class and an aircraft carrier, probably *Ark Royal*, came in right through the mist from astern, travelling at high speed. Bows to the right, inclination 170°. If only I had had a few torpedoes! I would not even have had to manoeuvre – I was just perfectly placed for an attack. No destroyers, no zig-zagging! I could have stayed where I was and got them both. Torpedo carrying aircraft observed operating from carrier. I might have been able to help *Bismarck*.

During the night a flotilla of five destroyers attacked the *Bismarck* and scored three hits with torpedoes. For a time she was stopped. Then she got under way again, steaming about eight knots, still capable of heavy and accurate gunfire.

At 0430 on 27th May the *Ark Royal* flew off a reconnaissance aircraft. The night was pitch black, the wind over the deck gusting to 48 knots, and there was still great movement on the ship. The carrier reduced speed to six knots and the Swordfish took off, rose vertically alongside the bridge, and immediately vanished into the darkness. It drove through the rain, but over the northern horizon was a great black cloud which covered the whole area of operations; the pilot failed to find the *Bismarck* and returned for further orders. He was told to search again. Again he failed, but was successful in the third attempt.

When dawn came the sky was clearer, the wind had gone to the north-west. Twelve Swordfish, which had been ranged before daylight, but had been struck below owing to the movement of the ship and the force of the wind, were flown off, their course being aided by sighting the destroyer *Maori* which was still in visual contact with the *Bismarck*. At 0710 she sent her last signal – 'Send U-boat to save War diary'.

By 0845 the *King George V* and the *Rodney* had closed the enemy. The air striking force reached the scene of action as the guns of the Fleet were opening fire. They flew over the *Bismarck* at 100 feet. According to one of the air-gunners she was then 'so battered that you couldn't distinguish her shape – she looked like a dark mass of junk floating on the water'. Some of the crews reported that they could distinctly smell the oil and cordite fumes.

The splashes from the shells made it impossible for the aircraft to dive on their target. They closed the flagship and watched the *Bismarck*'s end. By nine o'clock she was all but out of control, although her guns were still in action. Soon after ten o'clock she was silenced. She was a wreck, on fire fore and aft, and wallowing heavily. The striking force was about to finish her off when HMS *Dorsetshire* which had been ordered to torpedo her at close range, reported she was sinking and delivered only a token coup de grace.

The end came for this brave and mighty ship at 1040 on the 27th May. The heavy ships of the Home Fleet had done their worst pouring broadside after broadside into her at point blank range, then forming up in line ahead and steaming off to the north with only just enough fuel to get home. They left her with her upperworks reduced to a tangle of twisted, blackened and blazing wreckage, and below, a scene of horror and almost unbelievable devastation. Hatches were jammed by concussion, pipes were twisted and bulkheads buckled and smashed – hundreds of bodies lay broken and shattered in the debris. Perhaps mercifully, the tragic, hideous wreck with her battle ensign still flying, turned turtle, hovered keel upwards for a moment and then slid gently beneath the angry waves – *Hood* was avenged!

Throughout the long chase some 71 torpedoes had been fired at *Bismarck* and eight hits obtained, although it would seem from subsequent reports that they had little or no effect against the armour. *Rodney* fired two torpedoes in the latter stages of the action and became the first battleship to fire this type of weapon against another battleship. Although *Dorsetshire* was the last ship to engage the enemy with a torpedo hit on the port side, *Bismarck* was inevitably doomed. The crew had already opened the sea valves, exploded the scuttling charges and were abandoning ship.

Very heavy seas were running, but immediately the *Dorsetshire* and *Maori* commenced rescue work to try to pick up the dazed, helpless, stranded sailors from a bitterly cold water. The ships wallowed in a heavy swell and men were smashed against the ships' sides – many were too weak or injured to climb the ropes thrown to them or get up the scrambling nets. All the time the two rescue ships presented an easy target to any enemy submarine and then it happened: *U-74* was sighted by *Dorsetshire* and the two British ships beat a hasty retreat with 110 survivors. The submarine had been ordered to assist

Bismarck or at least save the war diary, but bad weather had delayed her and then she had been badly damaged and put out of action in a depth charge attack. She was on her way back to base and unable to attack the British ships. As she cruised through the battle area of oil, debris and bodies she managed to rescue three more survivors – a final total of 113 saved out of a ship's complement of over 2,300 men.

Prinz Eugen had parted company from the ill-fated *Bismarck* after nightfall on the 24th, to proceed independently while the *Bismarck* attempted to make for Brest. She reached the safety of Port on 1st June and there learned of the fate that had befallen her consort.

As *Ark*'s striking force were landing on a Heinkel 111 approached under the cover of low cloud. The ship was in an almost defenceless position, for she had turned into wind and her course could not be altered, nor could she use her 4.5 guns. The *Renown* and the *Sheffield* gave her protection, however, and her two after pom-poms also opened fire on the Heinkel, which dropped two large and five smaller bombs from 4,000 feet, then turned away into cloud with smoke pouring from her starboard engine. The bombs fell into the sea 400 yards from the ship, and all the Swordfish landed on safely.

During the operations the *Ark Royal* had flown off and landed on sixty-one aircraft, with three deck crashes but no serious casualties to personnel, contending with weather in which normally no aircraft would be expected to fly from a carrier. 'I cannot speak too highly of the courage and ability shown by the pilots in handling their aircraft, particularly when landing on in such conditions,' wrote Vice-Admiral Somerville in his despatch.

> It is not only skill that is needed to come in over the flight deck 'round down' when on occasions it is known to be rising and falling 56 feet.

In a message of congratulation to the Commander-in-Chief, Home Fleet, the Board of Admiralty stated:

> There can be no doubt that had it not been for the gallantry, skill and devotion to duty of the Fleet Air Arm in both *Victorious* and *Ark Royal* our object might not have been achieved.

The work for which Force H had been summoned was accomplished, but there was no respite. It turned south at once and

steamed back to Gibraltar. As the *Ark Royal* entered harbour on 29th
May the garrison hired every boat they could find and came out to
cheer her to her berth. Soon the small craft were clustering below her
as thick as floating wrack, and every rating, soldier and airman who
could find a foothold afloat stood shouting and waving up at the
carrier's decks to welcome her return.

'Some occasions in our profession', observed Lord Howe, 'will
justify, if not require, more hazard to be ventured than can by
systematically defended by experience.' Such hazard had to be
ventured in order to stop the *Bismarck*. The airmen of the *Ark* had
responded to the call made upon them and the result had justified
the risk.

The late Lieutenant Commander E. Esmond, VC, DSO, (second from the left) and other officers and men decorated for their part in the destruction of *Bismarck* in May 1941.

The mighty *Bismarck*. 50,900 tons fully loaded, 8 15 inch-guns, 12 5.9 inch-guns and 16 4.1 inch AA guns. Described by Hitler as the 'Pride of the German Navy', she was finally sunk by ships of the Home Fleet on 27th May 1941.

she was some 500 miles from landfall at Hamble in Hampshire which Blyth left on 18th October 1970.

(Below) *Ark Royal* after a three year refit and a £30,000,000 face-lift, is all set to serve until the late 1970s. The photograph shows conditions in one of her modern engine rooms.

Hurricane replacements on the deck of HMS *Ark Royal* en route from Gibraltar to Malta. One of her many aircraft ferrying sorties to the beleaguered island of Malta in World War II.

Chock men clear first Fulmar of 808 Squadron aboard HMS *Ark Royal* as aircraft prepares to take off. Skuas of 800 Squadron can be seen at the after end of the deck park.

21st September 1940 *Ark Royal* sailed from Freetown with 20 Free French flying personnel and 2 Luciole training aircraft for Dakar. Their mission was to win over French West Africa. The photograph shows French personnel and aircraft on *Ark*'s flight deck for Operation Menace eventually and cynically to be described as Operation Muddle.

CHAPTER 8

The Spirit of 'Old Ark'

The sinking of the *Bismarck* provided the one ray of encouragement in a picture of otherwise unrelieved gloom. In *Ark*'s favourite hunting ground of the Mediterranean, the strategic balance of power in the Eastern Basin had swung heavily in favour of the Axis powers. Crete had fallen and now the very existence of a British Force in Egypt and North Africa was threatened. Malta was daily becoming more isolated and untenable, since it could no longer be supplied from Alexandria, and the Mediterranean Fleet had suffered badly, with three cruisers, six destroyers, forty-four transports and fleet auxiliaries sunk and two battleships, one aircraft carrier, six cruisers and seven destroyers badly damaged.

It was a depressing story, but after the fierce fighting of recent weeks, June 1st ushered in the start of a summer lull and a chance to re-inforce Malta with more precious fighters. Everything hinged on our ability to supply our forces in Egypt and using Malta as the forward base, to prevent Rommel building up his strength across the central Mediterranean.

Admiral Somerville decided on a new plan for delivering Hurricanes to Malta. They would be led by Blenheim bombers taking off from Gibraltar, rendezvousing with the carriers at a pre-arranged launch point, and then escorting the fighters on to Malta. On June 4th, nine Blenheims duly arrived from England and the first of the new re-inforcement operations was successfully completed two days later, when forty-three Hurricanes landed on the island.

Ark Royal and Force H met the carrier *Victorious* bringing forty-eight Hurricanes out from England on 9th June, and the *Sheffield* said goodbye and headed for home and refit – the first of the famous trio to leave Force H. The two carriers arrived in Gibraltar on 11th June and *Victorious* transferred 24 Hurricanes over to *Ark*. On 13th they sailed once more with *Renown* and seven destroyers and slipped out of

La Linea Bay, turned left and headed at high speed towards a position to the south of the Balearic Islands. At the appointed time four twin-engined Hudsons from Gibraltar arrived at the rendezvous, and escorted forty-seven aircraft towards Malta. In the event only forty-five Hurricanes reached their destination and two of those crashed on landing. One of the Hurricanes got into trouble, broke formation and was last seen heading for the coast of North Africa, while another ditched in the sea en route.

The last re-inforcement operation in June resulted in thirty-five Hurricanes reaching Malta, to make a grand total of 145 fighters flown in during the month. Unfortunately *Furious* – accompanying *Ark* on this trip – had a minor disaster when one of the Hurricanes veered across the deck on take off, hit the bridge of the island and burst into flames. It caused quite a serious fire and some damage, as well as killing seven officers and seven men, including several RAF pilots waiting to take off.

The island of Malta now had the aircraft to strike at Rommel's supply lines to North Africa, but she needed stores, equipment, aviation fuel and men. But with the Mediterranean Fleet severely weakened and the sea route from Alexandria effectively closed to our convoys, any support would have to come from Gibraltar and the West. As a result Operation Substance was mounted in late July, to pass six storeships and a troopship through to Malta, and allow the fast auxiliary *Breconshire* and six empty merchantmen to sail west to Gibraltar.

The convoy sailed from Gibraltar on 21st July in company with Force H, but re-inforced from the Home Fleet by the battleship *Nelson*, the cruisers *Edinburgh*, *Manchester* and *Arethusa* and the fast minelayer *Manxman*. The convoy would provide 5,500 additional men and nearly 50,000 tons of stores for the island, but in the fog and poor visibility which covered the departure, the transport ship *Leinster* ran aground and over 1,000 troops had to be left behind.

The expected air attacks began on 23rd July soon after 0900, when a formation of nine S79 bombers were intercepted by seven Fulmars at 10,000 feet some 22 miles from the Fleet. In the ensuing battle, the enemy lost two aircraft and the rest were driven off for the loss of three Fulmars, but there was more to come.

While the attention was focussed on the high level bombers, seven more torpedo dropping aircraft came out of the sun, dived to sea level and delivered a very courageous and determined attack. Hits were scored on the cruiser *Manchester* and the destroyer *Fearless*, while the rest of the ships frantically put full helm over to try to dodge the torpedoes. After the attack was over, the *Manchester* with three of her four engines out of action, turned back for Gibraltar, while the *Fearless* was so badly damaged that she had to be sunk by our own forces.

So the attacks continued throughout the long day with one at 1645 and two more before dark. Though the convoy escaped unharmed, there was another warship casualty when the destroyer *Firedrake*, near missed abreast the boiler room, lost the use of her engines and had to be taken in tow and sent back to Gibraltar.

When the convoy reached the Skerki channel that evening at around 1900, Admiral Syfret's Force X took over the convoy and protecting Beaufighters from Malta relieved *Ark*'s hard pressed Fulmar fighters. Although there was an E-boat torpedo attack off Pantelleria in the early hours of the 24th, the convoy reached Malta safely on the morning of the 25th and Syfret returned west to meet Somerville and head for Gibraltar. The whole force reached there safely on the 27th.

The destroyer *Firedrake* had been escorted back by *Ark* and Force H and when she was safely secured alongside, one could see the extent of her damage. Next morning a small boat appeared alongside the destroyer. The boat was being pulled by an elderly man dressed in dungarees and a white sweater and as the Quartermaster watched, it floated into the gaping hole where the destroyer had once had a boiler room. The Quartermaster leaned over the side of *Firedrake* and shouted . . .

'Hey you! What the . . . do you think you're . . . well doing?'

'It's all right,' said the oarsman, 'I only wanted to be the first man to row a boat round a destroyer's boiler-room.'

The Quartermaster found out later that the oarsman was none other than his Commander-in-Chief, Admiral Somerville.

Over the weeks and months following her return from the *Bismarck* episode, *Ark* had been almost continuously at sea covering convoys to Malta and carrying out invaluable air reconnaissance. Her Swordfish carried out a night bombing attack on Alghero airfield on the west coast of Sardinia, obtaining direct hits on hangars, buildings and living quarters. The Fulmar fighters also had their share of success and managed to bring down a number of Italian shadowers, as well as a Junkers 52 transport aircraft. One

Italian pilot who was taken prisoner was convinced that he had been shot down by a Hurricane. The Fulmar pilots were pleased at their reputation, and that of their aircraft!

Operation Halberd on 24th September re-inforced Malta with yet more stores, men and ammunition and on October 16th, *Ark* sailed to deliver eleven Albacores of 828 Squadron into the Island. When she arrived at Gibraltar, she had steamed over 200,000 miles without a proper refit. Perhaps, just perhaps she would soon be going home. They had been away for eleven months and for many men, Christmas could be their first one at home for three years.

It was half past seven on 10th November when *Ark Royal* sailed with Force H and left Gibraltar for the last time. *Renown* had been replaced by *Nelson* and only *Ark* remained of the original trio. But *Ark* had to stay; 'Without her', Admiral Somerville remarked, 'I am like a blind beggar without his dog.' This time he flew his flag in the battleship *Malaya*, which replaced the battleship *Nelson* damaged by an aircraft torpedo during Operation Halberd, in September. As far as *Ark* was concerned, this was just another routine re-inforcement operation flying Hurricanes into Malta from herself and *Argus*.

That the British forces were having such successes and tipping the scales once more in the western and central Mediterranean areas, is borne out by the fact from German and Italian records we now know that from July 1941, the monthly losses in ships sunk and damaged rose steadily until it reached a staggering 70 per cent of the total Italian tonnage serving the North African theatre of operations. Supplies for Rommel fell below his requirements and with the successful build up by the Allies, the position of the Africa Corps became precarious.

At this point Hitler intervened and ordered the German Naval High Command to despatch U-boats to the Mediterranean. At the end of September the first six Atlantic U-boats passed through the Straits of Gibraltar and commanded by capable officers with experienced crews, they were to have an immediate and devastating effect.

Force H with the cruiser *Hermione* and seven destroyers passed north of Alboran Island, thence towards the Balearic Islands and after dark 10th, resumed heading for the flying-off position halfway to Malta. All day they had been shadowed, but with the carrier decks cluttered with Hurricanes, flying off fighter interception aircraft would be impossible unless an air attack was imminent. At

2130 that evening, a signal was received from No. 200 Group, RAF North Front, Gibraltar, stating that it was intended to postpone the operation for 24 hours owing to bad weather at Gibraltar. The 24 hour delay worried Admiral Somerville considerably, since he would have to kill time and steam around within enemy air coverage, and possible submarine patrol areas.

The weather on the morning of the 12th dawned fair and almost to the minute, four Blenheims appeared at 1004 to lead the first two flights of Hurricanes on their long journey over the sea to Malta. Seventeen minutes later, the first thirteen Hurricanes from *Ark* and six from *Argus* were on their way. At 1048 the next four Blenheims appeared and twenty four minutes later, the last of the thirty-six serviceable Hurricanes had lifted safely off the decks of *Ark* and *Argus*.

As soon as they had gone, Force H altered course to the west and zig-zagging at 16 knots, headed for Gibraltar and 'home' once more. *Ark* immediately launched a Swordfish aircraft for anti-submarine patrol and four of her Fulmars for fighter protection, hoping to intercept the interminable shadowers who seemed to watch her every move. At 1625 they received news that the Blenheims and thirty four of the thirty-six Hurricanes had reached their destination safely, the other two were reported by the enemy to have crashed in Sicily and North Africa.

That evening Admiral Somerville received two warnings of U-boat activity in the area close to the east of Gibraltar. At eighteen minutes to seven he was told by signal that the *Castello Oropesa*, a Spanish vessel, had been torpedoed and sunk by the Italian submarine *Dandolo* in Melilla Bay, west of Ceuta, on the African coast on 8th November. The second was a sighting from an aircraft on passage from Malta to Gibraltar, who reported a large submarine stopped on the surface, off the Spanish coast and some 35 miles north-north-west of Alboran island at 1048 that morning. Both these U-boats were close to the return track of Force H, but in the comparatively narrow approaches to Gibraltar from the east, there was little freedom in the choice of route.

During the night of 12th-13th November, the wind increased and Force H was compelled to reduce speed to avoid damaging the destroyers. Thirteen minutes after the morning watch had turned to at 0400, *Legion*, the starboard wing destroyer in the screen reported an underwater explosion in her wake. This was probably either an 'end of run' or premature explosion of *U-205*'s torpedo (Lieutenant-Commander Reschke), fired at the capital ships, and which a German broadcast claimed later to have hit the *Ark Royal*. In any case, it prompted everyone to be on their guard and alerted Force H to the fact that enemy submarines were very much in 'their area'. At 0817 Admiral Somerville warned all ships that submarines had been reported in the vicinity and great vigilance was necessary. An hour and a half earlier, *Ark Royal* had flown off six Swordfish to fly ahead of the ships and search for enemy U-boats, but nothing was detected and the force continued towards their destination at 19 knots.

All through the forenoon, *Ark* continued with her flying exercises, and because the prevailing wind was westerly or dead ahead, she had no cause to venture outside her protective screen of A/S destroyers. There were two submarine scares that morning. The first at five minutes to ten when the destroyer *Laforey* picked up a sonar contact and attacked with depth charges. The force carried out an emergency turn, but nothing came of the incident and soon the ships returned their original heading. At noon, when the ships were some 50 miles east of Gibraltar, the destroyer *Lightning* in the starboard screen reported a contact. Again the force made an emergency alteration of course, but a little later she reported that her contact was probably a mistake and normal course was resumed.

As the day wore on the weather improved and in the early afternoon, Somerville detached *Hermione* to act as a target for a throw-off shoot by *Malaya*. *Ark Royal* was busily operating her aircraft and following astern of the flagship with *Argus* astern of her. At 1515 *Ark* had a total of fourteen aircraft waiting to land on and others waiting to fly off, when *Laforey* again reported a submarine contact. The Fleet immediately turned, but six minutes later the contact was reported to be 'non-sub' and the ships altered back. 'Whales again', thought some of the spectators on *Ark*'s flight deck, who had gathered to watch the flying operations. Perhaps the *Ark Royals* took their immunity very much for granted and perhaps they had good cause. For over two years they had survived as the principal target of enemy bombs, mines and torpedoes. *Ark* was not just a happy ship, she was a lucky one!

The Fleet was now back on its westerly course and at 1529, *Ark* altered course to 286° to fly off eight aircraft – six Swordfish and two Fulmars – and land on five Swordfish. Nine minutes later, she altered course once more to land on more aircraft and was then 800 yards on *Malaya*'s starboard quarter, though still well inside the destroyer screen.

Undetected by any of the escorts, *U-81* commanded by Lieutenant Guggenberger saw *Ark Royal* in his periscope and fired three torpedoes. The destroyer *Legion*, who was the starboard wing ship picked up loud hydrophone effect at 1538, but thinking it was probably the destroyer *Ghurka*, did not report it. In fact it was probably the noise of the torpedo fired at *Ark Royal*.

Several officers and men on *Malaya*'s bridge were watching *Ark Royal* at 1541 that afternoon. Suddenly an enormous column of water shot into the air, up the carrier's starboard side abreast the island. In Admiral Somerville's own words he stated:

> At 1541, in position 36° 03'N., 04° 40'W. (098° Europa Point 30 miles) the *Ark Royal*, then still four cables on *Malaya*'s starboard quarter was struck by a torpedo on the starboard side. I observed an explosion apparently abreast of *Ark Royal*'s 'island', and noted it was so severe that the aircraft ranged before the barrier were thrown clear of the deck and bounced once or twice owing to the whip of the flying deck!

Almost immediately the *Ark Royal* took a heavy list of about 10° to starboard and still steaming at 22 knots, she started to swing to port between *Malaya* and *Argus*. All communications between the bridge and the rest of the ship were cut off. All the telephones were out of action, the ship's broadcast had failed and the engine-room telegraphs had jammed. It was vital for Captain Maund to get the way of the ship as soon as possible, in order to reduce the risk of spreading the damage further from the enormous pressures caused by the ship travelling through the water. Action stations were ordered by bugle and word of mouth, but it took a full fifteen minutes to get the machinery control room to act on verbal orders, reverse the engines and stop the ship. Below decks the situation was confused and in the semi-darkness and without communications, the position probably looked worse than it actually was.

It was not possible to assess the full extent of the damage and as the list seemed to be increasing, Captain Maund decided to evacuate all the surplus officers and men. About 1660, the destroyer *Legion* came alongside *Ark*'s port quarter, and cast off again at 1648 with 1,560 of the carrier's crew aboard. Most of the ship's company had

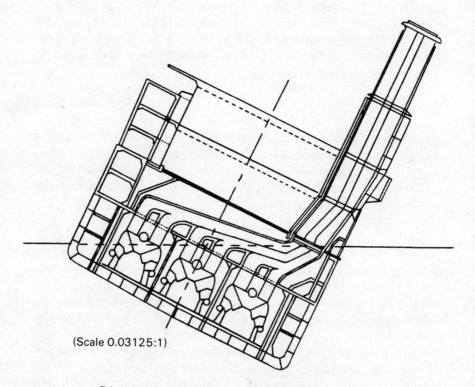

(Scale 0.03125:1)

Diagram showing list and relation to uptake trunking

been below decks, working in the hangars, on watch in machinery spaces or on the messdecks when the torpedo struck. Immediately lights went out, power failed and in areas adjacent to the explosion, smoke and fumes poured out of the ventilation trunking. The ship began to heel very quickly to starboard, so quickly that at first, many people thought she was going to turn right over. Obviously Captain Maund must have had this in the forefront of his mind when he gave the order to evacuate. With a ship's company of over 1,600 men on board, the loss of life would be enormous if she capsized as *Courageous* had done earlier in the war, with the loss of nearly half the ship's company and *Eagle* was to do just a few months later.

Many decks down below the waterline, four men were on watch in the main switchboard room, main telephone exchange and lower steering position. After the explosion, waist deep in fuel oil and water, choking in the fumes, they groped the way for the hatch which led to the compartment above and safety. Three men got out, but Able Seaman E. Mitchell was never seen again.

Lieutenant Commander (E) A.G. Oliver was the Senior Engineer and had just come off watch from below. He was sitting in his cabin looking at his stamp collection when the explosion shook the ship. He ran to the machinery control room and joined the Engineer Officer, Commander (E) H. Dixon, who at once sent him to investigate the extent of the damage. In the gloomy, half darkness of the auxiliary lighting, he moved along the steeply sloping decks to find the starboard boiler room flooding quickly. Closing hatches and fan intakes, he moved over to the centre boiler room. Here the story was the same, with water rising rapidly from below and pouring in from the uptake casing vents, it was already feet deep and had to be abandoned.

Signals were made at once to Gibraltar to send tugs with all available anti-submarine craft and aircraft. *Hermione* was recalled to join *Ark* to re-inforce the ring of ships forming a protective screen round the stopped, helpless and very vulnerable carrier. Admiral Somerville in *Malaya* with *Argus* in company carried on to Gibraltar at 18 knots and arrived at 1830 that evening, then he promptly re-embarked in the destoyer *Sikh* and at 32 knots, hurriedly returned to the scene where he arrived at about 2000.

Back on board the carrier, the situation began to look a little more hopeful. The Captain's order to reduce the list by counterflooding and pumping fuel oil from the starboard to port side was having its

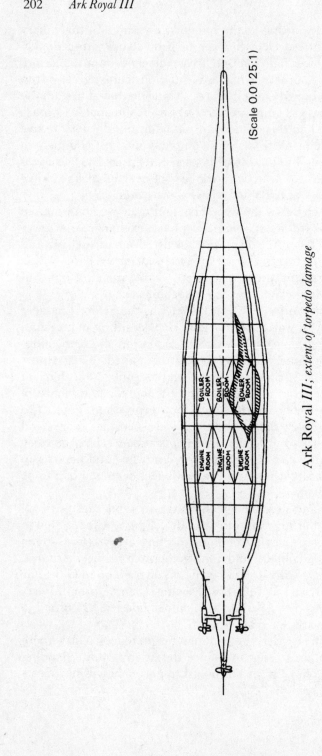

(Scale 0.0125:1)

Ark Royal III; extent of torpedo damage

effect, and by 1700 the list had steadied to about 17 degrees. Since the bridge was still without communications, an emergency conning position was set up on the flight deck, and communication established with the engine rooms using a field telephone. At 1730 the destroyer *Laforey* was ordered alongside to supply boiler feed water and electrical power and gradually, it was possible once again to raise steam in the port boiler room.

At twenty minutes to nine that evening, the *Ark Royal* was firmly secured to the tug *Thames* and proceeding at two knots towards Gibraltar. Slowly painfully, the carrier moved through the water and seemingly, the situation was getting better by the minute. At 2200 the electrical repair party from *Hermione* and *Legion* under the guidance of *Ark*'s Commissioned Gunner (T) Herring, managed to get two dynamos running, partly restore the lighting and provide power for the pumps and steam steering engine. Nowhere was the water actually gaining, and in the starboard engine room which had started to flood earlier, the water level was now falling quite steadily.

At 2224, Captain R.M.J. Hutton in *Laforey*, reported that he had left *Ark Royal*, which had her own steam and power, that the flooding was apparently under control and no more tugs were required until off the harbour. For nearly four hours until shortly before 0200 on November 14th, *Ark Royal* edged slowly towards the Rock now just under 30 miles away.

At 0200, the tug *St. Day* joined in the tow, but all this time, far below and out of sight, the insidious water was gaining and the damage spreading. Joints, bulkheads and watertight doors, already weakened by the explosion were giving way under the enormous pressure of the water. Compartments, hitherto undamaged, were slowly filling and the earlier counter-flooding had added to the problems. The list had not increased, but *Ark Royal* was now much lower in the water and water level was so high in the funnel gas uptake flat, that the port boilers had no outlet to the funnel. The steam pressure dropped back and shortly afterwards, the port boiler room had to be evacuated.

Without steam, the ship lost its lighting, but far worse, the pumps had stopped again. Although the *Laforey* was ordered alongside and supplied electrical power immediately, the list started to increase noticeably − slowly at first and then more quickly. Down below, loose articles started to move across the steep sloping decks. Aircraft broke free and slid across to the starboard side. Lockers shed their contents and all the time, the ominous rumble and crash told their own story, adding to the finale that everyone knew was about to happen.

Even the last moments had their touches of humour. A very newly promoted officer arrived on the deck with his brand new uniforms carefully wrapped in a bundle in his arms, then equally carefully tossed the lot into the sea.

A group of men waiting to slide to safety down a rope to a waiting rescue ship, were amazed to hear someone shout, 'Now then, no panic', then seize the rope and disappear rapidly out of sight.

Men grabbed their few precious possessions. One petty officer had time to snatch up twenty pairs of silk stockings he was taking home for his wife, and filled his pockets until they were bulging. Pet canaries were released and cats were grabbed by their owners and taken to waiting destroyers.

It was difficult to move about now as the ladders were swinging vertically on their hinges. Lieutenant Gardner had second thoughts about going below to collect his few personal possessions. He remembered the men in *Courageous* who had done just that, and had been lost in large numbers when the ship went over.

By four o'clock the ship had heeled to twenty-seven degrees. Her crew had done all that human resource and courageous endeavour could do to bring her to port, and now they could do little more. For the past half-hour the port boiler-room had been an inferno, the casings red-hot and the stoke-hold choked with fumes. The Senior Engineer, Lieutenant-Commander (E) A.G. Oliver, RN, who had been working unceasingly, was finally overcome by the fumes and the heat. Two of his men fainted and had to be given artificial respiration. Four times the stokers extinguished fires which had broken out. They continued to steam the boiler until further efforts were useless, and they were ordered up. Others had run the dynamo in the port and centre engine-rooms for many hours, working without ventilation in a mist of superheated steam.

Since there was now no hope of saving the ship every available rope was taken forward and secured inboard, abreast of the *St. Day*, so that the 250 men on board could leave quickly and cross over the *St. Day* to the *Laforey*.

The list was now a frightening 35 degrees. Admiral Somerville transferred from the *Sikh* to a motor launch and then to the *Laforey* still alongside the *Ark*. The last to leave was Captain Maund, his uniform covered in green slime and weed from the bilges of *Ark*, now lying almost on her side.

At 0613 on November 14, the end came for the ship the Germans had claimed to have sunk so many times. The *'Old Ark'* – turned over, remained bottom upwards for a few minutes, then, fourteen hours after she had been torpedoed, slid below the quiet, still and silent waters of the Mediterranean Sea. It was the final end of a famous, mighty and happy ship and the loss was announced in London on the one o'clock news that afternoon. Perhaps the news embarrassed the German Ministry of Propaganda, which had claimed the destruction of the carrier over two years before. It was not until twenty-four hours after the sinking that Dr. Goebbels announced the news to the German people and significantly, quoted the British Admiralty in confirmation.

Those officers and men who had sailed in the *Ark Royal*, and the many who had known her, mourned her loss. Gibraltar was silent and still that November morning. As the survivors stood on the jetty they looked forlornly at the empty berth, and the sight of its emptiness reminded them that the *'old Ark'* was gone forever. This time it was true that the Germans had sunk the *Ark Royal*, yet something of her remained which even they could not destroy. As the First Lord of the Admiralty said . . . 'She has paid a rich dividend'.

Put by herself a ship is nothing, it is her crew who make her great and cause her to be remembered. This is not fanciful nor is it a little thing. In the *Ark* the spirit was real if imponderable, and more enduring than the ship herself.

When the war was over a new carrier went to sea and took over the name *Ark Royal*. Many of the old ship's company were at the Commissioning Ceremony to present the new *Ark* with a silver bell which said quite simply:

'May the sound of this bell remind us of the power and harmony of men.'

CHAPTER 9

Ark Royal IV

'The Queen of the Seas'

The Second World War came to an end in August 1945, but the achievements of naval aviation during those five long bitter years were all and more than had been hoped for. The knell for the death of the capital ship was tolled in the Atlantic in May 1941, when the Swordfish from *Ark* left *Bismarck* a helpless cripple, unsteerable, far from her base and out of range of friendly air support, but within range of the Royal Navy's guns.

In March of the same year there had been a dress rehearsal when aircraft from the carrier HMS *Formidable* had crippled an Italian cruiser *Pola* at the Battle of Matapan. Torpedo-carrying planes proved that ships were vulnerable even in their base ports, with the *Richelieu* immobilised at Dakar, *Dunkerque* severely damaged at Oran and the Italian battle-line halved at Taranto. These exploits and the damaging of *Tirpitz* in Kaafjord in April 1944, represented the acme of Fleet Air Arm activity as understood before 1939, but they tended to distract from the more routine operations.

Headlines and glowing victories are all very creditable, but the solid though unspectacular achievements of the Fleet Air Arm during the Second World War must also deserve mention and recognition. The incredible efficiency and effectiveness of the shipborne aircraft, must be measured in the number of safe arrivals of merchant ships in convoys afforded virtual immunity by escort carriers to enemy air and submarine attack, and also by the establishment of numerous amphibious beach-heads under air protection of carrier aircraft.

All too often naval aircraft had to substitute for the lack of shore based air power, achieving splendid successes when Skuas from the Orkneys sank the light cruiser *Koenigsberg*, torpedo bombers from Malta helped to sever so effectively Axis sea communications in the central Mediterranean, and fighter and strike aircraft re-inforced the RAF in the Western Desert. When the virtual elimination of German surface sea power allowed the Royal Navy to deploy its Fleet carriers and their re-armed air groups to the Pacific, the new techniques developed in that war by the Americans were learned and mastered. In a very short space of time, the powerful British Pacific Fleet could fairly claim to have achieved an expertise at least equal to that of the originators, but at a speed and with an efficiency that the US Navy had been reluctant to believe possible.

By 1945, the Fleet Air Arm was almost unrecognisable. It had grown both in stature and size, possessing no less than 43 Air Stations, 31 operational carriers out of 49 in commission, and had 50 squadrons of aircraft and about 1,050 of them embarked. Another 15 squadrons, with 250 aircraft between them, were working up or operating with the RAF; while on top of this, there were another 10,000 aircraft for training, FRU and reserve duties. The personnel strength had reached a colossal 70,000 officers and men, making it both numerically and operationally a very large proportion of the Navy.

The aircraft carrier had more than proved itself and now reigned supreme as the new capital ship. Although the world was at peace, and the carrier was recognised to be of essential importance in the post-war Fleet, it did not prevent an immediate and disastrous run-down during 1945 and 1946. The escort carriers, which had given such good service in all parts of the world, were handed back to the US Navy under the terms of the Lend-Lease Agreement, and the thousands of Hellcat, Avenger and Corsair aircraft which remained were either broken up or dumped at sea.

This policy left the Fleet Air Arm of the Royal Navy with only Seafires and Fireflies with which to complement its few remaining operational carriers, and the Korean War was to provide the proof of such short-sighted policy. In addition to the six Fleet and five Light Fleet carriers which had been completed between 1940 and August 1945, there were two Fleet carriers under construction and five others programmed, as well as thirteen Light Fleet carriers under construction and four projected.

As the need for merchant ships to replace war losses was paramount, work ceased on all but one Fleet carrier and four of the Light Fleets – one of which was intended for the Canadian Navy. A year after the end of the war, the Royal Navy's carrier Fleet had dwindled to only five Light Fleet carriers, with 72 Fireflies and 48 usable Seafire XVs between them. One Fleet carrier was in commission as a trials and training ship.

It was indeed a sorry state of affairs, but gradually over the next four years there was an improvement in the state of aircraft equipment, although the manning situation remained critical throughout the Fleet. On the eve of the Korean War in June 1950, the Royal Navy possessed in its Fleet Air Arm four fully operational Carrier Air Groups comprising 104 Sea Furies, Seafire 47s and Fireflies between them. In addition, there were two Trials and Training Fleet carriers for which there were 45 RN front-line and 41 RNVR aircraft available. There was a moderate Fleet Air Arm expansion during the Korean War period and politically it was unavoidable, but thereafter, the pattern was one of reductions imposed by economic considerations of the growing cost of aircraft and ships and deliberate Government policies. There was the Radical Review in 1954, 'The Way Ahead Committee' in 1955 and thereafter, the Yearly Long Term Defence Reviews and Costings; with the RNVR Air Divisions disbanded in 1957 as part of the economies.

With the exception of *Victorious*, withdrawn for complete modernisation in 1950 and re-commissioned in January 1958, all the war-time Fleet Carriers had been scrapped or reduced to reserve by 1955 and had been superseded by *Eagle* (commissioned March 1952), and the new *Ark Royal* (commissioned February 1955). These 46,000-ton carriers were supplemented by three of 27,000 tons: *Albion*, *Bulwark* and *Centaur*, laid down in 1944-45 and completed in 1953-54.

Nevertheless there were other factors in the air, for the years 1945-56 brought far-reaching changes in the technique of deck-flying; changes which marched in step with the spectacular increases in aircraft performance as a result of the change-over from piston engines to jets. The period also provided in the Korean War (1950-53) and the Suez operation (1956) further evidence, if evidence were needed, of the unique ability of the aircraft carrier to provide effective mobile task forces in localised war situations.

The FAA led the world in experiments with pure jets aboard aircraft carriers. Within a few months of VJ-Day, on 4th December 1945, a specially modified Vampire had been successfully landed aboard the Light Fleet Carrier *Ocean*. It also led the world in introducing three inventions which enabled the aircraft carrier to deal efficiently with the faster jets: these were the steam catapult, the angled deck and the mirror landing-sight. The angled deck and the short-stroke steam catapult were to some extent complementary, in that they enabled flying-off and landing-on to take place simultaneously.

With the greater speeds and higher wing-loadings of modern aircraft, it was becoming increasingly difficult to follow the old system, introduced about 1939, of using the first third of the deck for catapult take-off whilst aircraft landing-on used the remaining two-thirds; the two areas being separated by a crash barrier. The crash or safety barrier as it was called was introduced to protect those aircraft in the forward deck park, so that they could strike down the forward lift as other aircraft were being landed on. To increase the deck area was impossible without making the carrier itself much bigger. The problem was solved by the ingenious method (invented by Captain D.R.F. Campbell, DSC, RN) of splitting the flight deck diagonally: this eliminated the need for a barrier, and meant that aircraft which failed to hook the arrester wires could take off again without encroaching on the space reserved for the forward parking, stowing and catapult area. It also had the incidental advantage of leaving an aircraft parking area forward of the super-structure. The first aircraft-carrier of the Royal Navy with an angled deck was *Centaur*, completed in September 1953, and its immediate benefit was to greatly speed up flying operations.

The mirror landing-sight, developed by Commander H.C.N. Goodhart, RN, was introduced to overcome the deficiencies of manual control of deck landing by a signals officer, known as the batsman. With the ever increasing approach speed of modern aircraft (the Sea Fury piston-engined fighter introduced in 1947 raised approach speeds to 90-95 knots – they had been less than 50 knots in the days of the Flycatcher) the old type of steepish descending approach at a speed little above the stall, followed by a flare-out and engine-cut, was modified in 1948 to a more nearly level approach at higher speed. The batsman technique, already severely strained by the new approach methods, became finally impracticable when Jet fighters lifted approach speeds still higher (not far short of 142 knots normal and up to 152 knots in emergency single-engine conditions for the phantom), and the introduction of the mirror-sight eliminated the time lag between the batsman's signal and the pilot's reaction to it which could prove disastrous at such speeds.

With the mirror stabilised to give a glide angle unaffected by the pitch of the ship, the pilot was provided with a visual glide-path indication and had merely to fly straight on to the deck with no flare out and no reduction of engine power until the aircraft engaged the arrester wire. A further refinement of this system was the incorporation of an audio airspeed indicator signalling in the pilot's earphones, which together with a head up display on his windscreen eliminated the need for him to watch his instrument panel and take his eyes off the mirror sight during the final approach.

The carriers were to some extent the new status symbol of a powerful maritime nation. The immense striking power of their aircraft gave them an effectiveness greater than that of any ship before, but perhaps to the post war world, their attractiveness lay in the fact that the sea was neutral – foreign policy could be exercised in a politically free medium. In the mid-1950s the Government supported the idea of a strong Navy built around the carrier.

'We believe', said the First Lord of the Admiralty, Mr. J.P.L. Thomas, 'that the carrier has a future as firm as any airfield', and in 1955 almost as if to give credence to his fervent belief, four carriers were commissioned: *Centaur, Albion* and *Bulwark* (all of the *Hermes* class, 27,800 tons) and *Ark Royal* of 50,786 tons.

By the time *Ark Royal* III was finally torpedoed off Gibraltar in 1941, the old *'Ark'*, as she was always called, had become a very emotive name. She was a household name up and down the country and even abroad the *Ark* was the best known ship in the Royal Navy, thanks largely to the Germans and 'Lord Haw-Haw', who posed the monotonous question: 'Where is Ark Royal?' in broadcast after broadcast, week after week. But now she was really gone. The incredible luck had finally deserted her, but the spirit of her ship's company and the legend lived on – it was worth keeping and the Admiralty decided to build another *Ark – Ark Royal* IV.

The keel was laid down in a secret ceremony by the Duchess of Kent in the Cammell Laird Shipyard at Birkenhead on 3rd May 1943. Originally she was to be one of four new 'Audacious' class carriers ordered under the 1942 programme, and her name – *Irresistible*. At the end of the war two of the four *Audacious* class were cancelled – as were the three much large 'Gibraltar' class ships ordered a year later under the 1943 programme – while *Audacious* herself was renamed *Eagle* and the *Irresistible* became *Ark Royal*.

The Admiralty finally announced in 1946 the fact that *Ark Royal*

IV was under construction, though it was to be another four years before she was launched and nine years to the commissioning. The glamour, the romance and publicity of her exploits, the memories, the emotion of her predecessor, still clung around the new *Ark Royal*. At the launching ceremony on 3rd May 1950, a staggering 50,000 people came to watch, to wave their Union Jacks and bunches of evergreen, or just to remember with pride. Very appropriately, *Ark Royal* IV was sent on her first journey to the sea by Her Majesty, Queen Elizabeth, the Queen Mother. The launching ceremony was performed with a bottle of Empire white wine and not champagne, since the early 1950s were still the years of austerity and shortages. Nothing however, could detract from the excitement and pride of those people at Birkenhead that day. *Ark,* their *Ark,* was at sea once more.

It took another five years to fit out and complete *Ark*. Progress on her completion was slowed down, it was officially stated, so that the improvements and developments which were being made in carrier flying techniques and associated equipment progress could be incorporated in the new carrier. There were ripples of cynicism, beginning to be heard, largely owing to the fact that since her keel was laid, her cost had doubled from £10,000,000 to £20,000,000, but partly to some gloomy prophecies that by the time she was commissioned she would be obsolete.

A song written by a Birkenhead cinema organist and sung to the tune of 'Old Fashioned Mother of Mine' during the Interludes, summed up the sceptical mood of the time. The verses ended with the chorus lines:

Though she's cost twenty million we have no regret,
For there's something that makes her divine;
But we doubt it as yet that she'll ever get wet,
Like an old fashioned ship of the line.

To which, the then First Lord of the Admiralty, somewhat obviously and perhaps testily replied: 'I think you will find she will get pretty wet soon now.'

In fact, *Ark* was completed in February 1955 and the total bill – £21,428,000. She was without doubt the biggest and most modern carrier to serve in the Royal Navy. She differed from her sister ship *Eagle* in that she was the first British carrier to have a side lift incorporated and a five and a half degree angled deck. Although she could not claim to be the first operational carrier to have an angled deck, she could certainly lay claim to being the first with everything fitted – the lot! She had an angled deck, deck edge or side-lift, two mirror landing-sights, new arrester gear, steam catapults, aircrew bar, excellent accommodation and a special search and rescue flight of two Whirlwind S.55 helicopters.

At 1830 on Saturday, 25th February, 1955 in the approaches to the Clyde, a bugle sounded the alert, the Red Ensign of the builders was lowered and the White Ensign was hoisted in its place. After twelve years in the Cammell Laird shipyard, HMS *Ark Royal* IV was provisionally accepted into Her Majesty's Service by her first Commanding Officer, Captain D.R.F. Campbell, DSC, RN.

How different she was from her predecessor *Ark Royal* III, now resting hundreds of feet down in the 'grave' of the Mediterannean Sea. But something of the old *Ark* lived on and was transferred to the new ship. At an impromptu meeting of survivors held in Gibraltar Dockyard soon after the sinking of *Ark Royal* III, it was decided to use the balance of the ship's fund to buy a silver bell for the next ship to bear the name. Two years later there was a casting ceremony at the works of Messrs. Gillet and Johnson of Croydon, attended by survivors and the then First Lord, Mr. A.V. Alexander. When ready the bell was kept in the Wardroom of RNB Lee-on-Solent, till the final stage in the story took place on 25th March 1955, when the bell was presented to the new ship in the presence of 250 members of the old ship's company. It was housed in a magnificent oak belfry, subscribed for by officers of the old ship and accompanying this splendid gift linking one ship's company with their successors in a continuous tradition was a framed vellum which reads:

This bell was cast at the behest of the company of the third *Ark Royal* in memory of a Great Commission.

They bequeath the bell to all who sail in the ships that bear her name in the belief that the bond of fellowship and the spirit and enthusiasm which inspired them will live on in the *Ark Royals* that are to come.

May the sound of this bell remind us of the power and harmony in the lives of men.

Ark Royal IV was 810 feet long overall, had a beam of 158 feet and displaced 36,700 tons, Captain D.R.F. Campbell, DSC, was proud of his new command. She had the new interim angled-deck which he had designed but there was another stronger link, he had commanded 803 Squadron in *Ark Royal* III at the outbreak of World War II. At long last her successor was ready for sea and the task of making her into an efficient fighting unit, begun during the sorting process in the commissioning office at Devonport and during the months of pre-commissioning training at Birkenhead, could go ahead in earnest.

After refuelling at the Tail o' the Bank, *Ark Royal* sailed for Loch Ewe in the north west corner of Scotland, for a week's 'shakedown' of the new ship's company away from the counter attractions of the more inhabited places; to enable them to get to know their way about and each other: to learn the routines, and practise harbour evolutions which so far they had only encountered in the lecture room.

The week successfully concluded, passage was made to the Portsmouth area to carry out those trials which come the way of all newly commissioned ships, and finally, at the end of March, *Ark Royal* arrived at her home port for the first time to spend eight weeks on catapult deadload trials, during which time much other work was carried out to improve the accommodation on board.

From Devonport, at the end of May, course was set for Gibraltar for a three-week spell of flight deck drills, seamanship exercises, gunnery practices and air direction exercises.

In this very first commission of the new *Ark*, one of the ratings serving in his first carrier was Leading Sick Berth Attendant J. Dongworth – now a warrant officer and senior medical rating at RN Air Station Yeovilton, Somerset, and Headquarters of the Naval Air Command. He recalls that it was their first trip abroad – the many young ratings in the ship's company were excited about going foreign – even if it was only Gibraltar.

'En route, we had a series of talks, advice and that sort of thing by various officers over the ship's main broadcast. I particularly remember the talk by the Principal Medical Officer, you know, telling us about the dangers of too much drink and then going with women of easy virtue. As he warmed to his theme, he became more explicit and ended with this dire warning:

' "I have heard all the stories there are about the various ways of catching venereal disease ranging from – please sir I never went with her, I must have got it from a seat, to, I don't know Doctor Sir, I think I've got a cold in it. Well, I can tell you I'm a very sympathetic man, but if it has got a cold I shall expect it to sneeze at me!" '

On her return to home waters *Ark Royal* began to feel at last like an aircraft carrier. So far, all her aircraft on board had been non-flyers but now, the period scheduled for her first flying trials had arrived. This in turn passed finally, and at the end of July, she again entered her home port of Devonport for docking, storing and to carry out a host of other tasks before she sailed to embark her squadrons.

After the usual work up trials for both ship and squadrons *Ark* said farewell to the west country for six months and sailed down the Hamoase, past Drake's Island and the breakwater on Monday, 26th September. One of the first tasks was to carry out a full power trial off Looe, and to remind everyone in the new ship's company where their action stations were and to let them hear the guns firing. During the next morning, ten Sea Hawks of 800 Squadron met their new home south of the Isle of Wight. As *Noah's News*, the carrier's monthly magazine, quoted the aircraft embarkation for the first time:

Nine of them flew past in formation and landed on. The wheels of the tenth were locked down and he was 'a lame duck'. They practised deck landings in the afternoon and later we anchored off Sandown. The next morning at 0900, as 898 Fighter Squadron of ten Sea Hawks were preparing to land on for the first time, a dove settled on the forward end of the Flight deck. As soon as the ten Sea Hawks had landed on and taxied up the deck and parked, the dove flew away.

As the editor of the time commented:

As an emblem perhaps Noah sent it to remind us that it is excellent to have a giant's strength, but it is tyrannous to use it like a giant.

809 and 891 Squadrons of Sea Venom all-weather fighter aircraft were delayed and 809 eventually flew out to join from Halfar at the end of the year whilst 891 embarked in early 1956. The last few months of 1955, *Ark* was plagued with problems with the new steam catapults and even had them both replaced in August.

No. 800 Squadron was the Fleet Air Arm's first operational Jet Squadron and they received the Supermarine Attacker in August 1951. By the time they embarked with Hawks in 1955 in *Ark*, the transition from piston to jet aircraft in first line fighter and strike squadrons had been completed. Piston-engined aircraft remained only in second-line squadrons and for specialised duties such as airborne early warning (Skyraiders) and anti-submarine (gannets) and from 1953 onwards the Wyvern turboprop strike aircraft.

Perhaps one of the most important and certainly one of the most useful facilities aboard the new *Ark* was its own shipborne television network.

The idea of starting such a system first came to mind shortly after the ship was commissioned in 1955, when it was realised that to enable the entire ship's company to see any one film it would have to be screened in the largest space available every night for at least a week. The answer to the problem seemed to lie in some method of splitting the audience for a film into groups in their own messes, and for this television was obviously the solution; especially as such a system could be made to serve a dual purpose and provide BBC or ITV programmes as well when the ship was within range of their transmitters.

Approaches were made to various firms, and in August 1955 after some preliminary experiments, a contract was signed for the supply of necessary equipment, including the receiving sets; ship's staff began laying the ring main cable in the ship, and in September the first show was transmitted over the circuit.

In October, just before the ship sailed for the Mediterranean, 50 representatives of the press came on board for a day and were welcomed by the Captain over the television system. When he answered their questions from the screen as well, they were so impressed that from their reports the next day one would have imagined that *Ark Royal* was a floating Crystal Palace!

Live shows were numerous: quizzes, talks, panel games, and on several occasions the camera went out and about, examples being a boxing match in the upper hangar at Gibraltar, and a walk round the hangar showing types of aircraft, including a close-up of a Sea Venom cockpit, with the commentator showing what each gadget was for.

On a more official level the system was linked with the Sound Reproduction Equipment for Rear-Admiral Pedder, the Flag Officer

Aircraft Carriers, to speak to the ship's company.

The Operations Officer was also able to brief on forthcoming exercises, and with the aid of charts and models, to tell the 2,600 odd officers and men where they were going and what they would be doing. These semi-informal briefings always aroused great interest, and one of the early Gallup-type audience research polls found that the Ops team had peak viewing figures and were 'Top of the Pops'.

Another great favourite in the first commission was a live mannequin parade held and televised in the upper hangar. This was extremely popular though strongly criticised by some, that the camera operator had very different views on comparative feminine charm than most of the male viewers.

A most interesting demonstration of the versatility of the equipment took place during a visit to Naples. A camera unit of the Italian Television service embarked for a day's flying prior to the ship going into Naples, and the following evening the ship's company watched the tele-recording on Italian TV newsreel. This was despite the fact that Italian TV transmits pictures on 625 lines, and the British on 405 lines.

One of the more amusing stories about the Fleet Air Arm concerns *Ark Royal* in her first commission, her fixed-wing fighter squadron, No. 898 Squadron, and the visit to Naples. It was the squadron's custom that each and every member maintained an individuality among flyers, that as each pilot climbed out of his aeroplane, he was seen to be wearing a black 'bowler' hat and the CO a 'topper'. Under the title of 'it pays to advertise – or, if you want to get ahead, get a hat', the *Ark Royal* news magazine published what must rate as one of the best leg pulls of all time, by the rival 800 squadron.

Astonished, dismayed or perhaps just bored by the brazen attempts of 898 Squadron to, in the words of 800 Squadron, 'obtain unfair publicity at any cost and appalled at their lack of honesty in the process', the CO of 800 Squadron and his merry men decided to find out just what lengths the 'peasants of 898' would go to. During the ship's visit to Naples, it was decided to write a letter to them purporting to have come from the Italian Television Authority. This letter invited them to come ashore, complete with bowler hats and is reproduced below. All names concocted in the letter except for Signor Casperolli and the Caleria Umberto are fictitious and the letter was otherwise a pure inter-squadron affair, delivered to *Ark* on her arrival:

Via Tia Maria
Napoli.

Dear –

Signor Carreli of the Italian Television Authority has asked me to write to you on his behalf.

It appears that he has learned from his cameraman, who was on your ship yesterday, that one of your squadrons embarked wearing 'bowler hats'. He would like to interview them for a news revue programme to round off the film of *Ark Royal* ... If this is possible, would the people concerned be on the Jetty at 1230, when cars will be available to take them to his studio in the Galeria Umberto.

He realises that the time is awkward, but he wants to complete the film so that it can be edited this afternoon. Lunch will be provided at the studio. If this is impossible, would you please telephone me at 93645. Will the Officers concerned please bring their bowler hats. This letter is brought to you by Signor Casperolli, whom you know.

Sgd. Peter Williams
Manager
British Information Service.

When the ship came alongside, a representative body of 898 stepped ashore for their debut on Italian Television. The perpetrators of the joke reported:

898 made a brave sight as they stepped out of the boat, complete with their personal flag at the dip. The cameras clicked. They looked like complete English Bookmakers on holiday! The cars drove up – they clambered in – the cars drove off. The deed was done.

And so we say farewell as the taxis, their meters clicking, slowly sink below the dockyard horizon with their load of lunatics seeking publicity from an imaginary producer in an imaginary studio, at an imaginary address, with imaginary film stars who are waiting to eat an imaginary lunch with our imaginary heroes.

The arrangements for the practical-joke were superb and the picture in the line book shows five stalwarts, complete with bowlers and dark suits waiting on the quayside – one can't reveal names, but I wonder how long it took to live that one down!

In July 1956, Egypt nationalised the Suez Canal and under the code-name 'Operation Musketeer', English and French Forces intervened on 31st October and five British and two French light fleet carriers operated in close support of the ground forces. In all probability it was the last time that five carriers would ever operate as one force and in the Seven Day War, showed its great value and impressive flexibility.

Ark Royal was in dock during this period, for a refit intended to bring her up to date with the latest technical developments, to improve living quarters and extend the flight deck and commissioned for her second commission on 1st November 1956. This time she was to carry 831 Squadron Wyverns in addition to Hawks, Venoms and Gannets. However, the Wyvern, or (Flook) as it was called was not particularly successful as a carrier Fighter Strike aircraft and the squadron disembarked and disbanded in December 1957, and was replaced by the much-travelled 898 Sea Hawk Squadron.

The post-World War II American carrier striking force was built up to include a new generation of super-carriers, so that by 1962 they had the *Forrestal, Saratoga, Independence, Enterprise, Constellation, Ranger* and *Kitty Hawk,* as well as three 'Midway' class and eight more of the modernised 'Essex' class. While on this side of the Atlantic, British policy was already changing direction. In the 1957 Statement on Defence, the UK Government pinned their faith in a nuclear deterrent strategy based on the RAF 'V-bombers' and the inter-continental ballistic missile Blue Streak. On the naval side, they had decided to have three carriers with the full-angled deck *Victorious, Hermes* and *Eagle,* with *Ark Royal* and *Centaur* continuing in service fitted with interim angled decks. Except for *Bulwark* and *Albion* converted into Commando helicopter carriers, all other carriers were either sold, scrapped or on the disposal list.

To add to the dilemma of the planners however, the Government Statement concluded that 'the role of naval forces in total war was uncertain. But as time went on, the case for the carriers seemed more and more directed towards the limited war concept.' Mention has been made already of the value of a carrier task force in providing air support in localised wars: the aircraft carrier's ability to operate where land bases were not available and the fact that it presented a moving target. Both factors were urged in its favour, by advocates who saw in it an alternative method of launching a nuclear-armed strike aeroplane against land targets. Whether for use against land-based targets or enemy fleets, it became Admiralty policy to equip the Fleet Air Arm with aircraft capable of delivering atomic bombs: the Scimitar was the first naval aircraft capable of delivering nuclear weapons and also the first swept-wing aircraft in the transonic class to enter service in the Fleet Air Arm. The first experimental flight of Scimitar aircraft was formed at Ford in 1957, to mark the beginning of a new era in naval air warfare.

Entering service shortly after the Scimitar, which replaced the Sea Hawk as the standard single-seat interceptor as well as being equipped for strike duties, was the two-seat Sea Vixen, a transonic all-weather fighter which superseded the subsonic Sea Venom FAW 21. Both Scimitars and Sea Vixens could carry air-to-air guided missiles, though the Sea Vixen proved to be a more versatile aircraft. Its ability to protect the Fleet was further enhanced by the introduction of improved radar surveillance carried in specialised air direction frigates surrounding the carrier task force.

From early in 1963, the Royal Navy's nuclear strike capability was greatly increased in the tactical role, with the arrival of Buccaneer Squadrons at sea in the carriers. New weapons and missiles were introduced to give the new generation of naval aircraft a much improved air-to-air and air-to-ground capability, but as ever, the major problem which confronted the planning staffs, was which way to go? What new equipment would be required to fulfil our commitments in 1970s and 1980s? How could they obtain a directive and then the necessary approval to purchase in a climate of ever increasing financial stringency?

In 1966, the 'Defence-axe fell': the British Government decided to put a ceiling of two thousand million pounds on the Defence budget and the carrier force was doomed. They stated that aircraft carriers would only be required to support an opposed landing against sophisticated opposition and outside the range of our shore-based aircraft, then neatly wrote the requirement out of any future Foreign Policy by stating that such intervention would be strictly by 'invitation only'. Against this background, it was decided to cancel the new carrier designated *CVA 01*, scrap *Victorious* and leave *Eagle*, *Ark Royal* and *Hermes* to continue into the 1970s.

From 1955 to the time of the controversial 1966 Defence Review, *Ark* completed five commissions. During that time, she had operated as our largest and most formidable strike carrier in almost every ocean in the world. On her last commission in 1964 to 1966 and prior to her major refit, she carried out two Beira patrols to intercept oil tankers carrying oil into Mombassa. It was on 10th May and just one month before her return to UK, that *Ark* had one of her more tragic air accidents. A Sea Vixen of 890 Squadron piloted by Lieutenant Alan Tarver with Lieutenant John Stutchbury as observer took off for a routine oil-tanker patrol. It was nothing out of the ordinary and the weather was good, but just as Tarver was returning to the carrier at the end of his sortie, a series of emergencies occurred which changed everything with dramatic suddenness.

The port engine flamed-out and the electrics failed but worse than that, he saw from his gauges that the fuel remaining for his good engine was being jettisoned at an alarming rate. Unless he could do something quickly, he would run out of fuel, his one remaining engine would flame out and they would have to abandon the aircraft. *Ark Royal* immediately launched a Scimitar tanker aircraft flown by Lieutenant Robin Munro-Davies, to rendezvous with and re-fuel the Vixen, which by this time was losing height and already down to fifteen thousand feet.

Ark was still forty miles away when he saw the Scimitar closing in his ten o'clock position. Quickly it banked round, streamed the refuelling hose and the two aircraft closed. Unfortunately Tarver was not able to hold his aircraft steady. Losing power on his one good engine and going slowly downhill, he found it was impossible to fly the Vixen's refuelling probe into the drogue on the end of the Scimitar's fuelling hose. Five times he tried to make contact and then his second engine failed as he ran out of fuel.

Ark Royal was now visible on the horizon, but his only hope was to get as near as possible and then eject. With the gliding characteristics of a brick, the Vixen wouldn't go very far, though perhaps he could stretch the glide for a few miles and thus reduce the time taken for a Search and Rescue helicopter to reach them.

At 6,000 feet, Tarver ordered his observer to eject. Sitting down in the 'coal-hole', below the pilot and on his right hand side, John Stutchbury reached up for his handle, then pulled it out and down over his face. The blind came down and nothing happened. The hatch cover was still in place, the seat hadn't fired and the aircraft was going down towards the sea like an express lift.

Over the intercom, Tarver yelled at the observer to bale out manually, while he reduced the airspeed as much as possible and fought to hold the plane steady. Tarver saw the hatch being jettisoned and a second or two later, the observer's head and shoulders appeared. He was a big man and had seemed to have got jammed in the narrow hatchway. Although down to three thousand feet and going dangerously slowly at about 200 knots, Tarver rolled the aircraft upside down and hoped the observer would fall clear. Still the observer hung there, upside down and firmly jammed. Again he rolled the aircraft, but it was no use. There was just one more chance. Lowering the flaps to reduce the speed still further to around 130 knots, he brought the aircraft almost to the point of stall in a last vain effort to allow the observer to struggle free. The tearing force of the slipstream was now very much less and more of Stutchbury's body slid out of the cockpit. It looked as though the plan would work. The observer was almost out and lying flat along the top of the fuselage, but something was still holding him in the cockpit. Frantically Tarver reached across and struggled to free the observer's feet, pushing and pulling as the waves rushed up to meet them. It was no use, the observer seemed to be unconscious, the aircraft was just on the stall at 400 feet and even if he got free now, his parachute wouldn't have time to open.

Circling in the Scimitar overhead, Lieutenant Munro-Davies watched everything happening as the stricken Vixen went down. He watched Tarver's last desperate effort to free his friend and then saw the aircraft stall, flick over to port and crash into the sea. In the very last seconds as the Vixen rolled and when it was almost on its side, he saw the pilot's ejection seat fire.

There was an enormous fountain of spray and that was that – all over. Munro-Davies reported to *Ark* that Tarver had left the aircraft almost as it hit and couldn't possibly have survived.

In fact he had. Miraculously his parachute had half deployed as he struck the sea and although stunned, he managed to struggle free and get into his dinghy. Twenty minutes later he was in the Planeguard Wessex helicopter and on his way back to *Ark*, and his only injury was a strained muscle in his back. For his outstanding courage in trying to save the observer's life and almost sacrificing his own life in the attempt, Alan Tarver was awarded the George Medal.

In October 1966, *Ark Royal* docked at Devonport for a major refit and modernisation that was to last three years. At the time, it was feared that the Government's new Defence Policy and their plans for a complete British Withdrawal from East of Suez would mean the scrapping of this famous carrier. During the next three years, she was in the words of one newspaper reporter, 'the biggest three-dimensional jig-saw in the world, and a bigger job than the building of the Q4'.

The background to the refitting of *Ark* is fairly well known, but the short-time scale and small amount of money available added to the enormity of the task facing the dockyard. Every modern method, including the use of computers, was brought to bear on the planning and administration of this refit. A small team of officers and ratings remained with the ship and their reliefs saw the refit through. Apart from hoisting the Ensign, as the ship was still in commission, they acted as recorders and advisers, and attempted to co-ordinate and answer the many and varied queries on the ship and its equipment.

The major task was the re-wiring of the ship. This involved everything except the ring main, and was estimated at something like 1,200 miles of cable. It was not just the length, but the connecting up of the countless cable ends which was such an undertaking. All of this had to be backed by thousands of drawings. The *Ark* was the first ship to have all cables marked for ease of identification. In addition, a new 440v 60cps three phase AC distribution system fed by two new turbo generators and two new diesel generators were installed.

The 'Phantomisation' of the flight deck and hangars was one of the major tasks. Part of the scheme involved converting the $5\frac{1}{2}$ degree angled deck into the full $8\frac{1}{2}$ degree, and then uprooting the starboard catapult and transferring it to the angle. Its length was increased to 199 feet long, but the port catapult remained at 154 feet long and was extensively refitted. Both catapults had the new jet blast deflector arrangements with the adjacent deck water-cooled to prevent excessive heating, otherwise the deck-plates would become very 'tacky' after being subjected to Phantom re-heat for about 15 seconds. Also, both catapults were fitted with the new Van Zelm bridle arresting gear designed to catch the very expensive wire bridles after each catapult shot. Other improvements included new arrester gear: a refit on the ship's main engines, boilers and auxiliary machinery, and an extensive modernisation of the messdecks and air conditioning.

As the days went by into weeks, and the weeks into months, slowly but surely *Ark Royal* was ripped apart and then put together again. As one newspaper put it:

> It was a race against time. The guts have been taken out of her and while the Politicians prevaricate, Devonport's white hope waits for rebirth. Stripped, mazed with cables and tubes carrying fuel for the cutting torches carving the ways for the new equipment to be eased in – the essentials to make her a fighting ship for the next ten years or so.

There must be thousands serving in the Royal Navy and literally millions of civilians, who have little or no idea that the three year long and 32 million pound refit and reconstruction of HMS *Ark Royal* – together with all the trials and work ups – were a far larger undertaking than the building of QE2. As has been said already, the most significant fact in the whole project, which was likened to a three year rugger match – was that there was no extra time!

Without doubt a major factor in this success story was the sustained and single minded effort of the ship's company as it built up throughout the final year. It was recognised that the long refit and final commissioning of HMS *Ark Royal* would be, perhaps, the toughest task that officers and ratings had to face during their time in the Service. If the majority were about to serve in their first – and perhaps their last commission in a Fixed-Wing aircraft carrier, there were others who could count many years' service in *Ark Royal* and/or her sister ship *Eagle*.

To commemorate the long refit of 1967-70, Commander G.V.P. Crowden, OBE, RN, the Marine Engineer Officer and his engineering department thought up the idea of an '*Ark Royal* Star and Bar'. The design of the star was based on the 1939-45 War Star for simplicity and had the ship's crest of *Ark Royal* as a centre decoration. The 'Bars' would represent each year, or part year, served in *Ark Royal*. As any time served in her sister ship *Eagle* would provide equally valuable experience, it was decided that bars for *Eagle* as well as *Ark Royal* would be produced.

Messrs. J.R. Gaunt Ltd. of Soho, London, willingly accepted the order and the Stars and Bars were struck in white metal suspended from a $1\frac{1}{4}''$ plain crimson ribbon. Just over 100 stars were produced, together with some 250 *Ark Royal* bars and 60 *Eagle* bars. The most interesting *Ark Royal* star without a doubt now belongs to a Chief Engineering Mechanic who has an unrivalled claim to 11 bars – all for Service in *Ark*. The NAAFI Manager, Ship's Barber and many others were eligible for the unique and much sought after souvenir of the *'Ark Refit'* medal.

'And now, Captain Lygo, splice the main brace!'

The long refit was over and with these words, Queen Elizabeth the Queen Mother ended her speech to the ship's company and some 4,000 guests aboard the *Ark* on the occasion of her recommissioning ceremony on 24th February 1970 at Devonport. The Royal Command was a welcome piece of news for the carrier's crew, for the days of the sailor's tot were numbered and another tradition was shortly to be scrapped.

Her Majesty said in her speech that since she launched the *Ark* in May 1950, she had missed only one of the six commissioning ceremonies, and had visited the ship on many occasions – the last time during flying exercises off the Aberdeen coast. The ship was now embarking on the 'most exciting and challenging commission of all', she said. With that, the Queen Mother cut the commissioning cake – a 420-lb. model of the ship – and said to be the largest cake ever baked in the Royal Navy.

The three year refit had given the carrier a further hull life of up to 10 years, but with the Phantom fighters and Sea King helicopters, backed up by the Buccaneer, Sea Vixens and Gannets, the *Ark Royal* would become one of our most formidable warships ever.

On sailing on the 10th October 1970, the catapults and arresting gear underwent testing and while the latter appeared much better, the bow catapult gave a lot of trouble. Nevertheless, *Ark* sailed for the usual hunting grounds of the Mediterranean and after a short ten day stop in Malta, sailed for Exercise Lime Jug in November.

On the evening of 9th November, an incident occurred which could have had disastrous results. From first light it had been a normal flying day for *Ark*'s aircraft and as usual, a witness to the operations was a Russian SAM *Kotlin* class destroyer. For many years, Russian spy ships disguised as innocent 'trawlers' have kept watch on British, American and NATO naval exercises. Recently however, Russian naval ships have shadowed and monitored Allied exercises and even the spy ships no longer pretend to be genuine trawlers, as loaded with every sort of electronic gadgetry, they tail RN ships and listen in for intelligence gathering purposes.

Kotlin 365 after the collision—damaged superstructure is covered by tarpaulin aft.

HMS *Ark Royal* in collision with Russian *Kotlin* GM Destroyer. Russian vessel close up to *Ark Royal*'s stern.

The need for air power at sea for the future? A Russian Badger reconnaissance aircraft flies over *Ark Royal* during Fleet exercises.

The Fleet Air Arm of tomorrow. RAF Harriers of No 1 Squadron carry out sea trials aboard HMS *Ark Royal* in the Moray Firth, May 1971.

The Marine Engineer Officer of the time recalls . . .

After a dog watch break, a fresh flight deck crew was ready on *Ark*'s flight deck, the night flying crews were briefed and the aircraft manned. Three miles on the starboard beam, the 2,500 ton *Kotlin* 365 travelled on a parallel course at 14-15 knots – watching and listening as *Ark* prepared to launch her jets.

Below decks *Ark*'s ship's company was relaxing. With work finished for the day or off watch for a period, some were watching closed circuit TV, writing letters, chatting, or sleeping. In the wardroom, the majority of officers had finished their evening meal, although some later arrivals were about to get their coffee.

Unconsciously each man on board noted the alteration of course and the increased tempo of the main engines as the speed of the ship was adjusted for flying operations. The reverberations of the first Phantom's engines on re-heat permeated the ship's ventilation systems and faded as the aircraft left the flight deck. The ship shuddered as the catapult piston was retarded at the end of the launch stroke. Everything was set for some good night flying. There was enough wind over the deck, not too much swell, and sufficient visibility to see the horizon and the clear navigation lights of the plane-guard destroyer in station on the port quarter. However, before the night was over the airborne Phantom was to be diverted ashore.

The noise and vibration of the second Phantom night launch never came. Instead, the throb and beat of the ship's engines changed suddenly, and it became clear that the carrier was actually working up to go full astern. Had the first Phantom ditched ahead of the ship? Inquiring glances were answered by the strident call of the alarm rattler for Emergency Stations. Clearly something serious had happened.

Reports after the accident state that *Ark Royal* was steering a straight course into wind in a position about 110 miles west of Crete, when the Russian destroyer altered course to port and crossed the carrier's bows. Lord Balniel, Minister of State for Defence, told MPs that the resulting collision could have been avoided by correct observation of the Rule of the Road of the Sea. 'Russia', he said, 'was a signatory to the 1965 International Regulations for Prevention of collisions at sea, which made it clear that ships must keep clear of a carrier when operating aircraft. From the nature of her work, a carrier was unable to get out of the way!

Lord Balniel said the destroyer approached from starboard immediately after the first aircraft had left the carrier. The ships struck each other on the port side. The *Ark Royal* was slightly damaged above the water line. The destroyer was badly scraped and her superstructure damaged.

Russian newspapers were loud in their condemnation of the incident, 'one would not like to think that the collision was the result of deliberate actions by the commander of *Ark Royal*', stated the Soviet Defence Ministry newspaper *Red Star*. Meanwhile the Soviet Government newspaper *Izvestia* quoted the destroyer Captain, Captain L. Gobysh, as saying that the *Ark Royal* only stopped to help in the rescue operation because Captain Lygo of *Ark Royal* 'evidently recognised his guilt'.

In fact had it not been for Captain Lygo's prompt action in cancelling the aircraft launch and going full astern for a full two minutes before the impact, the Russian destroyer would have been sliced clean in half and sunk with great loss of life. It must have been obvious to the Kotlin Captain that night flying was in progress. *Ark*'s flying lights were on, and the first Phantom had gone off the catapult like a 'ball of fire', with its reheat at full blast flying ahead of the Russian destroyer, then on *Ark Royal*'s starboard bow.

As the Russian turned to port and closed the *Ark* and when only a mile away, Captain Lygo signalled: 'You are standing into danger'. Although the engines were going full astern slowing the carrier from 18 knots to about four knots and the helm was put hard to port, *Ark*'s bow struck the Russian ship on the port side.

Seven Russian seamen either jumped overboard, or were hurled over the side by the impact of the collision. A sea and air search for them began immediately, headed by the frigates *Yarmouth*, 2,800 tons, *Exmouth* 1,456 tons and the RFA oiler *Tidesurge* 25,940 tons and Royal Navy helicopters. Another Russian ship also helped in the search.

Boats from *Ark Royal* and HMS *Yarmouth* picked up five of the seven missing Russian seamen and returned them to the Soviet destroyer, but they failed to find the other two. The Russians took no action other than an official protest, nor did they indicate why the Kotlin-class destroyer was sailing so close to the carrier. Referring to the continual 'snooping and harassment by Soviet forces', Rear

Admiral Morgan-Giles, Conservative MP for Winchester, said that 'an incident of this sort had become inevitable in the long run'.

The actual damage to the *Kotlin* may never be known, but the study of photographs and inspection of *Ark Royal*'s scars indicated that there were many points of contact. The SAM missile launcher seemed a likely cause of a small split in *Ark*'s side at for'castle level. Undoubtedly *Ark Royal*'s starboard anchor must have been embedded deep in the deckhouse below the missile launcher and there were other signs of heavy contact between the *Kotlin*'s port quarter and *Ark*'s bow. Before the carrier stopped, the Russian destroyer must have been heeled over heavily to starboard and then pivoted to port beneath the overhang of the flight deck. The *Kotlin*'s propeller guard – normally close to the water – must have been lifted clear of the water level, due to the large angle of heel and, being a solid and substantial piece of metal, had a 'tin opener' effect on the stem of the carrier.

In just eight hours, the shipwrights of *Ark* had repaired the damage to the bows and made her seaworthy, but the entanglement with SAM *Kotlin* 365 will be long remembered by the Royal Navy and by people everywhere, as the 'International Incident which was bound to happen one day!'

After a nine day self-maintenance period in Malta, the carrier sailed for exercises off the Island on 25th November. The short five day period included two notable events. The first was the Malta Sea Day on 28th when a most successful display was arranged for a number of local dignatories who had been invited on board. Then the next day – the 29th November – was Hot Air Balloon Day. Lieutenant Terry Adams of 849B Flight made the first launch ever from a British ship at sea in his red and white striped hot air balloon G – AVTL 'Bristol Belle'.

With full press and television coverage, the balloon lifted from the flight deck of *Ark* lying just south and upwind of Malta. The initial course taken by the balloon seemed to indicate that it might miss the small island and make a 'wet' landing in the sea. However, a judicious application of more heat carried it up to about two thousand feet, where the winds took the balloon inshore and over the island. This was also the first flight by a hot air balloon over Malta and the event promoted much interest and excitement by those who saw it. In fact, Terry Adams and his crew took only thirty minutes to 'drift' on their flight from *Ark* to land in the field of a very surprised farmer. After packing the balloon and basket, they delivered a pile of commemorative letters, specially franked to mark the occasion, to the local Maltese Post Office.

Throughout the next two years the carrier continued to operate from the Moray Firth to Puerto Rico, from the Mediterranean to the Seas off the North American Coast. Cross operating with mighty American carriers like the USS *F.D. Roosevelt*, she was again to prove that the Fleet Air Arm could hold its own in the field of carrier operations – that the best was not always in the largest packet.

Many naval warships have been adopted by various towns, cities and organisations over the years, but the association between the City of Leeds and *Ark Royal* is somewhat unique, for it stems back to World War II and the third *Ark Royal*.

During the war, various Government sponsored campaigns were mounted to encourage people to save in support of the war effort, buying savings certificates and war bonds. One of these schemes included a series of 'Warship Weeks' and the one in Leeds was arranged for 30th January to 7th February 1942. On 4th November 1941, in anticipation of the week and to add objective and incentive to the campaign, the City of Leeds, through its National Savings Committee decided to adopt HMS *Ark Royal*. A Target of £3 million was set. Ten days later, on 14th November 1941, *Ark Royal* was sunk. Immediately the target figure was raised to £5 million, but such was the enthusiasm that £9,301,293 was invested (equivalent to some £80 million at 1975 values.) The enormity of such an effort is still quite astonishing – and how right that, though many cities were anxious to adopt the fourth *Ark Royal*, the honour should remain with Leeds.

On 19th September 1942 the adoption became official when, at a ceremony in Leeds attended by the then First Sea Lord, Lord Chatfield, Captain E. Elgood, RN, received the City of Leeds Plaque and in return presented to the City the *Ark Royal* crest. This crest was diamond in shape and was replaced by the new round design when the present *Ark Royal* was commissioned. The City of Leeds plaque commemorating the adoption now has pride of place on the present *Ark Royal*'s quarterdeck, alongside that of Lloyds of London who also adopted the carrier at the time of her commissioning.

Over the years, the bonds between the ship and the City have been strengthened, and it was a most fitting climax to this unique relationship, that *Ark Royal* received the highest honour and was given the Freedom of the City on 25th October 1973.

The beginning of the 'seventies saw *Ark*'s sister ship *Eagle* paid off for the last time, *Centaur* sent for scrap, *Hermes* converted into a commando carrier, whilst ashore the Naval Air Stations of Brawdy and Lossiemouth were transferred to RAF control. Now, as we look to the end of 1976 only *Ark* remains as the sole survivor of the RN attack carrier fleet. Like the dreadnought battleships of an earlier age, she and her kind have enjoyed the reign and title as 'the queen of sea warfare'. In the Royal Navy it has been a brief interlude in the history and development of sea power – less than a life span of three score years and ten, but before the critics of naval aviation send *Ark* to her last resting place in the scrap-yard, perhaps we can see a new offspring on the stocks. Not the majestic, impressive attack carriers of today, but the new breed of cruiser capable of carrying a new generation of aircraft to sea.

Developed supersonic harriers with longer range and greater payload will probably replace *Ark*'s Phantoms and Buccaneers in the late 1970s. Despite the many advantages of operating sophisticated and specialised aircraft from large carriers, there is no doubt that V/STOL offers the best and probably the only long term solution to providing naval air power within a limited and ever decreasing budget. The Fleet Air Arm still provides Great Britain with a powerful part of its defence armoury. Its slogan of Fly Navy – once prominently displayed on the after end of *Ark*'s flight deck – is a wise choice for this country. It lends emphasis to that part of the naval prayer, applicable as ever today . . .

'It is upon the Navy, under the good providence of God, that the wealth, safety, and strength of the Kingdom do chiefly depend.'

In two – perhaps three years, *Ark* will leave her home of Devonport on her last voyage. The slow journey – hauled by tugs – to the breaker's yard. Gone will be her Air Group of noisy jets, the smell of kerosene and the rush of wind down her flight deck. Gone the hundreds of men, who for over two decades, toiled, sweated and strove to carry on the legend of the *Ark*.

As she passes Drake's Island, perhaps the ghost of Lord Howard of Effingham will be heard to mutter the same words he used – nearly four centuries earlier – in final and fitting tribute.

'I pray you tell Her Majesty from me that her money was well given for the *Ark Royal*, for I think her the odd ship in the World for all conditions, and truly I think there can be no great ship make me change and go out of her.'

Bibliography

Apps, Michael: *Send Her Victorious.* (Kimber)

Bragadin, Cdr (R), M.A.: *The Italian Navy in World War II* (Cornell)

Broome, Jack, Captain, RN: *Make Another Signal* (Kimber)

Brown, J.D.: *Carrier Operations in World War II* (Ian Allen)

Banbury, Philip: *Shipbuilders of the Thames and Medway* (David and Charles)

Callender, Geoffrey: *The Naval Side of British History* (Christophers)

Cameron, Ian: *Wings of the Morning* (Hodder and Stoughton)

Chatfield, Lord: *The Navy and Defence* (Heinemann)

Churchill, Winston, S.: *The Second World War Vols II and III* (Cassell)

Cunningham, Viscount: *A Sailor's Odyssey* (Hutchinson)

Doenitz, Admiral: *Memoirs, Translated by R.H. Stevens* (Weidenfeld and Nicolson)

Froude, J.A.: *English Seamen in Sixteenth Century* (Longmans)

Garrett, Richard: *Stories of Famous Ships* (Barker)

Graham, Winston: *The Spanish Armadas* (Collins)

Heifferman, Ronald: *World War II* (Octopus)

Hezlett, Sir Arthur: *Aircraft and Sea Power* (Davies)

Vice Admiral Howarth, David: *Sovereign of the Seas* (Collins)

Jackson, Robert: *Strike from the Sea* (Barker)

Jameson, William: *Ark Royal 1939-1941* (Rupert Hart Davis)

Rear Admiral Kemp, Peter: *The Fleet Air Arm* (Herbert Jenkins)

Lieutenant Commander, RN Kemp, Peter: *The Nine Vanguards* (Hutchinson)

Lieutenant Commander, RN Kemp, Peter: *The British Sailor* (Dent)

Killen, John: *A History of Marine Aviation* (Muller)

Laughton, Sir John: *From Howard to Nelson* (Heinemann)

Knox Lloyd, Christopher: *The British Seaman* (Collins)

MacIntyre, Donald: *Fighting Ships and Seamen* (Evans)

Marder, Arthur, J.: *From the Dardanelles to Oran* (Oxford)

Moore, Major G.W.: *Early Birds* (Putnam)

Poolman, Kenneth: *Illustrious* (Kimber)

Poolman, Kenneth: *Ark Royal* (Kimber)

Popham, Hugh: *Into Wind* (Hamish Hamilton)

Roskill, S.W. Captain RN: *The Naval Air Service Vol. I 1908-1918* (Navy Records Society)

Roskill, S.W. Captain RN: *History of Second World War, The War at Sea Vol. I, Edited by J.R.M. Butler* (H.M.S.O.)

Rutter, Owen: *Ark Royal* (H.M.S.O. 1942)

Russell, Sir Herbert: *Ark Royal* (John Lane)

Strabolgi, Lord, RN: *The Battle of the River Plate* (Hutchinson)

Taylor, John W.R.: *A History of Aerial Warfare* (Book Club Associates, London)

Tedder, Lord: *Air Power in War* (Hodder and Stoughton)

Warner, Oliver: *The Greatest Sea Battles* (Spring Books)

Winton, John: *The War at Sea 1939-45 Vol. I* (Arrow)

Woodward, David: *The Tirpitz* (Kimber)

Action of Cape Spartivento 5.5.48 (Supplement to the London Gazette, No. 32281)

The Air Battle of Malta (H.M.S.O.)

East of Malta, West of Suez (H.M.S.O.)

The River Plate Battle 17.6.47 (Supplement to the London Gazette No. 34989)

Sinking of the Bismarck 16.10.47 (Supplement to the London Gazette No. 38098)

Hutchinson's Pictorial History of the War Vols 1-25. Ark Royal Commission Books.

Ark Royal III –
Squadrons Embarked.

September 1939 to March 1940

800 Squadron	9 Skuas
803 Squadron	9 Skuas (to end of September 1939)
810 Squadron	12 Swordfish
820 Squadron	12 Swordfish plus one Walrus
821 Squadron	12 Swordfish

24th April to 7th June 1940

800 Squadron	12 Skuas
801 Squadron	6 Skuas and 6 Rocs (to 28th April)
803 Squadron	12 Skuas (from 30th April)
810 Squadron	12 Swordfish
820 Squadron	12 Swordfish

August 1940 to April 1941

800 Squadron	12 Skuas
808 Squadron	12 Fulmars (replaced by 803 squadron in October 1940)
810 Squadron	12 Swordfish
818 Squadron	9 Swordfish
820 Squadron	9 Swordfish

The 'Bismarck' Hunt

807 Squadron	12 Fulmars
808 Squadron	12 Fulmars
810 Squadron	9 Swordfish
818 Squadron	9 Swordfish
820 Squadron	9 Swordfish

April 1941 to November 1941
(torpedoed on 13th November 1941
by *U-81* and sank on 14th November)
807 Squadron
808 Squadron
825 Squadron
816 Squadron
812 Squadron

9 Swordfish (replaced 820
    in June 1951)
9 Swordfish (replaced 818
    • in July 1941)
12 Swordfish (replaced 810
    in September 1941)

Ark Royal IV
Squadrons and Aircraft Embarked

No. 809 Squadron – Formed at St. Merryn with Fairey Fulmar fighters on 15th January 1941, No. 809 Squadron embarked in HMS *Victorious* in July and was in action that month, covering a strike in Kirkenes, northern Norway, during which the squadron destroyed two Messerschmitt Bf 110s and a BF 109 for the loss of two Fulmars. Escort to Russian convoys was the next task and this continued for most of that year.

August 1942 saw No. 809, still aboard *Victorious*, in the Mediterranean and helping to fight a large convoy through the Malta (Operation Pedestal); 2 1/3 more enemy aircraft were added to No. 809's score. Then back home to St. Merryn, and at a succession of shore bases, the squadron was specially trained in Army cooperation work, after which it rejoined *Victorious* for the North African landings.

In April 1943 No. 809 re-equipped with Seafire IICs at Stretton and in August joined HMS *Unicorn* to support the Allied landings at Salerno. Returning to England again, the squadron was based at Andover where it became part of No. 4 Naval Fighter Wing (with Nos. 807 and 879 Squadrons); the establishment of each squadron was twenty Seafires. During the next few months some of No. 809's pilots were attached to the Desert Air Force, operating from Italian airfields.

In August 1944 aboard the escort carrier HMS *Stalker* the squadron took part in the invasion of Southern France and later that year flew 'seek and destroy' sorties over the Aegean islands. After the mainland of Greece had been liberated, No. 809 returned to the UK. In March 1945 the squadron rejoined *Stalker* in the Mediterranean and on her way to Trincomalee, Ceylon.

In the Indian Ocean No. 809 Squadron – whose establishment had now risen to thirty Seafires – provided support for the Rangoon landings and thereafter flew strikes against Japanese targets until VJ-Day. In October No. 809 was home again, at Nutts Corner, and the next month re-equipped with Seafire F.17s, but in January 1946 the squadron disbanded.

On 20th January 1949 No. 809 reformed at Culdrose with Sea Hornet NF 21s in the night-fighter role. After a prolonged work-up the squadron embarked in HMS *Vengeance*, a light fleet carrier, in May 1951 but was soon back at Culdrose. Eventually, in late 1952, No. 809 joined HMS *Eagle* and remained with this ship until going ashore in 1954 to re-equip with Sea Venom NF 20s (from May onwards) at Yeovilton. The next year the squadron received Mk. 21 Sea Venoms and took these to Hal Far, Malta, where it was stationed until disbandment in April 1956.

The next month No. 809 reformed at Yeovilton with Sea Venom FAW 21s and in September went aboard HMS *Albion*, proceeding to the Mediterranean. Then (October-November) came the Suez operation, in which No. 809 played a notable part, helping to neutralise Egyptian airfields and providing air cover for the landings at Port Said. In 1958 the squadron, still with *Albion*, flew strikes against terrorists in Cyprus and then saw service in the Far East, before disbanding at Yeovilton on 17th August 1959.

The 'Immortal Phoenix' (incorporated in the squadron's crest) rose again in January 1963, at Lossiemouth, when No. 809 was reborn to a new role, strike, by renumbering No. 700Z Flight, the IFTU for the Buccaneer S.I. Two years later the squadron reverted to second-line status and was renumbered No. 736 Squadron.

January 1966 saw No. 809 in business again, reformed at Lossiemouth with Buccaneer S.2s, and a year later (January 1967) embarked in HMS *Hermes*. Then followed a work-up in the Mediterranean, service off Aden and in the Far East, a return to Lossiemouth in October, and then back to Aden to cover the final stages of the British withdrawal.

No. 809 returned to Lossiemouth in February 1968 and later that year provided a notable aerobatic team – 'Phoenix Five' with their 20-ton Buccaneers – for the SBAC Show at Farnborough. Towards the end of 1969 there was a build-up in squadron strength and in May 1970 No. 809 embarked in HMS *Ark Royal*. Exercises in the North Atlantic and Mediterranean followed, and in December 1970 the squadron disembarked to Lossiemouth – with five years' accident-free flying to its credit.

Today No. 809, the Royal Navy's last Buccaneer squadron, goes where the *'Ark'* goes and when ashore has RAF Honington as its home 'port', Lossiemouth having been relinquished by the Navy. Squadron strength is fifteen Buccaneer S. 2s.

No. 824 Squadron – This unit was formed on 26th April 1933 by combining Nos. 440 and 460 Flights, equipped with Fairey IIIF spotter-reconnaissance aircraft, aboard HMS *Eagle*, then on the China Station. The following year, while still in the Far East, No. 824 was renumbered No. 825 but on the same day, 8th October 1934, a new No. 824 Squadron was formed for service in HMS *Hermes*. In December No. 824 re-equipped with Fairey Seals and operated from *Hermes*, transferring back to *Eagle* in 1937.

Swordfish replaced the Seals in 1938 and when war came in 1939 *Eagle* and No. 824 were in the Indian Ocean, based on Ceylon. They immediately set about searching for German shipping and also escorted convoys. In May 1940 *Eagle* joined the Eastern Mediterranean Fleet at Alexandria. Malta convoys occupied No. 824 initially, but on 9th July the squadron carried out a torpedo attack on Italian cruisers and destroyers off Calabria.

Eleven days later (20th July), No. 824, operating from a shore base, sank two Italian destroyers and damaged a merchant ship at Tobruk. On 22nd August the squadron sank a depot ship and a submarine in the Gulf of Bomba. Then, back aboard *Eagle*, No. 824 carried out further strikes in the Eastern 'Med', including a dawn bombing raid on Rhodes. *Eagle* was now in need of repairs and on 6th November two of No. 824's Swordfish were transferred to HMS *Illustrious*. On the 11th of that month they took part in the Taranto raid, as a result of which half the Italian battle fleet was crippled.

In March 1941 No. 824 moved down to Port Sudan in company with No. 813 (*Eagle*'s other Swordfish squadron) to support Commonwealth forces in the East African campaign. During April the two squadrons sank two Italian destroyers, shared a third and helped drive ashore two more which were finished off by RN surface ships. A sixth destroyer, damaged at Massawa, scuttled herself and the Italian Red Sea fleet was eliminated.

Back aboard *Eagle*, and on 6th June in the South Atlantic, No. 824 found and sank the German supply ship Elbe. *Eagle* returned to the UK in October and on the 26th the squadron disembarked to Macrihanish. In January 1942 No. 824 rejoined *Eagle*, with fresh

Swordfish, and escorted Malta convoys until the ship was sunk on 11th August; after which the squadron was combined with No. 813.

Reformed with nine Swordfish on 1st October 1942, No. 824 Squadron embarked in HMS *Unicorn* for operations in Home waters. In October 1943 six Sea Hurricanes were added to the squadron strength and No. 824 then transferred to HMS *Striker*. In the next few months the main task was escorting convoys to Gibraltar and across the Atlantic. In April 1944 the Sea Hurricanes were replaced by Grumman Wildcats and the scene of operations moved to Norway, followed by two Russian convoys, after which, on 10th October, No. 824 disbanded.

Nine months later, in July 1945, the squadron reformed at Katukurunda, Ceylon, with twelve Barracudas but did not become operational until after the Japanese surrender. No. 824 returned home in HMS *Activity* and re-equipped with Firefly Is at Ayr in October, but on 4th January 1946 was disbanded at Burscough.

In February 1952 No. 824 was reformed at Eglinton with Firefly AS6s which it took aboard HMS *Illustrious*, later transferring to HMS *Theseus*. By June 1953 Avenger AS.4s had replaced the Fireflies, at Lee-on-Solent, and the next eighteen months were spent mainly ashore, at Culdrose and also Gibraltar. No. 824 began to re-equip with Gannet AS.1s at Eglinton in January 1955 and later operated them from *Ark Royal* and *Albion*, but in October 1957 disbanded at Culdrose.

No. 824 was reborn as a helicopter squadron, at Eglinton on 21st April 1958, equipped with Whirlwind HAS7s. The next four years – minus a six-month disbandment in 1959 – saw service in *Ark Royal* and *Centaur*, and ashore at Portland and Hal Far, Malta. While aboard *Centaur* the squadron took part in the Kenya flood-relief operations in December 1961. On 22nd May 1963 No. 824 again disbanded.

On 24th February 1970 No. 824 became the Royal Navy's first operational Sea King squadron when it reformed at Culdrose with six of these advanced anti-submarine helicopters. From that day on, *Ark Royal* has been the squadron's home, apart from periods ashore at Culdrose, and recently No. 824's establishment has been raised to seven Sea King HAS1s.

No. 849 Squadron – Formed at Squantum, USA, on 1st August 1943 with twelve Grumman Avengers, No. 849 was ferried home in the escort carrier HMS *Khedive* to Hatston, where four Wildcats were temporarily added to the squadron's strength. After training in the anti-submarine role at Eglinton No. 849 moved to Perranporth for operations, starting on 20th April 1944, under RAF Coastal Command.

The squadron then turned its attention towards the Japanese, setting sail in HMS *Rajah* for Ceylon in September 1944. After working up in the strike role at Katukurunda and increasing its strength to twenty-one Avengers, No. 849 embarked in *Victorious* in December. During January 1945 the squadron took part in three devastating attacks on Japanese oil refineries in Sumatra – at Pangkalan Brandan on the 4th and Palembang on the 24th and 29th – which shortened the Pacific War by several months. From the end of March until 20th May No. 849's Avengers attacked targets in Sakishima Gunto and Formosa, and finally in July and August Japan herself. On 31st October 1945 the squadron arrived home and disbanded.

Nearly seven years were to elapse before No. 849 was born again. In November 1951 the Royal Navy began to take delivery from the USA of the Douglas Skyraider AEW.1, an airborne early warning aircraft with nearly a ton of powerful radar equipment which enabled the Skyraider to detect low-flying aircraft and provide early warning of an attack. Trials with the Skyraider were carried out at Culdrose by No. 778 Squadron, which on 7th July 1952 was redesignated No. 849 Squadron. The squadron consisted of a shore-based HQ Flight and four operational Flights ('A'-'D') for service aboard the aircraft-carriers.

The Skyraider gave excellent service for eight years until superseded in 1959 by the Gannet AEW.3, initially in No. 700G Flight. On 1st February 1960 No. 700G became 'A' Flight, No. 849 Squadron, and gradually the whole unit re-equipped. In January 1965 the squadron moved from Culdrose to Brawdy and during that year its Flights were involved in the Indonesian Confrontation, followed by the Beira blockade in 1966.

During the next few years the number of operational Flights diminished as the Labour Government's decision to scrap aircraft-carriers began to take effect. No. 849 Squadron moved to Lossiemouth in August-November 1971, where, in addition to providing two seagoing Flights for the last two carriers ('D' on *Eagle* and 'B' on *Ark Royal*), it began training RAF radar operators for the

Shackleton AEW.2s of No. 8 Squadron. Now, apart from its HQ Flight, No. 849 Squadron – a unique and irreplaceable unit – consists only of 'B' Flight with four Gannet AEW.3s aboard *Ark Royal*.

No. 892 Squadron – Formed on 15th July 1942 at Norfolk, Virginia, with Wildcats, this squadron operated initially in defence of Atlantic convoys, flying from the escort carrier HMS *Archer*. Disbanded in August 1943, the squadron was reformed in April 1945 with Grumman Hellcats as a night-fighter unit and embarked in the light fleet carrier HMS *Ocean*, but saw no further action in World War II and was disbanded in April 1946.

Then came a gap of nine years until, on 4th July 1955, No. 892 reformed at Yeovilton with D.H. Sea Venom FAW 21s. The following year while embarked in HMS *Eagle* the squadron took part in the Suez operation, but disbanded on 5th January 1957. On 2nd July 1959 No. 892 was reformed, by renumbering No. 700Y IFTU, at Yeovilton to become the first operational Sea Vixen squadron.

The squadron took its Vixen FAW.1s aboard *Ark Royal* on 3rd March 1960 for sea trials and later served in *Victorious* and *Hermes*. During 1963, by which time No. 892 had transferred to *Centaur*, the Sea Vixens were involved in the Indonesian Confrontation, the Radfan fighting, and the Dar-es-Salaam crisis. On re-equipping with Sea Vixen FAW.2s, the squadron re-embarked in *Hermes* in July 1966 and sailed to Aden, where trouble was still brewing, before returning to Yeovilton in February 1968. While ashore No. 892 formed a five-Vixen aerobatic team, 'Simon's Sircus', which took part in many displays before the squadron was disbanded in October 1968.

On 1st March 1969 No. 892 was reformed at Yeovilton as the Royal Navy's first – and, as it has turned out, only – front-line squadron to be equipped with McDonnell Douglas F-4K Phantom FG.1s. In July 1964 the British Government placed an order for 140 Phantoms for the Royal Navy, but after Labour had got into power and decided that carriers should be phased out, the RN order was cut to a mere twenty-eight. After gaining sea-going experience in the American carrier USS *Saratoga* in the autumn of 1969, No. 892 embarked in *Ark Royal* in June 1970. Squadron strength is twelve aircraft and when not at sea in the '*Ark*', No. 892 is nowadays based at RAF Leuchars.

Ark Royal I

The *Ark Royal* was acquired by the Crown from Sir Walter Ralegh, who was presumably having her built for the colonisation of Virginia. She was launched at Deptford on 12 June 1587, with the name *Ark Raleigh*, and in the subsequent campaign against the Spanish Armada the Lord High Admiral, Lord Howard of Effingham, flew his flag in her. Writing to Burghley on 28 February 1587/8, Howard says:

I pray you tell her Majesty from me that her money was well given for the ARK RALEGH, for I think her the odd ship in the world for all conditions; and truly I think there can be no great ship make me change and go out of her.

Lord Howard of Effingham calls her 'Her Majesty's good ship the *Ark*' – the name *Ark Royal* only came into use later. The cost of her purchase, £5,000 was deducted in 1592 from Ralegh's debt to the Crown.

In the expedition to Cadiz in 1596 she again wore the flag of Lord Howard of Effingham; and in 1599 that of Sir Walter Ralegh, during the threat of invasion.

In 1608 she was rebuilt and her named changed to *Anne Royal* in honour of the then Queen, wife of James I. The *Anne Royal* was broken up in 1636 at the East India Company's dock at Blackwall, after going aground in the Thames.

The following details about her are given by Oppenheim in his '*History of the Administration of the Royal Navy*' (1896):-

Length of Keel	100 feet
Beam	37 feet
Depth of hold	15 feet

Rake forward	33.6 feet
Rake aft	6 feet
Burden	555 tons
Ton and Tonnage	692 tons
Weight of masts & yards	18.4 tons
Weight of rigging tackle	15,300 lbs
Canvas for sails in bolts, ¾ths of a yard broad and 28 yards long	84 bolts
Anchors, seven	13,500 lbs
Cables, seven	24,000 lbs
Weight of ordnance	50 tons
Men in harbour	17
Men at sea	400
Mariners	268
Gunners	32
Soldiers	100
Cost per month at sea: wages and victualling	£606.13.4
Demi-canon (brass)	4
Cannon periers (brass)	4
Culverins (brass)	12
Demi-Culverins (brass)	12
Sakers (brass)	6

HMS Ark Royal II

Summary of Service

HMS *Ark Royal* was commissioned at Blyth, Northumberland, as a Seaplane Carrier, by Commander R.H. Clark-Hall, RN on 9th December 1914. She left Blyth on 10 January 1915, and calling at Harwich and Chatham, arrived at Sheerness on the 30th January.

Equipped with 1 Short, and 2 Wight, seaplanes (200 HP Canton-Unne engines), 3 Sopwith Seaplanes (100 HP Monosonpape engines) and 2 Sopwith Tabloid aeroplanes (80 HP Grome engines), the *Ark Royal* sailed from Sheerness on 1 February 1915 and arrived at Malta on the 12th.

On the 17th, having arrived at Tenedos, to take part in the Dardanelles operations, she hoisted out her Short Seaplane to reconnoitre the enemy coast.

On the 5th March, off the entrance to the Dardanelles, one of her Sopwith Seaplanes (No. 808) which had been sent up to observe fire for HMS *Queen Elizabeth*, crashed into the sea out of control, the pilot and observer being rescued by HMS *Usk*. The second Sopwith went up later in the afternoon and spotted for the *Queen Elizabeth* until bad light made further observation impossible.

The 10th March found the *Ark Royal* at Xeros Island where her aircraft were sent up to reconnoitre the fortifications at the Bulair Isthmus. On the 28th, the ship was attacked by an enemy aeroplane which dropped two bombs but without doing any damage.

On 31st March she accompanied a small allied squadron to Mitylene and her planes examined the northern coast of the Gulf of Adramyti. Returning to Mudros for refuelling, and embarking a new Wight seaplane, she proceeded to the Gulf of Smyrna and on 4th April two flights were made for the purpose of mapping the defences there. After calling at Tenedos the *Ark Royal* sailed north to the Gulf of Enos and carried out a seaplane reconnaissance. She returned to Mudros the next day and having embarked two Sopwith 'Schneider Cup' seaplanes, sailed for the Gulf of Xeros, where she arrived on

12th April. On the 16th, one of her seaplanes spotting for HMS *Lord Nelson*, helped to blow up a section of the magazine at Taifur Keui. On the same day Gallipoli was reconnoitred by two of her Sopwiths which dropped bombs on the Turkish battleship '*Turgud Reis*' achored there.

The *Ark Royal* returned to Mudros on 17th April. The landings on Gallipoli commenced on 25th April, the ship being then off Gaba Tepe. From dawn of that day her aircraft were up spotting for the ships covering the landing, and continued on these duties until the 30th April.

On 10th May *Ark Royal* left Gaba Tepe for Kephalos Bay, Imbros, where she remained until 1st November, carrying out reconnaissance, spotting and photography flights. She then proceeded to Salonica (arriving on 8th November) where she remained until 27th March 1961, carrying out reconnaissance flights. 1st April 1916 found her at Mudros, where she remained until 3rd April 1918, when she left for Syra. During this long period at Mudros, *Ark Royal* was attacked by hostile aeroplanes on 1st November 1916; bombed by a Zeppelin on 1st March 1917, and by hostile aircraft on 1st September 1917. She was at Syra from April to October 1918 and was at Piraeus from when the war ended, arriving back at Mudros on 31st December.

In the early part of 1920 an Air Force contingent of 12 DH9 machines, which was despatched from England in the *Ark Royal*, took part in the Somaliland campaign in co-operation with a small force of the Camel Corps.

In 1922, when an international crisis arose in the Near East, the *Ark Royal* took No. 4 Squadron RAF to Kilia Bay in October, to strengthen the British garrison in the Dardanelles Zone.

She returned to England in 1923 and passed the rest of her service in the Reserve Fleet at Chatham. She was re-named *Pegasus* in December 1934, and after a period as a trials ship for catapults, aircraft recovery and training, she was recalled to active service in the early days of World War II. From December 1940 until July 1941 she was equipped with three Fulmar fighters and acted as a catapult carrier escorting nine Atlantic convoys.

On 26th July 1941, *Pegasus* returned to her routine catapult training duties in the Clyde area, and survived the war to be finally sold in 1946. Renamed *Anita I*, she was finally broken up at Gray's Yard in Essex in 1950.

HMS *Ark Royal* III

Summary of Service

HMS *Ark. Royal* was commissioned on 16th November 1938, and replaced HMS *Courageous* as flagship of the Rear-Admiral, Aircraft Carriers, Home Fleet.

When war began on 3rd September 1939, she was at sea with the Home Fleet from Scapa, and on 14th September was attacked by two torpedoes from *U. 39*. Both missed, and *U.39* was hunted and sunk by destroyers – the first U-boat to be sunk in the war.

On 26th September, the *Ark Royal* was attacked by German aircraft. The pilot of a Heinkel 111, Lieutenant Adolf Francke, claimed to have sunk her. He was promoted and awarded the Iron Cross. For some time, the German radio continued to ask 'Where is the *Ark Royal*?', despite repeated denials by the Admiralty that she had been damaged. Even when she appeared in Rio several weeks later, Dr. Goebbels kept up the legend, and the German colony there protested that she must be another ship of the same class.

Between October 1939, and February 1940, the *Ark Royal* operated in the South Atlantic, searching for enemy raiders. In March, she proceeded to the Mediterranean, but was recalled to the Home Fleet after the German invasion of Norway in April, leaving Scapa on the 23rd to give fighter protection over the Namsos and Andalsnes area. She continued to operate off Norway until after the Allied forces were evacuated in June.

On 18th June 1940, the *Ark Royal* left Scapa to join Force H which was formed under Admiral Sir James Somerville at Gibraltar. She arrived on the 23rd, by which time Italy had entered the war and France had capitulated. Her first duty was to take part in the attack on French ships at Oran on 3rd July, to prevent their falling into German hands. In September 1940, she took part in the expedition of General de Gaulle to Dakar.

Between July 1940, and November 1941, the *Ark Royal* took part in some 30 operations by Force H in the Western Mediterranean. They included the ferrying of aircraft into Malta; cover for naval and troop reinforcement convoys for Malta and the Piraeus; air attacks on Sardinia, Pisa and Leghorn; the bombardment of Genoa and mining of Spezia; and the action with the Italian Fleet off Cape Spartivento on 27th November 1940.

Every time Force H covered the passage of a convoy it had to meet determined opposition, but each time the convoy went through. The reconnaissance work of the *Ark Royal*'s aircraft was an essential part of the protection of the Force. 'If I haven't got the *Ark* with me', said Admiral Somerville, 'I feel like a blind beggar without his dog.'

On 24th May 1941, when the German battleship *Bismarck* and heavy cruiser *Prinz Eugen* broke out into the Atlantic, the *Ark Royal* left Gibraltar with Force H and steamed north-westward at high speed. On the evening of the 26th, she flew off a striking force of torpedo aircraft which scored two hits, one on the port side amidships, the other on the starboard quarter. The latter damaged the *Bismarck*'s propellers, wrecked her steering gear and jammed her rudders. This hit sealed her fate, as it ensured her being brought to action and sunk next morning by the Home Fleet under Admiral Sir John Tovey.

On 13th November, 1941, returning from an aircraft ferrying operation into Malta, the *Ark Royal* was torpedoed by a U-boat* when 30 miles from Gibraltar. By midnight she was in tow by two tugs, proceeding at two knots, but at 0215 on the 14th fire broke out in the port boiler-room, and could not be controlled. With a heavy list, she had to be abandoned, and at 0613 turned over and disappeared, 14 hours after being hit. Only one rating was lost of her complement of nearly 1,600.

HMS *Ark Royal* was awarded the following Battle Honours:

Norway	1940
Spartivento	1940
"Bismarck"	1941
Mediterranean	1940-1
Malta Convoys	1941

* *U.81*

HMS *Ark Royal* IV

In November 1934 it was announced that the new aircraft carrier would be called the *Ark Royal* and she was laid down on 16th September 1935, at Cammell Laird, Birkenhead and launched on 13th April 1937 by Lady Maude Hoare, wife of the First Lord of the Admiralty.

Originally designed to carry 72 aircraft, her nominal displacement was 22,000 tons with a length overall of 800 feet, a beam of 94¾ feet and a mean draught of 22 feet. She carried 16 4.5-inch dual purpose guns, six multiple pompoms and eight multiple machine guns. She commissioned on 16th November 1938, under the command of Captain A.J. Power (later Admiral of the Fleet Sir Arthur Power) and was flagship of Vice-Admiral Carriers, Vice-Admiral G.C.C. Royle, and then Vice-Admiral L.V. Wells.

Her war career was celebrated by repeated German claims to have sunk her. She joined in the search for the Graf Spee; took part in the attack on the French Fleet at Mers-el-Kebir (Oran), and the expedition to Dakar. The *Ark Royal* then joined Force H at Gibraltar and took part in many successful operations, including the sinking of Bismarck. On 14th November 1941, after being torpedoed the previous day, she turned over and sank in sight of Gibraltar.

Two large carriers were included in the 1940 Supplementary Programme and on 7th February 1942, HM King George V approved renaming the second of these ships – (the *Irresistible*) – *Ark Royal*. At the same time the ship was adopted by the City of Leeds. Laid down at Cammell Lairds on 3rd May 1943, she was launched on 3rd May 1950, by the Queen Mother. She was 810 feet long overall, had a beam of 158 feet and displaced 36,700 tons. Four feet longer than the *Eagle*, she was the largest carrier in the Royal Navy. The fourth *Ark Royal* – fitted with the interim angled flight deck – was commanded by Captain D.R.F. Campbell who designed it, and also commanded No. 803 squadron in the third *Ark Royal* at the outbreak of World War Two.

The *Ark Royal* recommissioned on 1st November 1956, after a long refit during which she was fitted with all the latest aids for operating aircraft. These included the necessary Command facilities for a Task Force Commander in operations involving the new generations of aircraft, and radars for plotting enemy movements. The angled flight deck was extended over the port side forward, by removing two 4.5-inch gun turrets, which also increased accommodation space.

Turbo generators replaced the diesel electric ones and the lubrication system of the steam catapult was re-arranged to minimise servicing. An interesting development was *major improvements* to the television system with a ring main system through 60 messes running over 50 receivers. The system could also be used for air crew briefing or instructional lectures.

On 24th February 1970, after a £30 millions refit, the *Ark Royal* recommissioned under the command of Captain R.D. Lygo RN. The Queen Mother, who launched her in 1950, attended the ceremony. The refit which started in 1966 provided for air conditioning, modifications to the port catapult and the resiting and rebuilding of the starboard one with jet blast deflectors; new communications and revised hangar stowage for Buccannear Mk. 2s and Phantom aircraft. New radars were fitted and a fully angled flight deck was incorporated as in the *Eagle*. The upper portion of the hangar deck was stiffened to accept bigger loads and there was a 199 feet catapult on the port waist.

The increased power of the catapult due to the lengthened stroke allowed the Phantom to be launched under 'nil' wind conditions. Another feature was the bridle arrester. Previously the bridle, linking the aircraft to the catapult, was lost every time an aircraft was launched. The arrester gear retrieves it with significant economies and the elimination of a logistic problem.

New directaction arrester gear was fitted with greater energy absorption enabling bigger aircraft to be landed at higher speeds. On May 11th and 12th 1971, successful Harrier trials were conducted.

HMS *Ark Royal* arrived at Devonport at the end of July 1973 for a further refit starting in September and completing by the Spring of 1974. This continued her operational life for some years and she is expected to remain in active service until 1978.

Index

Ships Index